"What a delight to see an updated edition of this comprehensive and useful book! Lorri and Ken continue to share their experience and the development of their model. The Play Therapy Dimensions Model provides us with a thoughtful, structured method to understand the intricacies and depth of the play therapy process. Perhaps as important, it allows us to look to understand ourselves as play therapists and the way we interact and engage with our clients. This is an excellent book to assist play therapists of all levels of experience to continue our own development!"

—Linda E. Homeyer, PhD, LPC-S, RPT-S, Distinguished Professor Emerita, Texas State University, USA

"Lorri and Ken's *Play Therapy Dimensions Model* fills a gap in the literature for clinicians who work from an integrative approach to play therapy. They provide a systematic and process-oriented framework for tailoring treatment approach to clients' needs and to aid therapists in identifying and assessing therapeutic movement within and across sessions."

—Sue C. Bratton, Professor and Director, Center for Play Therapy, University of North Texas, USA

"*Play Therapy Dimensions Model* is the most brilliant contribution to the play therapy literature published in the last ten years. Read this book if you want to (a) learn about play therapy, (b) deepen your understanding about how and why play therapy works, and/or (c) become more intentional and efficacious in your therapeutic work with children."

—Terry Kottman, PhD, LMHC, NCC, Registered Play Therapist-Supervisor and Director, The Encouragement Zone, Cedar Falls, Iowa, USA

"[This book] provide[s] both novice and seasoned clinicians with a[n]...invaluable framework, and excellent resources, to conceptualize the multi-dimensional practice of play therapy and inform decision-making... All play therapy training courses should include this book on their required reading lists."

—Eileen Prendiville, CEO and Course Director of the Master of Arts in Humanistic and Integrative Psychotherapy and Play Therapy, Children's Therapy Centre, Ireland

"I am fascinated by the clinical basis and multi-dimensional framework that the *Play Therapy Dimensions Model* provided me as a play therapy practitioner, particularly the understanding of the child's uniqueness, as well as the dynamics of psychic movement during the play session. Furthermore, I acquired a profound and flexible view of the therapist's role and accompanying skills for tuning in to and addressing the child's unmet needs. Through the case discussions, I have come to realize the importance of underlying change mechanisms in the process of play therapy, and the utility of the Play Therapy Dimensions Model tracking tools and forms for assessment purposes."

—Dr. Amjed Abojedi, Psychology Department, Al-Ahliyya Amman University,

by the same authors

Turning Points in Play Therapy and the Emergence of Self
Applications of the Play Therapy Dimensions Model
Edited by Lorri Yasenik and Ken Gardner
ISBN 978 1 78592 388 3
eISBN 978 1 78450 747 3

of related interest

Theraplay®
Innovations and Integration
Edited by Rana Hong and A. Rand Coleman
Foreword by Phyllis Booth
ISBN 978 1 78775 591 8
eISBN 978 1 78775 592 5

Play Therapy in the Outdoors
Taking Play Therapy out of the Playroom and into Natural Environments
Alison Chown
Foreword by Sara Knight
ISBN 978 1 84905 408 9
eISBN 978 0 85700 805 3

Rhythms of Relating in Children's Therapies
Connecting Creatively with Vulnerable Children
Edited by Stuart Daniel and Colwyn Trevarthen
ISBN 978 1 78592 035 6
eISBN 978 1 78450 284 3

PLAY THERAPY DIMENSIONS MODEL

New Insights for Integrative
Play Therapists

Lorri Yasenik and **Ken Gardner**
Forewords by Athena A. Drewes and Karen Stagnitti
3rd Edition

Jessica Kingsley Publishers
London and Philadelphia

This edition first published in Great Britain in 2024 by Jessica Kingsley Publishers
An imprint of John Murray Press

First edition published in 2004 by Rocky Mountain Play Therapy Institute™

2

Copyright © Lorri Yasenik and Ken Gardner 2024

Foreword to the second edition copyright © Athena A. Drewes 2012, 2024
Foreword to the third edition copyright © Karen Stagnitti 2024

The right of Lorri Yasenik and Ken Gardner to be identified as the Author of the Work has
been asserted by them in accordance with the Copyright, Designs and Patents Act 1988.

Play Therapy Dimensions Model™ is a trademark of Rocky Mountain
Play Therapy Institute Inc. (Calgary, AB, Canada).

The cover image is for illustrative purposes only, and any person featuring is a model.

All rights reserved. No part of this publication may be reproduced, stored in a retrieval system,
or transmitted, in any form or by any means without the prior written permission of the
publisher, nor be otherwise circulated in any form of binding or cover other than that in which
it is published and without a similar condition being imposed on the subsequent purchaser.

All pages marked with ✳ and supplementary videos and transcripts may be downloaded
at https://library.jkp.com/redeem for personal use with this program, but may not be
reproduced for any other purposes without the permission of the publisher.

The clients presented in the book represent fictional composite
cases and are therefore not real people.

A CIP catalogue record for this title is available from the British Library and the Library of Congress

ISBN 978 1 83997 653 7
eISBN 978 1 83997 654 4

Printed and bound by CPI Group (UK) Ltd, Croydon, CR0 4YY

Jessica Kingsley Publishers' policy is to use papers that are natural, renewable and recyclable
products and made from wood grown in sustainable forests. The logging and manufacturing
processes are expected to conform to the environmental regulations of the country of origin.

Jessica Kingsley Publishers
Carmelite House
50 Victoria Embankment
London EC4Y 0DZ

www.jkp.com

John Murray Press
Part of Hodder & Stoughton Limited
An Hachette UK Company

Contents

Foreword to the Second Edition by Athena A. Drewes **8**

Foreword to the Third Edition by Karen Stagnitti **11**

Acknowledgments **13**

1. Introduction **15**
The Journey to Case Conceptualization   15
A Road Map: Organization and Use of Materials in this Book   17
What is the Play Therapy Dimensions Model?   19
About This Book   22
Appendices   23
Videos   24
Case Studies   25

2. Integrative Decision-Making **35**
Do Play Therapists Need an Organizing Framework?   35
Integrative Play Therapy: The Need for a Framework for Decision-Making   38
Play Therapy Dimensions Model: A Decision Guide for Integrative Play Therapists   41
How Do Integrative Therapists Make Decisions?   42
Do Decision-Making Theories Designed for Adults Fit for Play Therapists?   43

3. Play Therapy Dimensions Model: An Overview **47**
Consciousness Dimension and Pre-Imaginative Play Skills   49
Two Primary Dimensions   50
The Four Quadrants   54
Factors Related to Movement between Quadrants   57
Degree of Reorganization: The Child's Process   58
Level of Therapist Interpretation   61

4. The Consciousness Dimension in Play Therapy **63**
What's So Mysterious about Consciousness? Historical and Current Perspectives   63
Are We Playing a Game of Hide-and-Seek?   67
Learning to Embrace the Game of Hide-and-Seek   73

5. The Directiveness Dimension in Play Therapy **76**
So, What Kind of Therapist Are You?   76

The Compass and the Gauge	79
The Observer-Participant Role	83
Tapping the Therapeutic Powers of Play	83

6. Non-Intrusive Responding: Quadrant III **86**

The *What*: The Defining Features of Quadrant III	86
The *How*: Therapeutic Roles and Activities	88
Illustrative Case Study: Video Quadrant III Segment—Ellis	90
The *When*: Considerations for the Play Therapy Process	92
The *Who*: Clinical Applications	96
Should I Stay or Should I Go? Indications For Working in Quadrant III	98
Illustrative Case Study—Haley	100
Movement Within This Quadrant	101

7. Co-Facilitation: Quadrant IV **104**

The *What*: The Defining Features of Quadrant IV	104
The *How*: Therapeutic Roles and Activities	105
Illustrative Case Study: Video Quadrant IV Segment—Ellis	108
The *When*: Considerations for the Play Therapy Process	111
The *Who*: Clinical Applications	113
Should I Stay or Should I Go? Indications for Working in Quadrant IV	114
Movement Within This Quadrant: Illustrative Case Study—Haley	117

8. Active Utilization: Quadrant I. **120**

The *What*: The Defining Features of Quadrant I	120
Illustrative Case Study: Video Quadrant I Segment—Ellis	123
The *How*: Therapeutic Roles and Activities	126
The *When*: Considerations for the Play Therapy Process	127
The *Who*: Clinical Applications	129
Should I Stay or Should I Go? Indications for Working in Quadrant I	130
Illustrative Case Study—Haley	133
Movement Within This Quadrant	134

9. Open Discussion and Exploration: Quadrant II **137**

The *What*: The Defining Features of Quadrant II	137
The *How*: Therapeutic Roles and Activities	141
Illustrative Case Study: Video Quadrant II Segment—Ellis	142
The *When*: Considerations for the Play Therapy Process	143
The *Who*: Clinical Applications	144
Should I Stay or Should I Go? Indications for Working in Quadrant II	146
Movement Within This Quadrant: Illustrative Case Study—Haley	147

10. Preparing Parent Feedback **151**

Conceptualizing Parent Feedback: The Four Steps of Preparation	152
Parent Presentation Styles	156
Consider Future Needs and an Ongoing Treatment Plan	162

11. Case Conceptualization: The Case of Ellis **164**

Purpose and Use of the Case Conceptualization Form 164

Process and Guiding Questions: Eleven Areas for Supervision 165

Summary 179

12. Utilizing the Play Therapy Dimensions Model: In Supervision **181**

Why Use the Play Therapy Dimensions Model for Supervision? 181

How to Use the Videos 183

Aiding Supervisees to Use Videos/Video Review 185

Using the Play Therapy Dimensions Model to Review Videos 186

A Developmental Model of Supervision 187

Utilizing the Tracking and Observation Form 197

Utilizing the Child Moderating Factors Scale 198

Utilizing the Degree of Immersion: Therapist Use of Self Scale 200

13. Therapist Use of Self **202**

What Are We Looking For? 204

1) Verbal Use of Self 205

2) Emotional Use of Self 212

3) Physical Use of Self 215

4) Self-System 217

5) Cultural Use of Self 218

14. Setting the Compass: The Journey to Self-Awareness **220**

Play Time: Know Yourself as a Player 220

Know Yourself and Your Temperament 224

Know Yourself Culturally and Ethnically 226

Know Yourself when Working with Parents 228

Making Meaning 231

Appendix A: Child Moderating Factors Scale **236**

Appendix B: Degree of Immersion: Therapist Use of Self Scale **244**

Appendix C: Tracking and Observation Form **256**

Appendix D: Parent Feedback Conceptualization Form **262**

Appendix E: Case Conceptualization Form **266**

Appendix F: Playtime Exercise **268**

References **270**

About the Authors **279**

Subject Index **280**

Author Index **286**

Foreword to the Second Edition

Play therapists over the past ten years have felt more and more challenged in being able to address the growing complexity of referral issues in their practices, notably complex trauma. Because psychological disorders, especially for children and adolescents, are multi-layered, complex, and multi-determined, a multifaceted treatment approach is needed. Indeed, many clients come with not one clearly defined diagnosis, but rather several overlapping problems due to the co-morbidity of issues, such as in the case of complex trauma resulting in overlapping anxiety and attention problems, along with phobias and sexualized behaviors, attachment issues, and domestic and environmental violence. Consequently, play therapists have been seeking alternative ways to conceptualize and conduct, as well as supervise, play therapy with their diverse populations from their initial training in one theoretical and/or treatment approach. Thus, play therapy and child clinicians are finding that "one size" cannot possibly and successfully fit all of the presenting problems with which they are being faced today.

Because of this multi-dimensional aspect, play therapy calls for the unique demand that the therapist should wear many different hats and be skillful in changing from one therapeutic stance to that of another in order to meet the needs of the child and the various other people in the child's life. One moment, the play therapist is intensely involved in deeply evocative, often very conflicted, play therapy with the child client. At that moment, the therapist needs to deal with the child's internal struggles and a non-directive approach may be necessary in allowing the child to play out their inner concerns and conflicts, with the therapist leaving the material on an unconscious level. Reflective non-directive tracking skills would be needed to allow the material to unfold. In the next moment, the therapists may find themselves having to set limits or offer psycho-education around anger management or experiences of being bullied. The play therapist then has to quickly change hats and become more directive and involved in the child's play in dealing with conscious material and behaviors. Flexible switching is required between the various degrees along each of these continuums. As a result, these often conflicting and rapidly changing roles require play therapists to adopt an eclectic prescriptive style in which therapeutic interventions are chosen and then changed according to the most pressing external demand.

In addition, in direct contrast to linear models of psychopathology, integrative theories of psychopathology assume a weaving of various aspects of the client's personal experience, thereby conceptualizing psychopathology from the viewpoint of multi-causation. Rather than just jumping from one type of treatment to another, the play therapist can develop an integrative and prescriptive approach to treatment which broadens the therapist's concept of what is appropriate from the various theoretical points of view and can offer a wider array of tools and treatment stances with which to work.

As a result, we need now, more than ever, a model of treatment and supervision that can be clearly articulated for the play therapist in how to move easily from a non-directive approach to a directive approach as well as move flexibly within the child's conscious and unconscious expressions through their play, while being developmentally sensitive to the child, their play, and the therapy process. Quite a tall order to fill! Luckily for the reader, and the field of play therapy, such a model exists which is clearly articulated and conceptualized. Lorri Yasenik and Ken Gardner offer the reader a uniquely conceptualized integrative model of play therapy treatment and supervision in *Play Therapy Dimensions Model: A Decision-Making Guide for Integrative Play Therapists*.

In a clearly articulated approach, the model contains a vertical continuum, identified as the *consciousness* dimension of the child's conscious and unconscious expressions of play within the session. On the horizontal continuum, identified as the *directiveness* dimension, the therapist's degree and level of immersion is reflected. Thus, the therapist moving along this horizontal line would be non-directive to directive, as needed in their immersion in the child's play. The circular diagram, which is a clear visual representation of the integrative possibilities of the model, is divided into four quadrants: *Active Utilization*, *Open Discussion and Exploration*, *Non-Intrusive Responding*, and *Co-Facilitation*. The reader is able to follow along and begin to formulate how they would work within a session and across sessions as therapy progresses. It is a flexible model which allows for a circular way of working rather than the often more rigid linear approaches to treatment in which only one model is used. A wonderful video is included with the book, which allows the reader and viewer to see the model in action as the authors clearly narrate the events, and the various components of the continuum of treatment are labeled. It is a great teaching tool for supervisors, as well as helping beginning play therapists to stretch their thinking and become more integrative and prescriptive in their treatment conceptualization and approach. The therapists and children in the video are realistic and authentic in their interactions and reactions, making for a believable and useful tool.

Play therapists have finally obtained a model of conceptualizing treatment and supervision that allows for a creative and flexible approach to be integrative in meeting the needs of their clients. So, reader, be prepared for the Play Therapy Dimensions Model to become a much-used tool in your treatment and supervision. Sit back and enjoy!

Athena A. Drewes, PsyD, MA, MS Ed, RPT-S
Founder and President Emeritus of the New York Association for Play Therapy,
Former Director of the Association for Play Therapy, Semi-Retired, Private Practice
Ocala, Florida, 2012

Foreword to the Third Edition

It is an honor to write this foreword to the third edition of *Play Therapy Dimensions Model*. In this edition, Lorri Yasenik and Ken Gardner have articulated, in more depth, the considerations that play therapists need to make for individual children within the complexity of available approaches in the field of play therapy. Charles Schaefer would consistently emphasize the point that play therapists should be thinking: what is the appropriate and effective play therapy for this child for this moment? The third edition of *Play Therapy Dimensions Model* provides advanced nuanced knowledge to think through such a question as a play therapist. The Therapist Use of Self Scale has received an overhaul and has been expanded to include self-system and cultural use of self. These new areas, together with verbal use of self, emotional use of self, and physical use of self, will guide therapists in self-reflection. This revised scale goes hand in hand with the updated Play Therapy Dimensions Model, which now includes pre-imaginative play. In my early readings of Axline, many years ago, I realized that she assumed that children had the ability to pretend play, that is, the ability to play in the metaphor. This was curious to me as I had been working with children who did not possess pretend play ability. Many years later, when I began to understand pretend play and, consequently, pre-imaginative play skills, I was able to articulate the importance of pretend play ability for children and their place in their worlds. I came to understand the importance of scaffolding a child's ability to pretend in play. For many children, this necessitated scaffolding pre-imaginative play skills into the higher level of pretend play ability. In the updated Play Therapy Dimensions Model diagram this is symbolized as the half-moon (pre-imaginative play) cradling the four quadrants and the grayscale-bleed into Quadrants III and IV. In scaffolding children's play so they were able to spontaneously initiate their own pretend play, I observed children who began to spontaneously play in the metaphor, children who became more present in the playroom and began to articulate what they had been doing (that is, autobiographical narrative, sense of self), and children who used narrative and language and began to have friends over to their homes to play. The addition of pre-imaginative play skills as the cradle for the four quadrants, with grayscale-bleed into Quadrants III and IV acknowledges the hierarchical nature of play, is consistent with our current understanding of the neurobiology of play, and opens up the Play Therapy Dimensions Model so it can be applied for all children. The new Play Therapy Dimensions Model includes crossed arrows in each quadrant, indicating the nuanced nature of play therapy, with the therapist moving across a quadrant or even between quadrants. Moving across and between Quadrants III and IV, in my experience, is in response to the child's ability in complex pretend play, with movements from Quadrant IV to III occurring when children are able to play spontaneously in the metaphor. This new model also illustrates that the therapist's therapeutic use of self may require scaffolding of pre-imaginative play skills to pretend play skills, which puts demands on their physical use of self, self-system, and cultural use of self. I am delighted to highly recommend this third edition. This book explains in much more depth the nuances that are required in play therapy so that all children can receive appropriate, individualized, and effective play therapy.

Karen Stagnitti
Emeritus Professor, Deakin University,
Creator of Learn to Play Therapy

Acknowledgments

Nineteen years have passed since writing the first edition of this book. Initially encouraged by our colleague Dr. Joyce Mills to write the book in 1996, it still took us eight years to formally publish in 2004. We are forever grateful to you Dr. Mills, for your initial encouragement and belief in us!

Seven years after 2004, we published the second edition as we continued to be inspired by university professors, professional trainers, and play therapists who saw the utility in the Play Therapy Dimensions Model in their teaching and in conceptualizing their play therapy practice. We incorporated new ideas, thoughts, and concepts that elaborated our original ideas. In particular, Dr. Athena Drewes offered her support and positive feedback and referenced the Play Therapy Dimensions Model in her own work. Dr. Drewes, we deeply appreciate your openness and collegial friendship you offered us that helped direct us in writing the second edition.

It is with great admiration and gratitude that we have Eileen Prendiville as a dear colleague and friend. The Children's Therapy Centre in Ireland has been a significant supporter of us as well as the Play Therapy Dimensions Model. The Centre incorporated the model into their training programs, and students in the program have significantly forwarded the use of the Play Therapy Dimensions Model.

We would also like to honor Professor Emeritus Karen Stagnitti, who brought the Play Therapy Dimensions Model into Deakin University in Victoria, Australia. Dr. Stagnitti forwarded the thinking of the directiveness and consciousness dimensions in Quadrant IV, in particular, in her work with children on the autism spectrum. She has considered the therapeutic use of self and has incorporated the Play Therapy Dimensions Model in her academic and clinical work "Learn to Play." Dr. Stagnitti has challenged our thinking and encouraged the elaboration of the model. Students at Deakin University have also used the Play Therapy Dimensions Model to forward the thinking, as they used it as an organizing framework for continuing research projects and dissertations.

Our colleagues at Wroxton International Study Group are acknowledged as part of the mosaic of multicultural and international support we have enjoyed in relation to the Play Therapy Dimensions Model. Over the 20 years of attendance at the

International Study Group, the Play Therapy Dimensions Model has been referenced and included in conceptualizing the play therapy process and decision-making in play therapy.

There would be no book without the many contributions made by the students who have attended the Rocky Mountain Play Therapy Institute™ training programs over the past 25 years. Every time we thought we really knew it, we were challenged once again. It was the collaborative learning environment that helped create the basic constructs that support the Play Therapy Dimensions Model. This model of thinking about play therapy is a tribute to the idea that it takes many approaches and philosophies to create a truly inclusive learning and treatment environment.

Thanks to our brave and talented past staff members, Susan James and Lynde Hill, the video turned out to be an excellent learning tool that is timeless. They jumped right in and, with little scripting and no practice runs, demonstrated the play therapy segments as they related to the four quadrants. We endlessly appreciate their readiness to take on the challenges thrown their way and we are grateful to have had them as members of our team.

Our original videographer Rein Evelein could be described as logically creative! The combination of order, sequential thinking, and creativity is more than we could have asked for as he helped to conceptualize the clinical video sessions that have become well-known accompaniments to the second edition of the book. Two other creatives joined us in this newest edition: Ward Cameron and Jonathan Graham. Ward offered his expertise in camera work and sound and then handed over multiple camera takes to Jon who spent many hours weaving all the angles and sound together. From there, our requests for inserting additional images resulted in two new videos on case conceptualization and parent feedback. Thanks to both Ward and Jon for your expertise!

We cannot begin to name all our colleagues with whom we have trained and worked. They have influenced our thinking and professional development and challenged us so that professional growth was possible.

Many thanks to Jessica Kingsley Publishers for all of their support and technical expertise!

Finally, but most importantly, we want to thank our family members who endlessly and continually support us through each and every new project that demands our time. They have provided nurturing and caring home environments in which to seek refuge when we were less than nurturing to ourselves, and have made the writing of the third edition of this book possible.

Lorri A. Yasenik and Ken Gardner

◉ **Chapter 1** ◉

INTRODUCTION

Step inside, you will always find a place.

THE JOURNEY TO CASE CONCEPTUALIZATION

The *Play Therapy Dimensions Model* was initially published in 2004, approximately eight years after Dr. Joyce Mills suggested that our concepts about a decision-making framework for play therapists be formalized and published (Yasenik and Gardner, 2004). Reaching further back in time, the impetus for the model came from supervisee questions such as, "What should I do next?" No doubt this is a familiar question for supervisors, along with the question, "How directive should I be?" Questions such as these spoke to the need for a framework or model that supported the development of case conceptualization skills. As we often worked with supervisees trained in different models of therapy, we realized that a broad perspective was required. Naturally, this fits with our inclinations to work from an integrative perspective. However, it was also important that practitioners working from a single model could benefit from a framework that encouraged reflective practice and emphasized therapist use of self.

Since the Play Therapy Dimensions Model™ was first developed, advances have of course been made within the field of psychotherapy, particularly in relation to treatment planning and case conceptualization. Sperry and Sperry (2020) note that case conceptualization has over the past 30 years come to be recognized as an essential clinical competency for mental health practitioners, yet graduate training programs have been slow to integrate case conceptualization skills in their training programs. This often leaves mastery of this skill set to the supervision process. Unless the supervisee and supervisor have a model to draw upon, the end result is less than ideal, not only from the perspective of clinical outcomes but also because the ability to conceptualize provides the therapist with a sense of confidence in their work (Hill, 2005).

◉ 15 ◉

Sperry and Sperry (2020) highlight that case conceptualization functions as a bridge to connect assessment and treatment with clinical outcomes. Essentially, it is a way to organize information and guide or focus treatment. It is also a process that unfolds over time, moving from provisional to full-scale case conceptualizations. These authors differentiate too between low-level conceptualizations, which are more akin to case descriptions, and high-level conceptualizations, which include specific statements related to clinical/diagnostic parameters as well as cultural formulations. Over time, the tools connected to the Play Therapy Dimensions Model have expanded to include parameters such as cultural formulations.

Case conceptualization is not just something we strive to do well because of clinical outcomes; it is increasingly linked to evidence-based practice. In 2005, the American Psychological Association's Presidential Task Force on Evidence-Based Practice recognized this link (Sperry and Sperry, 2020). Bringing this matter closer to our field, a Delphi study conducted in relation to the introduction of a phase model for credentialing by the Association for Play Therapy (APT) examined specific competency indicators (Turner *et al.*, 2020). A consensus was reached amongst 11 leaders in play therapy for the identification of 27 indicators under three predetermined areas of competency. Interestingly, case conceptualization is not identified as a distinct competency. However, several elements of case conceptualization are represented under the competency area of clinical play therapy skills, such as ability to articulate and explain the play therapy process and the ability to apply assessments that highlight aspects of the child and/or system and the play therapy process. Importantly, there is also one distinct indicator of cultural competence.

Moving from the past to the present, there remains a need for supervisors to support supervisees in their development of case conceptualization skills. As this is one of the more complex skill sets for practitioners to develop, it leads us right back to where we began—the need for a decision-making framework that contributes to high-level case conceptualizations tailored to the client.

Gil (2019) notes that our field is facing a plethora of models and we may be at a stage where very few original theories will be created. The impetus to "brand" new models of play therapy runs the risk of outpacing our capacity to help practitioners solidify their case conceptualization skills, as new and untested models provide little direction in terms of how to conceptualize the treatment process. In contrast, evidenced-based play therapy models, such as Adlerian Play Therapy, provide the practitioner with several tools. For example, there are tools that help create a lifestyle conceptualization, and, more recently, a therapy skills checklist has been developed that supports reflective practice (Dillman Taylor and Kottman, 2019).

Sperry and Sperry (2020) suggest there are three ways of constructing a case conceptualization. The first route, which we believe is least preferred, is the seat-of-the-pants method whereby the clinician uses trial-and-error thinking and ends up with little more than a case summary. The second route is to learn and apply a structured or theory-based method. This route is exemplified by Adlerian Play Therapy, whereby the identification of phases of treatment assists the clinician in understanding the manner in which an active or directive stance, particularly in the latter phases of treatment, supports client insight into their lifestyle (Kottman and Meany-Walen, 2016). A third way is to use an integrative model that incorporates common elements from various models, while allowing unique and distinctive elements of specific approaches to be integrated. The Play Therapy Dimensions Model aims to provide the practitioner with tools for taking an integrative approach to case conceptualization and treatment planning, while avoiding the seat-of-the-pants methodology!

The book and accompanying videos provide a breakdown visually and descriptively of the Play Therapy Dimensions Model. Included in this chapter are two detailed case studies that familiarize the reader with the background and presenting concerns of the child clients who are represented in the primary video accompanying this book. The reader should view this video for a concise introduction to the model. The video should also be viewed while reading chapters on each quadrant, as the video illustrates decision-making and movement specific to each quadrant, in relation to the cases. For the third edition we have elaborated case descriptions of family/parent functioning and, as noted above, two additional videos have been produced. The first video includes: 1) use of the Case Conceptualization Form (Appendix E) focusing on Ellis; and 2) use of the Parent Feedback Conceptualization Form (Appendix D). The second video includes parent feedback delivered to Ellis's parents. The second and third videos should be viewed after reading Chapters 10 and 11.

A ROAD MAP: ORGANIZATION AND USE OF MATERIALS IN THIS BOOK

Building case conceptualization skills is a journey for clinical practitioners, and most journeys require some type of road map. The following diagram provides an overview of the conceptual frameworks and tools used in this book.

Road Map to Play Therapy Case Conceptualization

Integrative Play Therapy: Multitheoretical Approaches

Play Therapy Dimensions Model: A Decision-Making Framework

Case Example 1: Nine-Year-Old Ellis	Case Example 2: Ten-Year-Old Haley

Six Conceptualizing Tools

Child Moderating Factors Scale	Degree of Immersion: Therapist Use of Self Scale	Tracking and Observation Form	Parent Feedback Conceptualization Form	Case Conceptualization Form	Playtime Exercise

Organizing and Delivering Parent Feedback

We begin with a discussion of why a decision-making framework is needed and the distinct features of four integrative approaches to psychotherapy. Next, we delineate what the Play Therapy Dimensions Model is and how it functions as an integrative decision-making framework that assists the play therapist to understand complex client–therapist–treatment interactions. The two primary dimensions, consciousness and directiveness, are discussed in detail, both from a historical standpoint and from a practitioner perspective, so that tracking movement along these dimensions forms a central part of case conceptualizations and treatment planning. Following this, each of the four quadrants is discussed to deepen the practitioner's understanding of movement within and across quadrants. Therapist use of self, which we view as a critical change mechanism, is explored in depth in Chapter 13 and during discussions about two cases. An addition to the third edition is Chapter 10 and a video on parent consultation, which exemplify how to organize and deliver feedback to parents. The ability to succinctly deliver a conceptualized treatment plan is a hallmark of excellence in case conceptualization and is a skill set that we believe is bolstered by the tracking and conceptualization tools.

The book and accompanying videos provide a visual and descriptive breakdown of the Play Therapy Dimensions Model. Included in this chapter are two detailed case studies that familiarize the reader with the background and presenting concerns of the child clients who are represented in the primary video accompanying this book. The reader should view this video for a concise introduction to the model. The video should also be viewed while reading the chapters on each quadrant, as the video illustrates decision-making and movement specific to each quadrant, in relation to the cases. For the third edition, we have elaborated case descriptions of family/parent functioning and, as noted above, a second video on parent consultation has been produced. The second video should be viewed while reading Chapter 10.

The journey would not be complete without providing specific tools that support integrative thinking. The book offers six specific tools to aid play therapists in their professional development and can be used regardless of their phase of development. The tools are included as Appendices and are considered an essential part of the case conceptualization process. Regular use of these tools should assist the practitioner in developing a template for organizing and conceptualizing essential components of the play therapy process.

WHAT IS THE PLAY THERAPY DIMENSIONS MODEL?

The Play Therapy Dimensions Model diagram is defined as a "bottom-up" model for practitioners. Now expanded to include pre-imaginative play at the base of the diagram, the model emphasizes the need to consider a child's play skills. We must follow child development and therefore understand pre-pretend play. Stagnitti (2021; Stagnitti, Wadley, and Sheppard, 2012) claims that pretend play looks simple on the surface, but she notes it is a "melting pot of ability" that includes: narrative, cognition and metacognition, social competence, problem-solving, divergent thinking, understanding context, self-regulation, creativity, language and metacommunication, and emotional understanding. Before a child can drive and direct pretend play, many discrete play skills need to be mastered. The Play Therapy Dimensions Model diagram is no longer only representative of children who can engage in imaginative pretend play. Not all children who come to see a play therapist can drive and direct play. Some children will be missing critical play skills through developmental interruptions, trauma, or neurodiversity. Gaskill and Perry (2014) and Perry (2009) describe brain development as hierarchically organized from brainstem to midbrain to limbic system and cortex, and emphasize the need to work with children at their level of play development. Stagnitti (2021) encourages play therapists to whenever possible engage in a play assessment and notes:

> When we engage with a child at a level of play that the child does not understand, then the child will disengage because our play actions fall outside the child's zone of proximal development. The child does not understand what we are doing. We are neurologically ineffective. (p.26)

Pre-Imaginative Play Skills: An Addition to the Play Therapy Dimensions Model Diagram

It is clear that there can be no imaginative, metaphorical play without the accumulative development of discrete play skills. The Play Therapy Dimensions Model diagram (see Figure 1.1) is therefore anchored by a band at the bottom that identifies the foundational necessity of "pre-imaginative play skills." Children can't enter play using symbols and materials metaphorically without collective play skills being in place. The diagram displays a grayscale bleed from the pre-imaginative play skills band into Quadrant III and Quadrant IV, indicating the therapist may engage in play activities with a child to potentially both observe the child's drive and interest in certain materials (Quadrant III) and then purposefully scaffold a child's play (Quadrant IV) in an effort to increase the child's play skills toward the goal of increasing the ability to work in the metaphor (Quadrants III and IV).

The model will appeal to individual treatment-focused practitioners as well as those who are practicing from a systemic framework. It is our view that play therapy is an efficacious form of treatment and is most productively embedded in parent work and systems-based consultations and interventions. It is a widely held belief that parents should contribute to the formulation of goals for therapy and must be informed as to treatment progress. Through helping parents learn more effective ways to deal with their child's emotional needs, personality, and developmental or adjustment issues, therapists can secure their support and enhance therapeutic outcomes (McGuire and McGuire, 2001). The third edition has broadened this scope by discussing these facets of treatment in greater detail and through the case example of Ellis.

While recognizing that there are fundamental philosophical differences between schools of play therapy, as well as shared viewpoints, the Play Therapy Dimensions Model conceptualizes the play therapy process according to *two primary dimensions*:

directiveness and *consciousness*. These dimensions help define the therapeutic space in a manner that most practitioners will recognize as fundamental to the change process. The *consciousness* dimension reflects the child's representation of consciousness in play and is represented by the child's play activities and verbalizations. The second dimension, *directiveness*, refers to the degree of immersion and level of interpretation of the play therapist (therapeutic use of self).

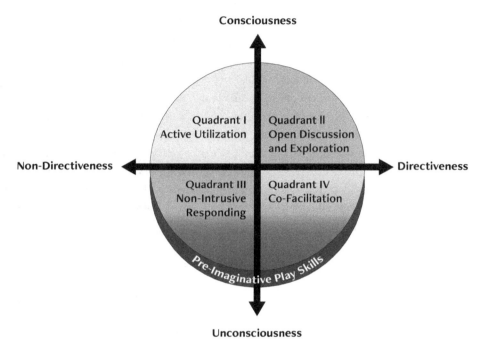

FIGURE 1.1: PLAY THERAPY DIMENSIONS MODEL DIAGRAM

Figure 1.1, the Play Therapy Dimensions Model diagram, depicts a circumplex model where each dimension is represented as a continuum with end points. Consistent with the American Psychological Association's definition of circumplex (*APA Dictionary of Psychology*, n.d.), elements or variables having opposite values or characteristics are displayed at opposite points, while those elements having highly similar characteristics are displayed close to each other on the circumplex. Accordingly, the similarity or correlation between elements declines as the distance between them on the circle increases. Practically speaking, the use of a circumplex model helps the practitioner understand that even subtle movement along either dimension is noteworthy as we are impacting variables that are associated with that dimension. For example, raising consciousness by putting forth a more direct comment about how a play metaphor relates to the child's experiences may impact the child's capacity to verbalize or express a thought or feeling, in either a positive or inhibiting manner. During play therapy, there is likely to be movement or weaving along each dimension, in relation to specific therapist–child–treatment interaction factors, rather than a static positioning on either continuum. If a practitioner can make use of this circumplex representation to articulate when, why, or how movement occurred, they are well on their way to conceptualizing the play therapy process. As illustrated in Figure 1.1, the two dimensions intersect to form four quadrants.

Consistent with a circumplex approach, each quadrant is unique in relation to the primary client–therapist variables that comprise the space along the dimensions. While certain models or approaches to play therapy may primarily operate within one quadrant, the quadrants do not represent specific models of play therapy.

Depending on the case conceptualization, and the theoretical approach of the therapist, a therapist might choose to focus therapy activities primarily in one quadrant. Alternatively, there may be a number of indicators that suggest movement is required within or between the quadrants. Furthermore, movement may occur within a session, or across sessions, as the therapy process evolves. As will be discussed, this conceptualization assists therapists in navigating the complex client–therapist–treatment interactions to tailor treatment approaches and optimize effectiveness. This integrative approach also offers a process-oriented framework, providing guidance for tracking important change mechanisms.

ABOUT THIS BOOK

Chapter 2 introduces integrative decision-making and offers a basis for understanding the core elements of the Play Therapy Dimensions Model. Chapter 3 provides an overview of the model, and for this new edition, the role and importance of pre-imaginative play skills is highlighted. Chapters 4 and 5 outline important theoretical constructs in relation to the consciousness and directiveness dimensions, placing each of these in a context for decision-making by integrative play therapists. Chapters 6–9 are dedicated to a description of each of the four quadrants: *Non-Intrusive Responding, Co-Facilitation, Active Utilization*, and *Open Discussion and Exploration*. Chapter descriptions are organized in such a way that therapists can answer the *who, what, when, why*, and *how* questions for each quadrant. In each of the chapters describing the quadrants, six indicators help therapists to decide whether they should stay working in a particular quadrant or should go. Additionally, Chapters 6–9 refer directly to the video case examples and describe the therapist activities and child responses when working in each quadrant. The quadrants are presented in the order in which they occur on the video so that the reader can follow the therapy sequence.

Chapter 10 is new to the third edition and includes many considerations for the role of parents and parent feedback in the play therapy process. This chapter is supported by an organizing tool (Appendix D). A video demonstration using the

INTRODUCTION

Parent Feedback Conceptualization Form is exemplified during a supervision session in Part 2 of the second video. Part 3 of the video provides a full parent feedback session related to the case of Ellis. Chapter 11 is also new to the third edition and offers a new tool for strengthening case conceptualization skills from an integrative perspective. Specifically, the case of Ellis is discussed, using the Case Conceptualization Form (Appendix E), deepening our understanding of what has transpired in play therapy and paving the way for consulting with Ellis's parents. This chapter is supported by Part 1 of the second video where the practitioner receives supervision using the Case Conceptualization Form. Because the Play Therapy Dimensions Model is an integrative approach to play therapy, it is a sound supervision tool.

Chapter 12 is dedicated to the use of this model in supervision. Play therapists and play therapist supervisors are given introductions on how to use the video in clinical supervision, how to aid supervisees in making videos, and how to use the model to review the videos. A specific developmental model of supervision for play therapists is presented, and bridging activities for the supervisee and supervisor are discussed for each phase of play therapy development. Chapter 13 examines the therapist use of self and raises the play therapist's awareness to the various ways one makes use of the self in a play therapy session. Further direction is provided for using the Degree of Immersion: Therapist Use of Self Scale (Appendix B), by examining in detail five areas of immersion.

Knowing yourself is an essential underpinning to working with people, but in working with children, your inner child is instantly awakened and present during therapy sessions. We believe this work cannot be done without significant self-exploration, since working with children triggers another level of emotional and spiritual vulnerability. Chapter 14 outlines a number of critical matters worth exploring such as, "Know yourself and your temperament," "Know yourself culturally and ethnically," and "Know yourself when working with parents." Issues related to vicarious trauma and the importance of making meaning in therapy are also explored in this chapter.

APPENDICES

The book offers six specific tools to aid play therapists in their professional development. Therapists can use the tools, regardless of their phase of development. All Appendices can be downloaded from https://library.jkp.com/redeem using the code RTECPZF.

- *Appendix A*: Child Moderating Factors Scale. This scale helps the therapist to identify client moderating factors to appropriately plan, set goals, and intervene with clients.

- *Appendix B*: Degree of Immersion: Therapist Use of Self Scale. This self-reflective tool helps play therapists rate the ways and degrees in which they immerse themselves in play. Therapists can evaluate the client response in relation to their immersion and subsequently make decisions as to whether the use of self should alter or stay the same.
- *Appendix C*: Tracking and Observation Form. This comprehensive scale is designed for therapists to use after each play session. It assists therapists to evaluate: the developmental stage of play; play process including initiation of play activities, play skills, inhibitions/disruptions, and endings; relational and affective markers including emotional range, self-regulation, and engagement; and thematic representations.
- *Appendix D*: Parent Feedback Conceptualization Form. This form is a quick reference to how to provide feedback to parents. It provides a template for managing and organizing therapist observations and areas of focus.
- *Appendix E*: Case Conceptualization Form. This is a tool that can be used at the beginning and throughout the supervision process. It is an integrative tool that captures several core concepts essential to case conceptualization, such as child moderating factors, thematic representations in play, and therapist use of self.
- *Appendix F*: Playtime Exercise. This is a self-exploration exercise that helps play therapists to examine their personal history of play—both individually and with their families of origin. This exercise can also be used with parents in preparation for Family Play Therapy.

VIDEOS

There are three videos that should be viewed along with reading the book. These can be downloaded, along with transcripts, from https://library.jkp.com/redeem using the code RTECPZF.

- *Case examples video*: Two examples of clinical cases are provided—the case of Ellis and the case of Haley. Each case example is approximately 30 minutes in length and introduces readers to the possibility of movement along the two primary dimensions. Therapists working from specific theoretical orientations may have chosen different entry points and may have fostered movement at different points, for various reasons. This simply reflects the "art" of therapy. By offering a decision-making guide that is mapped on to two dimensions, the play therapist may escape what Norcross (1987) refers to as "kitchen-sink eclecticism." Therapists will expand their theoretical frame and repertoire of interventions by utilizing the Play Therapy Dimensions Model.

INTRODUCTION

- *Case conceptualization video*: This supervision video is in two parts. The first part demonstrates case conceptualization of Ellis using the Case Conceptualization Form. The second part of the video uses the Parent Feedback Conceptualization Form and provides an example of preparing to give feedback to Ellis's parents.
- *Parent feedback video*: This is a demonstration of Ellis's therapist delivering feedback to his parents. This video is meant to accompany Chapter 10 and offers an example of how an integrative play therapist might work with parents around the midpoint of the therapy process.

CASE STUDIES

Models tend to remain academic exercises unless they are brought to life and a therapist can see how the model is implemented. To this end, the accompanying one-hour instructional video includes two case studies. The first case, of a nine-year-old boy named Ellis, demonstrates each quadrant of the Play Therapy Dimensions Model through four brief play segments lasting five to ten minutes each. The segments are chronologically ordered, representing what therapy might look like if one were working with Ellis over the course of several play sessions. This unique view through the playroom window allows us to observe movement across play sessions, in conjunction with hearing about the underlying decision-making points that contributed to movement amongst the four quadrants.

The second case illustrates a single session in a condensed format lasting approximately 30 minutes. The young person is a ten-year-old girl named Haley. This case offers a different view through the playroom window, one in which the play therapist constantly tracks the play and, at certain points, strategically moves along the play dimensions. The decision-making points and outcomes of movement are discussed in the context of the Play Therapy Dimensions Model.

To establish an understanding of the context for the referral issues and the accompanying therapeutic goals, detailed case descriptions are provided for each child.

Video Case Study: Ellis

PRESENTING PROBLEM

Download the case examples video and transcript from https://library.jkp.com/redeem using the code RTECPZF.

Ellis is a nine-year-old, cisgendered, Grade-4 student referred to therapy by his mother, Donna. During the telephone intake interview Donna reported that she and her husband, Don, have three children. Ellis is the middle child; there is a younger four-year-old brother, Sam, and an older 12-year-old sister, Janet. Donna reported

25

that Ellis had become increasingly "destructive" and "angry" at home. For example, Donna reported that Ellis broke several of his own toys when he could not get one to work. She further noted that Don observed Ellis yelling at teammates on his baseball team, claiming this was very uncharacteristic of Ellis. Furthermore, a teacher who has had Ellis in her class for the past two years recently reported that Ellis has been bossy with certain peers and seemed to overreact to helpful feedback from adults. It was also the teacher's impression that Ellis appeared unusually angry.

Historically, Donna indicated that Ellis was usually cooperative and accepting of rules and routines. However, lately Donna had noticed that Ellis was frequently argumentative and somewhat challenging of her authority. While this is less obvious during interactions with his father, Donna emphasized that Ellis has always had a special relationship with Don as he enjoys many of the "guy things" they do, such as repairing household items or tinkering in the garage.

Given his age, Ellis spends little time playing with his younger brother, although he was described as generally behaving in a kind and gentle manner toward him. Donna reported that Ellis and Janet seldom play together. However, Donna noted that their relationship is a positive one, emphasizing that Ellis sometimes looks up to his older sister. As Ellis is bussed to school, he has a separate group of friends near home that he plays with regularly. While Donna indicated that Ellis has never had a best friend, she said that he seemed to be well liked by his age mates. Ellis had two close friends at school. Unfortunately, both children moved last year, and Ellis has yet to report that he has a consistent group of friends that he plays with this year. Compounding this was a recent report from school that Ellis had been subjected to bullying on at least three occasions. On the first occasion Ellis was cornered in a washroom stall and two children refused to let him out. Another student reported the incident to a teacher as he heard Ellis's crying. The two playground incidents involved physical pushing and teasing. Both times, a group of three students, all of whom were older and bigger than Ellis, ganged up on him. The actions taken by the older children appeared to follow a clear bullying profile, and this group of children were known to the school for having targeted another student who had previously been significantly harmed. It was unknown with what frequency the aggressor children had been targeting and purposefully harming Ellis. Ellis had not directly disclosed what was happening although his behaviors began to change. While immediate steps were taken to sort out these issues, Ellis soon began to report that he didn't like school. During the intake interview, Donna reported that Ellis had not reached a point where he outwardly refused to get on the school bus each morning. However, Donna was concerned that Ellis was very slow at getting himself ready for school and seemed to be stalling during every step of his morning routines.

A primary concern raised by Donna was that Ellis had never been very talkative when it came to expressing or sharing his feelings. To repeated questions concerning why he seemed to get upset so easily, or why he argued, Ellis often responded, "I don't know." Given this context, Donna requested that Ellis be seen individually for play therapy. Donna also asked that she and Don be included in a parent consultation process to strengthen and support their parenting strategies. When asked about specific desired outcomes for therapy, Donna identified the following three goals.

- To help Ellis identify and cope with a range of feelings, including anger and frustration.
- To examine the impact of incidents of teasing and bullying at school.
- To assist Ellis in expressing his feelings.

BACKGROUND

Donna and Don reported they were both employed on a full-time basis. No significant changes in family life were reported. Further, Don and Donna reported low levels of stress in their parenting and work roles. Don was actively involved in coaching sport activities and had been Ellis's soccer coach for the last two seasons. Donna regularly volunteered at Ellis's school and had accompanied his class on several outings. Each parent presented with a different style during the meeting with the therapist. Donna was observed as being a Collaborative Parent (CP) and Don, although willing to be involved, presented more with a Solution-Focused Parent (SFP) style. The therapist considered how she would keep these styles in mind for any parent feedback or parent involvement suggestions. The cultural nuances of the family system were also relevant: the parents were both born and raised in Eastern Canada and had moved across the country from Newfoundland to Alberta for work. They reported getting used to living in Alberta as initially difficult. They were used to living in a smaller community of 5000 people and they missed the open-door approach of their hometown where people just came by without invitation. They also reported a lifestyle that was linked to ocean activity, and Don's family had always been a part of the fishing industry. His father, a hard worker, was a commercial fisherman. The parents both attended a community church when they lived on the coast, but they had trouble finding a church that they felt comfortable to attend after they moved. Both shared that they had strong Christian values. Close friends and family all continued to live in Newfoundland. Donna's parents had immigrated from Ireland, and the family followed several Irish traditions related to rituals and celebrations. Both parents came from working class families and believed that it was important to work hard. Their parenting practices were authoritative, and both parents had relatively high expectations that their children would perform at school, work hard, and "do the right thing."

Ellis's delivery was described as normal. As an infant and toddler, Ellis had frequent ear infections. Donna remembered Ellis as a loving and active infant and toddler, but also a colicky one. His early motor skills, such as sitting up, crawling, and learning to walk, developed normally. Ellis's early language development, such as first words, asking simple questions, and talking in sentences, seemed to be typical.

Ellis attended preschool, beginning at age four. He seemed to learn things at about the same rate as other children. No unusual or atypical behavior management problems were recalled for this time period. However, Donna reported that Ellis seemed to have more difficulty developing social skills than most other children.

At the point of referral, Donna described Ellis as angry and aggressive as well as somewhat "perfectionistic." While Donna described Ellis's mood as typical of others his age, she said that he shows intensely high levels of energy followed by periods of anger or sadness. Donna also commented that Ellis is somewhat small for his age. As Ellis seems to be very sensitive about this issue, and has been teased about his size, Donna now wonders whether Ellis struggles with feelings of low self-esteem. In support of this, Donna overheard Ellis tell his grandparents that he wanted to be the biggest student in his class, remarking, "then no one would pick on me!"

During a modified play-history interview, Don and Donna indicated that Ellis was a very imaginative and creative individual who enjoyed activities such as playing cars and building with Lego. As Ellis is an active child, they noted that he also enjoyed outside, rough-and-tumble play activities with Don. Although Ellis has a tree house and used to have friends over to play fantasy war games, Don and Donna reported that this stopped abruptly, equating this to the time that Ellis was being bullied at school. Prior to this time, Ellis seemed to take an active role when playing with other children in his neighborhood. For instance, Donna remarked that Ellis used to phone other children and invite them over to play.

Finally, a discussion about Ellis's emotional adjustment indicated that he has always displayed an "independent style." Don elaborated on this by stating that if Ellis really didn't like what the other kids were playing, and couldn't convince them to try things his way, he would either move on and play with other children or engage in his preferred play activity alone. Donna emphasized that Ellis's tendency for self-direction is a strength, although he never appeared to take advantage or dominate other children in play.

During the initial parent consultation, Donna and Don were shown the play therapy rooms. Don remarked that Ellis might find certain activities, such as puppets, "boring" or "childish." Accordingly, the therapist took additional time to learn about Ellis's play interests and capacities. The therapist also provided Donna and Don with an overview of the play therapy process, highlighting the parent consultation process as well as the nature of the parents' involvement in treatment activities. At the end of the meeting, ideas were jointly discussed concerning how the parents could prepare Ellis for coming to play therapy.

INITIAL IMPRESSIONS

During the first session, Ellis sat by himself, fidgeting with his hands. Donna was the initial spokesperson for the family, commenting that Ellis was "unsure" about coming to meet the therapist. The therapist openly acknowledged Ellis's feeling of uncertainty and then briefly provided a framework to help Ellis get a sense of what might unfold. As planned, the therapist stated that when Ellis's parents met with her, they wondered how it was that children and parents could raise their "fun-meter." This wording appeared to grab Ellis's attention; the therapist then quickly demonstrated with her arms a gauge-like meter, emphasizing that it could go up and down or sometimes could become stuck. Next, the therapist had family members guess where each other were on the fun-meter, using their arms as gauges. Ellis immediately asked to go first. In making a gauge representing his father's fun-meter, Ellis placed his gauge in the high range, remarking that it went up because his father just got a new tool for woodworking. The discussion soon moved toward fun experiences for each family member. As Don and Donna were prepared for this analogy, they also asked the question of what people do when their fun-meter becomes stuck. When asked in which ways they noticed the fun-meter getting stuck, Donna stated that she thought Ellis's meter became stuck after he was bullied at school. This provided an opening for the therapist to briefly comment on what other kids had told her about such experiences. She also emphasized that these same children were able to get "unstuck" through play activities they did together. This idea seemed to intrigue Ellis. The therapist elaborated that the playroom was a place where children get to try out all sorts of ideas and activities.

During this animated discussion, Ellis began to shift his focus to the various play objects in the therapist's office. The therapist took the opportunity to introduce her role to Ellis and explained that coming to counseling was "private but not secret." She would always check with Ellis first if she was going to talk to his parents to update them about how he was doing and that his time was private. Ellis seemed pleased with this idea. It was further explained that it was not secret time and that he could tell his parents anything he would like to about his special play time. The four hurts[1] were then shared with Ellis as the things that could not stay private, and it was explained that it was important to the therapist that Ellis was safe. Within a few minutes Ellis asked, "So do kids get to go to the playroom right away?" The therapist asked if Ellis would like to go and look around the playroom, to which he immediately said, "Yes." After a cautious start, it appeared that Ellis was ready to begin his journey in play therapy.

---

1   Lorri Yasenik coined the term the "four hurts" to refer to a way of explaining the limits of confidentiality for children and youth. The therapist can't keep the following hurts confidential if shared in a session by the child. The hurts include: 1) someone is hurting you; 2) you know someone who is being hurt; 3) you are hurting yourself; 4) you are planning to hurt someone else.

Video Case Study: Haley

PRESENTING PROBLEM

Download the case examples video and transcript from https://library.jkp.com/redeem using the code RTECPZF.

Haley is a ten-year-old, cisgendered, Grade-5 student. Sarah, Haley's mother, referred her to therapy after school staff alerted Sarah that Haley appeared increasingly "withdrawn" and seemed reluctant to go outside for recess. Teachers reported that Haley seemed lost and preoccupied. Although Haley has always been a strong student academically, teachers noted that she was completing less schoolwork during class and frequently made errors.

At home, Haley was described as a quiet child who spent long periods of time playing alone in her room. Although Haley had always enjoyed playing with her six-year-old brother, Jonathon, Haley had recently become bossy and controlling in her play. Sarah noted that this was uncharacteristic of Haley, and the situation had reached the point where Jonathon often came crying to Sarah stating, "Haley is being mean again."

Sarah reported that Haley had never been a discipline problem. During the intake interview, Sarah commented that Haley was always a "pleaser" and seemed to defer to other children's ideas when playing. Sarah also described Haley as a very sensitive child, emphasizing that she overreacts to negative feedback. Sarah further commented that Haley seemed to absorb all sorts of information. For example, Haley recently heard about a tornado warning in another part of the country and became fearful that a tornado was about to occur in her city. This worry lasted for several weeks.

During the intake interview, Sarah commented that she and her husband, Mike, parent in different ways. Sarah described herself as "tougher" than Mike. However, Sarah indicated that they work closely together as a parenting team. Further, since Haley seemed to have few behavioral difficulties, Sarah emphasized that, "There is little to manage except Haley's occasional overreactions."

Daily communication between home and school was reported. At the beginning of the Grade-5 school term, the school contacted the parents stating that Haley had been subjected to verbal teasing in class and on the playground. This was discovered one day when a teacher observed Haley standing by herself on the playground. When the teacher approached her, Haley was crying and hiding her face. Haley was reluctant to discuss this incident with her teacher. When she returned home, Sarah gently raised the issue, noting that Haley was very quiet and reserved. Eventually, Haley began to cry and informed Sarah that she had been teased since the beginning of the school term (approximately three months earlier). Once this information came to light, the parents and school put an action plan together. Part of this plan included buddying Haley with a Grade-6 student at recess, followed by periodic check-ins with Haley's

INTRODUCTION

teacher. As well, follow-up discussions occurred at home on a regular basis. As far as both the teaching staff and parents were aware, there was only one other mild teasing incident. This occurred during a line-up and Haley reported it directly to her teacher. Accordingly, the buddy system was phased out and Haley began going out for recess on her own.

Currently, Haley's teachers reported that she plays well when she is involved with just one other student. However, this tends to break down in group play situations as Haley experiences difficulties joining in. In these circumstances, Haley often moves to the periphery and either watches or plays alone.

When asked to specify desired outcomes for therapy, Sarah identified the following three goals.

- To help Haley find ways to engage her peers.
- To help Haley become stronger emotionally by taking greater risks.
- To help Haley cope with overwhelming feelings and situations.

BACKGROUND

Sarah and Mike are the biological parents of Haley and Jonathon, with Mike employed on a full-time basis. When Jonathon was school aged, Sarah began a part-time position with flexible hours. Sarah reported enjoying her re-entry into the workforce, although she found herself tired in the evenings. As weekends are often devoted to household management activities, Sarah found that she has less time to play with her children. However, Sarah noted that Mike has "really stepped up" by taking the children out for walks or to other activities in the nearby community.

Sarah was born in Canada and Mike was born in Australia. They met during a vacation when they were both in their later twenties. They come from different parenting and cultural backgrounds. Sarah reported a history of trauma (physical abuse) until her father moved and left her, her mother, and her younger sister. Mike reports no history of trauma and comes from an intact family system. The parents attend the Catholic church and Sarah is quite active in church activities. The family attends church on Sundays. Sarah is not as close to her family as she is to Mike's family. The group spends summers in Australia with Mike's family. He is the eldest of two boys and his brother is in a long-term relationship with a man named Greg. Mike's brother and partner have a close relationship with Haley and Jonathon.

During pregnancy, Sarah had no significant health problems. Immediately following the birth, Haley was healthy. As an infant and toddler, Haley experienced frequent ear infections. Sarah remembered Haley as an affectionate, observant, and calm infant and toddler. Haley's early motor skills, such as sitting up, crawling, and learning to walk, developed earlier than for most other children. Haley attended preschool, beginning at age three. Sarah recalled that Haley appeared to learn things at about the same rate as other children but seemed very slow to warm up to new situations. Under these circumstances Haley would cry easily and often refused to join the activity. Haley's reaction to the arrival of her brother, Jonathon, was described as difficult, as she became more clingy and needy of her parents' attention.

At the point of referral, Sarah and Mike described Haley as a kind and gentle child but also one who seems shy, emotional, irritable, and somewhat unhappy. Their descriptions suggested that Haley's mood varied normally. She could play quietly when asked to do so and often chose solitary play activities. Haley reported liking most school/learning activities and consistently stated that she would rather stay in and work during recess so that she didn't have to take work home. Sarah was concerned that this was becoming a pattern of avoidance for Haley.

During a modified play-history interview, Sarah and Mike indicated that Haley appeared to have a limited repertoire of play activities. She uses her dollhouse and play characters to engage in fantasy play scenarios. Together with her younger brother, Haley has also used dress-up for make-believe play. Although there are children her age who live close by, Sarah and Mike reported that Haley often chose to play with her younger brother, or alone. The exception to this is when her cousins come to visit. Sarah emphasized that Haley always followed the lead of the other children and never became the initiator. This trend was noted throughout the play history, as in preschool Haley was described as a follower during play-center activities.

The play history also revealed that Haley loved art-making activities and often drew about her experiences, positive or negative. For example, around the time of the teasing incidents, Haley's teacher found that Haley had drawn several pictures depicting children pushing and fighting.

Finally, a discussion about Haley's emotional adjustment through the play-history interview indicated that she was clingy and experienced difficulties separating when she first entered playschool. Specifically, Haley cried and became uncommunicative for over an hour when Sarah left her for the morning preschool program. This pattern did not abate for approximately three months. Mike recalled that for those occasions when he dropped Haley off at school, Haley seldom fussed and was able to transition to program activities after a few minutes.

During the initial parent consultation meeting, Sarah and Mike were shown the play therapy rooms, and the therapist provided them with an overview of the play therapy process. This included a discussion of parental roles and their involvement in treatment. Toward the end of the meeting, ideas were jointly discussed concerning ways of preparing Haley for coming to the first session.

INITIAL IMPRESSIONS

During the first session, Haley sat on the couch, positioning herself close to her mother. Mike sat on a nearby chair and made several light-hearted comments,

INTRODUCTION

interjecting humor and comfort into the meeting. After spending time during intake with Mike and Sarah, Haley's therapist Susan observed Mike as a Collaborative Parent (CP) style while Sarah seemed to be more of a Process-Focused Parent (PFP) style. Haley appeared shy and reserved, often avoiding eye contact. As discussed in the preparatory meetings, Haley brought one of her stuffed animals along for comfort; during the meeting, she focused primarily on this object.

Following a warm-up discussion about some of Haley's special activities and interests, the therapist introduced her role as one of helping parents and children, particularly when they have been trying to figure out some "tricky feelings." An analogy of feelings being like clouds was provided. Sometimes they blow in, and out again, without anyone even noticing. At other times, they kind of sneak in and stay put, because they need something to push them along. As planned, the parents took this cue and briefly stated that Haley appeared to get similar tricky feelings, and they would like to figure out ways that they, as a family, could move them along. The therapist next asked when the parents first started to notice the settling of the clouds. Sarah reported that they might have "blown in" at the beginning of Grade 5, but she didn't really notice them until she learned that Haley had been teased at school. The discussion swung around to include Haley's view of when the clouds thickened. Haley's response was polite but succinct; she quietly stated, "I don't know. It seems like they've been there for a while."

Tightly gripping her stuffed dog, Haley joined the therapist for her first look at the playroom. En route, Haley inquired about where her parents would be, even though this had been discussed prior to leaving the therapist's office. Once in the playroom, Haley tentatively looked around and visually explored some areas of the room. Once she spotted the dollhouse she remarked, "I have one almost exactly like this at home." She immediately went to the dollhouse and spent several minutes looking through the baskets of characters nearby. Haley's journey was about to begin.

KEY POINTS

- The Play Therapy Dimensions Model aims to provide practitioners with a range of tools that support an integrative approach to case conceptualization and treatment planning.
- The Play Therapy Dimensions Model diagram presents two primary dimensions: directiveness and consciousness. The two dimensions help define the therapeutic space and contribute to decision making regarding the *who, what, when, why,* and *how* of the play therapy process.
- The model has been expanded to include pre-imaginative play at the base of the diagram. Thus, there is a "bottom-up" view of the child, emphasizing

the examination of the child's development and the importance of under-standing pre-pretend play skills.

- The videos should be viewed while reading the book. The two case exam-ples videos, along with a new video demonstration of a parent feedback session, illustrate the conceptualization process and use of the clinical tools (found in the Appendices).

◉ Chapter 2 ◉

INTEGRATIVE DECISION-MAKING

The blended picture forms into a unified whole.

DO PLAY THERAPISTS NEED AN ORGANIZING FRAMEWORK?

Currently, there are burgeoning new approaches to and theories of play therapy, which creates a decision-making dilemma for play therapists. Prior to an increase in focus on integrative practice in the general field of psychotherapy, practitioners selected, from various theories, those strategies and techniques that, in the moment, appeared to be best for the client (Schaefer, 2003). This historical trend also occurred in the field of play therapy, paralleling the proliferation of theories and techniques in the literature. Historically, in a survey of play therapists, Phillips and Landreth (1995) found that an eclectic, multitheoretical orientation was, by far, the most common approach reported by respondents. Many practitioners did not adhere to a purist, one-size-fits-all orientation, and decision-making guidelines were lacking. This is similar for general psychotherapy practitioners, because they have had to work out how to integrate multitheoretical approaches as models and theories have developed (Behan, 2022; Scaturo, 2012). A confounding factor is that if play therapists continue to be truly multitheoretical, they require a model for conceptualizing and monitoring the primary therapeutic change mechanisms. LaBauve, Watts, and Kottman (2001) developed a tabular overview for approaches to play therapy to assist play therapists to understand the basic tenets of contemporary play therapy approaches and to identify the focal points of change for each. This overview provides play therapists with a comparative framework for examining the similarities and differences of play therapy approaches. This summary provides a starting point for therapists who wish to adopt an integrative versus a purely eclectic approach, as it helps identify the commonalities amongst various schools of play therapy.

Even with a comparative overview, unless there is an organizing framework, the play therapist runs the risk of adopting an atheoretical approach to treatment,

◉ 35 ◉

applying techniques in a haphazard manner which disregards underlying theory and ignores the importance of mediator and moderator variables. However, when an integrative perspective is firmly placed within a decision-making model that offers a clear conceptualization of the change mechanisms, the practitioner can flexibly and mindfully operate within several schools of play therapy.

In a therapeutic climate that increasingly focuses on time-limited and evidence-based treatments, many would argue that there is mounting pressure to become goal-focused at the expense of acknowledging the child's inner direction and drive as a central feature of the play therapy process. Others suggest that play therapists should develop practice guidelines and matching specific treatment interventions to referral problems, based on available empirical studies (Schaefer, 2003). Research lends support to the use of play therapy across a range of presenting problems. For example, LeBlanc and Ritchie (1999) conducted a meta-analysis of play therapy research, indicating that play therapy was an effective intervention regardless of the presenting problem of the child. The results suggested that two primary variables have an impact on the efficacy of play therapy: the involvement of parents in the play therapy process, and the number of therapy sessions. Bratton and Ray (2000) examined over 100 case studies documenting the efficacy of play therapy. They reported that participants consistently demonstrated more positive behavior and fewer symptomatic issues after play therapy interventions, as compared to their behavior before the play therapy interventions. A limitation of these studies is controlling the complex client–therapist–treatment interaction. Bratton *et al.* (2005) conducted a meta-analysis of 93 controlled outcome studies to assess the overall efficacy of play therapy and to determine factors that might impact its effectiveness. The effects were more positive for humanistic than for nonhumanistic treatments, and using parents in play therapy produced the largest effects. As noted by Schaefer (2003; Drewes and Schaefer, 2015), what lies at the core of this issue is our ability to define the underlying change mechanisms in successful play therapy, as well as client and therapist variables that influence treatment. This does not mean that therapists should refrain from anchoring their work to one school or model of play therapy. However, what links us together is an understanding of the importance of the therapeutic process and the underlying change mechanisms. As noted by Schaefer (2003):

> Change mechanisms are not theories—they are descriptions of observed relationships. They are more general than techniques and they are more specific than theories. They are the "if…then" relationships that tell us when to do, what to do and whom to do it to. (p.309)

The Play Therapy Dimensions Model assists the practitioner to consider the complexities inherent in change mechanisms and encourages decision-making concerning the *possible* applications of a number of theoretical approaches and techniques, tailoring these to the child.

In the field of play therapy, it has long been recognized that play, in itself, will not ordinarily produce changes for hurt or troubled children. Rather, it is the therapist's interventions and utilizations of the play that are critical (Chethik, 2000). How the therapist and child share the *therapeutic space* is central to many models of play therapy. In some models, such as Cattanach's (1992) multi-dimensional model of play therapy for working with abused children, this space is viewed as the transitional space between the child and therapist. It is described as a psychic space in keeping with Winnicott's (1971) views where the child discovers the self, and the space is used to define *me* and *not me*. In child-centered models, the use of the relationship is a defining characteristic of this space (Landreth, 2002). In other models, the use of this space and the underlying change mechanisms are conceptualized in substantially different ways. For instance, in Adlerian Play Therapy, emphasis is placed on building a relationship, as well as reorienting and re-educating the child, helping them gain insight into their lifestyle (Kottman, 2003b). In this therapeutic context, the role of the Adlerian therapist is described as active and directive.

Commonalities in goals and principles exist across the various models of play therapy. For instance, Wilson, Kendrick, and Ryan (1992) point out that there is general recognition that play therapy occurs in the context of a therapeutic relationship and that the function and symbolic meaning of children's play is central to the way children express their wishes, fantasies, conflicts, and perceptions of the world. Further, there is widespread agreement that play therapy often provides a corrective emotional experience for children, along with opportunities to develop mastery over disowned feelings. These results follow from what many recognize to be the major therapeutic powers of play, such as its communication power, its teaching power, its ego-boosting power, and the propensity for self-actualization through the safety and freedom to be oneself in play (Schaefer, 2003).

Unfortunately, debate continues to surface over the *correctness* of one model over another, placing the practitioner in the position of "choosing" one approach over another at the expense of losing sight of the child as well as the therapist's own personal orientations toward psychotherapy. The latter factor must not be underestimated; many would argue that the "personal fit" between the individual therapist and the theoretical approach is critical to the successful implementation of that approach (Cattanach, 2003; Landreth, 2002).

While an integrative approach to play therapy is of great value in guiding and informing our practice, it is simply not enough to ensure effective practice. Play therapists work in various settings and are often part of a collaborative team. In this context they are able to offer unique insights and understanding of the child or family system. This speaks to the need for the play therapist to have a solid understanding of other therapeutic modalities as well as a firm grounding in child development. Most important, the play therapist needs to constantly work on knowing themselves and use that self-understanding in the most appropriate and meaningful ways, therapeutically. Accordingly, it is assumed that most readers will have extensive academic background and experiential training in areas related to child development and family work. It is also assumed that as a practitioner in play therapy the reader will be familiar with various theoretical approaches to play therapy and is actively involved in a supervision process; if acting as a supervisor, it is assumed that a range of support mechanisms and monitoring tools are in place. To strengthen practitioner and supervisory skills, this book provides a number of tools for self-development and supervision.

INTEGRATIVE PLAY THERAPY: THE NEED FOR A FRAMEWORK FOR DECISION-MAKING

There has been much written in the adult psychotherapy literature about integrative approaches to therapy. Through the 1970s there was a proliferation of writing that contributed to the thinking about what the terms "integrative" or (as many described themselves) "eclectic" mean. Eclecticism was harshly criticized as, "a hodgepodge of inconsistent concepts and techniques" (Smith, 1982, p.802). The random use of techniques and theory was discouraged. At the same time, the use of a single school of practice was also viewed as being limited. Integrative therapy is considered to be a purposeful weaving of theory, techniques, and common factors identified across therapies (Norcross, 2005). Although being integrative requires an approach and a way to decide how to work with a client, Garfield (1994) noted that those who described their work with clients as "integrative" said that they followed what was best for their clients but described differing decision-making processes and differing theories and techniques from one another. Even with the current availability of defined integrative practice approaches, there is not enough outcome research that shows what integrative therapists do and if what they do is really that different to purist therapists (Garfield, 1994; Glass, Victor, and Arnkoff, 1993). The question is, "Do integrative therapists follow a decision-making model for their client work and if so what is it?"

The current status is that there are four main approaches of psychotherapy integration in the adult psychotherapy literature:

- *Common factors approach*, which focuses on the common underlying factors shared by different therapies, and which generally include catharsis, acquisition and practice of new behaviors, and the client's positive expectancies (Grencavage and Norcross, 1990).
- *Technical integration*, which is prescriptive in nature in that it focuses on the best treatment for the client and the presenting problem. The treatment

choice is based on research about others who present with similar issues (Lazarus, 1976).

- *Theoretical integration*, which draws on two or more theoretical approaches to therapy. Essentially, the practitioner attempts to weave different theories and techniques together to best serve the client (Wachtel, 1977).
- *Assimilative integration*, which is when the therapist begins with their core training approach to therapy, but they may borrow or select from other approaches to incorporate a new way of working with the client. The therapist is viewed as grounded in *a* theory while being flexible in their use of a range of other theories and techniques, perhaps creating new ways of working (Norcross, 2005).

Much of the play therapy literature on integrative approaches to therapy is anchored in reported case studies. This being said, some play therapists appear to be making use (knowingly or not) of the above integrative approaches to working with children. Drewes (2011) identified Kenny and Winick's (2000) use of technical eclecticism with an 11-year-old autistic girl where a sequential treatment approach was utilized; Kevin O'Connor's (2001) use of Ecosystemic Play Therapy was noted as an example of theoretical integration where he incorporates components of analytic, child-centered, cognitive, Theraplay (Jernberg, 1979) theories, as well as concepts of personality and psychopathology in his treatment planning and goal setting; Weir's (2008) use of common factors in work with an adoptive family where commonalities across play therapy treatment techniques for Reactive Attachment Disorder were utilized; and Fall's (2001) case study using assimilated integration to treat a child in a school setting. Fall used the core theory of Child-Centered Play Therapy but blended this approach with Adlerian and cognitive-behavioral theories and techniques.

Following the common factors approach to integrative therapy, Drewes (2011) points out that (in addition to therapeutic alliance, opportunity for catharsis, acquisition and practice of new behaviors, and the client's positive expectations; Grencavage and Norcross, 1990), play therapists should consider the therapeutic powers of play in work with children. Drewes (2011) included potential change agent factors such as:

self-expression, access to the unconscious, direct/indirect teaching, abreaction, stress inoculation, counterconditioning of negative affect, positive affect, sublimation, attachment and relationship enhancement, moral judgment, empathy, power/control, competence and self-control, creative problem-solving, fantasy compensation and reality testing. (p.29)

Identifying common factors across theoretical approaches to play therapy is still in process. More research will be needed to unveil commonalities. Schaefer (1999) supports the notion that the curative factors and change mechanisms in work with children are highly important to the overall effectiveness of the therapy. This being said, it would be important to examine common factors that lead to change in play therapy and any other intervening variables that increase treatment effectiveness.

Are play therapists moving closer toward integrative thinking? Rapid theory development may be encouraging play therapists to think in integrative ways. Learning a theory or two, however, does not make an integrative play therapist. There are now over 25 approaches to play therapy (and counting). It has already become overwhelming for students of play therapy to incorporate the multiple ways there are to work with children. Many play therapists who attend the Rocky Mountain Play Therapy Institute™ arrive for training without a core training approach to play therapy. At the Institute, they receive an overview of at least 12 models of play therapy with a practice/experiential focus on at least three models. This is, for some, the first exposure to the variety of ways in which play therapists approach therapy. There is little encouragement to seek comprehensive training, as the play therapy associations continue to accept hours earned at workshops that have been cobbled together to count as hours toward formal "play therapy" training requirements for certification. An eclectic approach to training will likely lead the play therapist to learn about one or two models of play therapy and a variety of techniques. The problem with this approach to training in the private sector or in universities is that, as Drewes (2011) states:

> Therefore, students graduating will call themselves eclectic, but what they are really saying is that they have been taught two different approaches (usually cognitive behavioral and Rogerian). Consequently, they are not fluid in thinking between the two theories and approaches and they do not feel well-grounded in either approach, resulting in an inability to truly integrate them. Thus, a truly integrative approach is lacking. (p.33)

Those who have been trained in a pure play therapy approach in a university setting are few, as there are not many comprehensive programs offered. Those who have come from a specific play therapy model of training tend to be clustered geographically due to living near training centers or universities that offer full training programs such as the University of North Texas. Otherwise, it is more often that those seeking training in play therapy arrive with their adult-focused academic training backgrounds, many of which have been influenced by postmodernism. These therapists generally claim to be eclectic practitioners. Coscolla *et al.* (2006) make the controversial claim that psychotherapies were developed during a culture of modernity and there has since been a cultural shift to postmodernism, which influences the psychotherapists' attitudes regarding theory. They state that eclecticism is postmodern and that integration has roots in modernism. Coscolla *et al.* use the work of Norcross and Newman (1992) to delineate the ways the two words are characterized. The terms used to describe integration include a belief in theory, a seeking to find agreement between theories, and a focus on developing better approaches and legitimization through scientific methods, while eclecticism focuses on functionality, no "grand" narratives, and everything goes, and it is based on clinical needs. This is one conceptualization and there are others who may find different anchors to differentiate the two terms. It is an interesting discussion as we are amid cultural change in the ways we philosophically view the world and how we go about understanding problems, processes, approaches, and outcomes in therapy.

Regardless of which theory, approach, model, or world view you come from, decision-making frameworks are lacking for integrative therapists. As previously noted, there are at least four approaches for integrative therapists who work with adults, which provide basic guidance without providing standard approaches to decision-making. However, the ways in which the integrative approaches are viewed differ greatly from therapist to therapist. Stricker (2010) argues that the current categorizations for integrative therapies (although helpful) have blurry boundaries for research purposes. The more detail that is put forward, the more complex and hazier the boundaries between the integrative approaches become. Stricker claims that there may be two ways to move ahead: 1) expand the categories, or 2) abandon the categories. In other words, provide more clarification categorically or simplify the way to view integrative therapy. Practitioners and researchers are looking for ways to explore integrative therapy in order to identify common pathways to this way of working with clients. Without a decision-making process that is relatively standard, integrative play therapy may continue to be at risk of slipping back to looking more like eclecticism.

PLAY THERAPY DIMENSIONS MODEL: A DECISION GUIDE FOR INTEGRATIVE PLAY THERAPISTS

The Play Therapy Dimensions Model provides a fluid process for decision-making. There are a number of scales and tools for the play therapist to use to track their continual decision-making process. These tools provide all play therapists with a way to identify and manage their ongoing clinical decisions. Appendices A, B, and C assist in regular systematic tracking. One of the main obstacles to research in integrative therapy is that integrative psychotherapy can be highly complex and that decisions regarding treatment are being made on a continual basis throughout therapy (Beutler, Consoli, and Williams, 1995). Beutler *et al.* (1995) also note that the client characteristics change over the course of treatment, which shifts the way in which treatment is delivered. The Child Moderating Factors Scale (Appendix A) helps the play therapist to track these ongoing shifts and changes in their child client. The Degree of Immersion: Therapist Use of Self Scale (Appendix B) tracks session-by-session ways the therapist makes use of the self with the client and also asks for a description of the client's response to the therapist's use of self. Because the tool is not about techniques, it helps a range of play therapists to be aware of the *how* of the process rather than the *what*. Additionally, Figures 1.1 and 3.1–3.3 provide a visual template of the dimensions of consciousness and directiveness, which assist the therapist to identify therapeutic movement during sessions and across sessions. Visual mapping of therapy activities raises the awareness of the presence of integrative play therapy decision-making.

The Play Therapy Dimensions Model is useful for qualitative, quantitative, or mixed-methods research due to the establishment of a way of systematic recording of the play therapy processes at four levels: 1) child characteristics, 2) therapist characteristics (including therapist skill level), 3) therapist use of self (and corresponding child client responses), and 4) session tracking and observation form (including play skills, identification of work in consciousness and directiveness dimensions, development, play process, relational and affective markers, play themes, and a summary). Each of the recording forms looks at a different part of the play therapy process and identifies when changes in direction, intensity, directiveness, or consciousness in play therapy should shift. How does the therapist "decide" to be more integrative? The child client directs the changes (verbally, non-verbally, or metaphorically through the play). Although adult models of therapy have addressed a client-driven focus (Miller, Duncan, and Hubble, 2005) whereby the wishes and needs of the client ascend the theoretical and technical approaches of the therapist, this has not been as clearly identified in the child therapy literature. A possible explanation for this difference is the developmental and inherent power differences between the therapist and child and the assumption that the child cannot express themselves in the ways an adult client can.

HOW DO INTEGRATIVE THERAPISTS MAKE DECISIONS?

There is no research to support whether therapists consciously shift from utilizing a primary model of therapy to working in an integrative way (Schottenbauer, *et al.*, 2007). Specific guidance in therapeutic decision-making was one of the goals of the Play Therapy Dimensions Model for those working with children. In the adult literature, authors concur that a common theory for decision-making processes for therapists would be valuable (Beutler and Clarkin, 1990; Beutler *et al.*, 1995; Street, Niederehe, and Lebowitz, 2000), but currently there is no common adult-based decision-making process for psychotherapists. Schottenbauer *et al.* (2007) note that there are a few factors that assist the adult therapist to make decisions to be more integrative, such as if the client becomes stuck during treatment or if the therapist thinks there is a more efficient way to meet the same goals to cut the cost of therapy; or as Marmar (1990) adds, "individual patient differences, phase of therapy, patient state, patient capacity for absorption of process, or related contextual problems" (p.267) may influence more integrative ways of working with a client. The Play Therapy Dimensions Model is based on these types of contextual considerations for the child client. We concur with Zuber (2000) who refers to patients' varied ways of describing their problems, which in turn affects the decision-making of the therapist regarding how to work with the patient. The importance of client input regarding clinical intervention is highlighted. The same thinking can be applied to work with children, except their "explanations" of their problems are presented in verbal, non-verbal, and metaphorical ways in play and their input is often more non-verbal. Early on, we realized the skill set for the play therapist needed to be broadened from that of being an adult therapist to working with children. Therapists needed assistance to know what they were looking for in their work with the child so that they could address the unique presentations and preferences of the child. Otherwise, the therapy interventions would likely be driven by therapist preferences and parent or third-party expectations.

DO DECISION-MAKING THEORIES DESIGNED FOR ADULTS FIT FOR PLAY THERAPISTS?

There are well-known and emerging decision-making theoretical frameworks for adult integrative therapists. The well-known subjective *utility theory* consists of analyzing decisions by reviewing all possible outcomes, assigning probabilities to each, and choosing the best decisions with which to proceed. The problem with this approach is that it is biased, it can be overly inclusive, it is not based in the moment, and therapeutic decision-making is not always a rational task to be sorted in advance of the process (Schottenbauer *et al.*, 2007).

Emerging decision-making approaches identified by Schottenbauer *et al.* include information-processing theory and bounded rationality theory. *Information-processing theory* uses symbolic and qualitative reasoning derived from transcripts from therapists that provides, as Elstein (1988) states, "what knowledge structures, cognitive operations, and rule structures are necessary and sufficient to produce clinical reasoning" (p.19). Through this analysis, therapists may be able to understand how their original theoretical orientation and the theories and techniques that were brought into the therapy interact. Schottenbauer *et al.* ponder, "whether clinicians using psychotherapy integration use more strategies, or more complex strategies, than clinicians using pure-form therapies" (2007, p.233).

Bounded rationality (although not a new construct) as discussed by Gigerenzer (2001) is a decision-making process that takes note of the practical limitations for therapists such as resources, time and knowledge, and computational capacities—which differs from the boundlessness of utility theory. The term "satisficing" is used to describe the process of gathering information in a timely way and making decisions. The decisions are made using search rules (determining alternative actions and gathering cues), and stopping rules (one or more criteria is met before a search for alternatives is sought and a different course of action or decision is made). Medical model diagnostics use stopping rules by listing criteria or characteristics to choose from in order to make a diagnosis or move on to another way of viewing the client situation. Decision rules are made based on heuristics and on the limitations of time and information available about the client. "The theory of bounded rationality considers three basic elements relevant to the decision-making task: psychological plausibility, ecological rationality and domain specificity" (Schottenbauer *et al.*, 2007, p.235).

Psychological plausibility is a reasoning process that takes into consideration the therapist's cognitive and emotional factors that contribute to decision-making when time, knowledge, and computational capacity are limited. The review by Schottenbauer *et al.* (2007) is of interest as they comment on the emotional factors that play a part in decision-making. It stands to reason that therapist use of self-evaluation must be included in a conscious way, which is (in part) why Appendix B (Degree of Immersion: Therapist Use of Self Scale) was developed. If therapist emotionality is viewed as one of the decision-making factors, the therapist must make sense as to how they are making use of themselves. Seymour (2011) points out, "Considering the importance of therapist factors identified in common factors research, one possible method would be to include the incorporation of self of therapist work with studies on integrative psychotherapy" (p.13).

Ecological rationality describes a decision-making element that meets the environmental situation. Because play therapists work with children, parents, and systems, there is a continual interaction between the therapist, the client, and client system. Constant adjustment to the environment and the needs of the client is necessary. The Play Therapy Dimensions Model provides a method for the therapist to collect this information through a tracking system. This frees the therapist to move freely in the moment and to evaluate the process along the way. Appendix A (Child Moderating Factors Scale) helps the therapist to evaluate child characteristics, therapist characteristics, and the interactions between them. The focus on client characteristics can assist the integrative play therapist to be discerning about the techniques they choose to use. Schottenbauer *et al.*'s (2007) reflect on the work of Beutler and Martin (2000): "More recent research has shown that variables relevant to choosing therapeutic techniques can be grouped into four categories, including patient predisposing variable, treatment context, relationship qualities and interventions, and selection of the strategies and techniques that best fit the patient" (p.230).

According to Schottenbauer *et al.*, domain specificity is related to how assessment and treatment generalizes from client to client and focuses on the degree of therapist integration. Domain specificity is based on heuristics and tailoring approaches of therapy to the client. Domain specificity is addressed in the Play Therapy Dimensions Model. Appendix C (Tracking and Observation Form) is more than just a checklist, as it leads the therapist through several considerations that allow for deeper conceptualization, client to client. Comparing various client profiles and clinical interventions as related to presenting issues is possible with this tool. Play therapists who regularly use the tool deepen their conceptualizing ability and increase their ability to tailor their interventions in a more effective, less time-consuming way with their child clients.

The above decision-making theories may be familiar to play therapists due to initial training exposure to therapy with adults. The theories provide useful guidelines for therapists to draw on when considering integrative play therapy. Of particular interest to us is how these theories fit with the Play Therapy Dimensions Model's structured tools. The bounded rationality theory of decision-making appears to offer some theoretical direction to the Play Therapy Dimensions Model's decision-making structures. The difference that theory makes is that it suggests where to focus. The point that bounded rationality theory makes is that therapists could not possibly process all the information about a person or situation—even if they had access to it all. Given time and different pieces of information, a person may make different decisions, but they would still have to select information and use some rules to do so. Bounded rationality theory supports the development of techniques, habits, and standard operating procedures to facilitate decision-making. The theory also sheds light on the cues therapists use to consider one direction over another in their work with clients. Elements of the theory appear to drive the intended use of the Play Therapy Dimensions Model's structured tools. The therapist can optimize their treatment decisions through the ongoing recording of observations of self and other, the tracking of the play therapy process across the dimensions of consciousness and directiveness, and the therapeutic interaction between these areas.

Generally, we have found that play therapists bring a wide variety of therapy skills and experience to their work with children. As trainers, it became clear to us that it was difficult for play therapists to "hold" and later process the incoming information gathered during play therapy sessions without the use of tools to anchor their experience. Therapists needed a way to observe and record the play therapy process in order to feel that they could evaluate the decisions they were making (either intuitively or consciously). The result of consistent use of the structured forms is that therapists began to make better decisions because they had a framework through which to evaluate their work. They could get feedback in supervision in new ways once they could use a shared language with which to speak to the supervisor about what was happening. They could make better plans and provide broader feedback to third parties. The best part of the process is that the Play Therapy Dimensions Model found a way to be inclusive to all theories and models of play therapy.

In summary, when you shift the way you are working with a child, it is important to consider the particular play therapy theories you are drawing on so that you can identify *how* you are following an integrative approach. It is equally important to look to the literature to identify an approach to integrative therapy and to identify your decision-making theory. The Play Therapy Dimensions Model provides a number of tools and structured forms (see Appendices A, B, and C), as well as a conceptualization diagram (see Figure 1.1), to assist you to be systematic in your work with children. The information gathered from these tools may also be used for evaluative or research purposes. It will not matter what approach to integration you choose; the structure will help you become a more effective practitioner and decision-maker.

KEY POINTS

- Practitioners are encouraged to consider the complexities inherent in change mechanisms and to make use of an organizing framework, such as the Play Therapy Dimensions Model.
- There are four main approaches to psychotherapy integration: common factors approach, technical integration, theoretical integration, and assimilative integration.
- There are both well-known and emerging decision-making frameworks for adult integrative therapists. The Play Therapy Dimensions Model draws upon the bounded rationality framework. This framework assists play therapist in examining structures and tools, such as the Tracking and Observation Form (Appendix C) for case conceptualization and decision-making in the realms of ecological rationality, psychological plausibility, and domain specificity.

◎ Chapter 3 ◎

PLAY THERAPY DIMENSIONS MODEL

An Overview

The crossroads intersect and lead us in new directions.

The Play Therapy Dimensions Model is an outgrowth of many years of clinical experience and is our attempt to integrate various models, approaches, and theories to child and play therapy. Our philosophy is that children's needs are best met through specialized child therapy approaches, versus adapting adult models to children. We strongly believe in the inner wisdom of the child, while at the same time recognizing the central role of the therapeutic relationship in facilitating change and optimizing growth. A diagram of the Play Therapy Dimensions Model is shown in Figure 3.1. A copy of this diagram can be downloaded from https://library.jkp.com/redeem using the code RTECPZF.

The model is defined as integrative and is intended to provide a way for the therapist to conceptualize the play therapy process. It is useful to most play therapists in that it allows for the reflection on and the use of numerous play therapy theories and models. The Play Therapy Dimensions Model is a decision-making and treatment-planning tool. It guides the therapist to identify the critical elements of the play therapy process. There are three fundamental overriding assumptions: first, each child is unique regarding their skills and abilities; second, all children follow a common developmental pathway; and third, the play therapist has a central role in facilitating change and optimizing growth. Specifically, the goal of the model is to aid play therapists to answer the *who, what, when, why,* and *how* of the play therapy process.

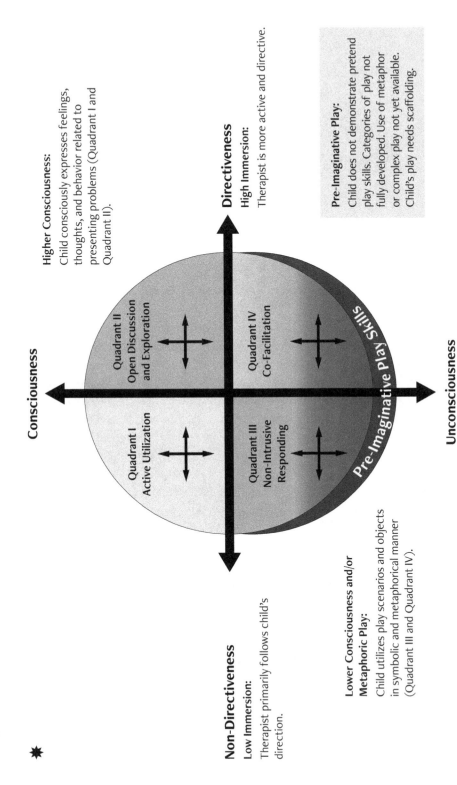

FIGURE 3.1: FULL PLAY THERAPY DIMENSIONS MODEL DIAGRAM

CONSCIOUSNESS DIMENSION AND PRE-IMAGINATIVE PLAY SKILLS

We can't assume all children have fully developed imaginative play skills. As an added feature to the Play Therapy Dimensions Model, consideration has been given to children who for reasons related to developmental issues, neurodiversity presentations, and/or trauma-related interruptions may be considered to be working at the bottom part of the diagram. Some children are missing discrete play skills. To fully "play" using metaphor, children need to have mastered a series of early play skills. Discrete skills such as sensory play, exploratory play, manipulative play, construction play, relational play, cause and effect play, imitative play, etc., all build somewhat hierarchically to create a cumulative skill set that when put together creates the foundation for imaginative play (Linder, 2008; Stagnitti, 2021). Some children present with limited ability to use play materials which means that the play therapist would work differently and not expect that a child may drive and direct metaphorical complex play in a play therapy setting.

The Play Therapy Dimensions Model is a bottom-up model of thinking (Gaskill and Perry, 2014). Some children will need their play purposefully scaffolded and therefore there is a grayscale bleed in the diagram that filters up from the Pre-Imaginative Play Skills half-moon cradle at the bottom of the diagram. The bottom of the diagram is the foundation for all play. Children presenting with limitations in their play skills will require a play therapist who will assess what may be missing and then purposefully intervene, for example by demonstrating play actions and waiting for the possibility for imitation play. A play therapist may also provide sensory materials for children who have had interruptions due to trauma and adopt a follow-lead-follow approach to working with a child. For children diagnosed with Autism Spectrum Disorder (DSM-5: American Psychiatric Association, 2013), a careful assessment of play skills would be indicated so the therapist could identify what materials would be most helpful to assist in the scaffolding process (Stagnitti, 2021). This would lead the therapist into immediately thinking about degrees of directiveness in terms of use of self as well as what materials to have available for the child.

Children who need their play scaffolded with the assistance of a play therapist are working at lower levels of consciousness and are therefore observed working with a therapist at the bottom parts of the diagram. The emergence of "self" and self in relationship with others where shared meaning is necessary may not be present yet for the child. This awareness is necessary for children to be observed as playing at higher degrees of consciousness. Stagnitti (2021) refers to the critical play skills that increase a child's development of self, such as understanding play scripts, sequencing of play actions, object substitution, doll/teddy/character play, role-play, and social pretend play. Children also need to be able to, "describe their play, attribute properties

● 49 ●

to objects in play, refer to absent objects, problem-solve in the play and predict what will happen next" (Stagnitti, 2021, p.14). Play leads all development.

TWO PRIMARY DIMENSIONS

The Play Therapy Dimensions Model identifies two primary dimensions: consciousness and directiveness. The *consciousness* dimension reflects the child's representation of consciousness in play, while the *directiveness* dimension relates to the degree of immersion and level of interpretation of the play therapist. Each dimension will be explored.

The *consciousness dimension* (Figure 3.2) is represented by the child's play activities and verbalizations. For many children there is a need for emotional distance from the issues they are attempting to reorganize. There is often a weaving process, representing movement up and down this dimension, moving from greater levels of consciousness to lesser levels or vice versa. The child's play could be very direct and literal, accompanied by verbalizations, indicating that the child is working with a certain level of conscious awareness. At other times, the child needs distance and protection from troublesome thoughts or feelings and utilizes play scenarios and objects in a less conscious and more symbolic manner.

Wilson *et al.* (1992) refer to the dimension of consciousness in relation to symbolic play and its role in play therapy. They refer to Piaget's (1977) developmental theories of adaptation, assimilation, and accommodation in relation to symbolic play. When children experience disruption through an outside experience, their mental schemas may be distorted and conflicted in relation to the way they see themselves and/or others. Through symbolic play, dissociated thoughts and feelings can be made conscious. Symbols used in play can assist in the organization of cognitive schemas, and the child may begin to assimilate new possibilities into a past representation, which in turn, helps the child grow and change. The capacity for conscious "awareness" for children must be viewed from a developmental perspective. The younger the child, the less likely it is that the child will represent awareness in a direct manner because language and cognitive schemas are still developing. Wilson *et al.* (1992) note:

> the level at which therapeutic insight occurs in young children (and indeed, in older children and adults at times) will be largely at a semi-conscious or experiential level, rather than a cognitive level; often the symbols will have private meaning rather than social meaning. (p.35)

We would be remiss to refer to the consciousness dimension without acknowledging the psychodynamic theorists and Jungian Analytical Play Therapy (Peery, 2003). Although children may not always be consciously aware of it, they project internal energy onto the play objects. The objects or play materials may then symbolize those energies. What the therapist chooses to do with those representations is another question. A play therapist influenced by Jungian constructs will identify conscious and unconscious influences and, at times during the play, make interpretive comments and identify various themes. The term "deintegration" would be used to indicate a possible regression to access deeper unconscious material. Whether a therapist adheres to a theoretical perspective that fully explores the level of consciousness of a child client or not, all therapists make decisions about initiating facilitative comments in addition to deciding if, when, why, and how to enter the play with the child.

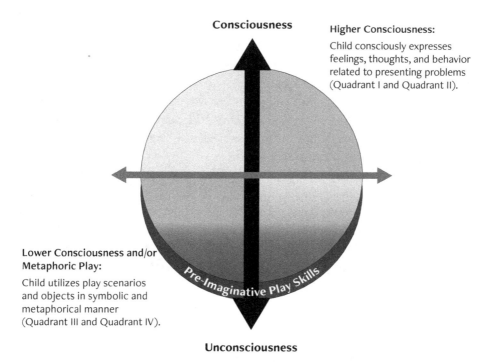

FIGURE 3.2: CONSCIOUSNESS DIMENSION

Those working with the consciousness dimension need to be aware of the coping strategies utilized by children who have experienced traumatic occurrences, for instance, life-threatening experiences. Pynoos and Eth (1986) outlined the following observable coping strategies in their study of children who had witnessed homicide: repression, fixation on the trauma, displacement, denial-in-fantasy (child imagines a positive outcome rather than the traumatic one), and identification (child identifies themselves with a parent or helper figure). Terr (1994) observed compulsive repetition of the abduction scene in her description of sessions with the children of Chowchilla, who had been buried alive in their school bus.

Decisions about facilitating greater degrees of conscious representation of dissociated thoughts and feelings in the play are critical. Very directive play therapists may stay with the symbolic representation of the play but begin to name possible feelings, behaviors, and future actions during the play session. Others may structure play activities for the child as related to the interrupting events. Some children enter therapy and alert the therapist to the fact that they need to openly explore and directly talk about their worries or concerns as in the case of Annie. During the sessions, Annie would often stop her play activities and tell stories about how her sister was mean and hurt her. The therapist decided to help Annie directly explore her feelings about her sister by asking her to draw a picture of a time she remembered her sister acting in a "mean way." Annie's first drawing was a picture of her in her bed and her sister touching her in a sexual way. If the therapist had not followed Annie's lead in wanting to talk about her sister, the therapist may have missed an opportunity for her to fully disclose what was happening with her sister.

Those working on the lower end of the consciousness continuum (Figure 3.2) would not interrupt the child's process; rather, they would follow the child's lead and trust the inner drive of the child to reorganize their experience(s) without using interpretive comments to bring the issues to consciousness.

The *directiveness dimension* (Figure 3.3) represents the therapist's activity with respect to the degree of immersion and level of interpretation. Immersion relates to the degree to which the therapist enters and directs the play. At the lowest level of directiveness, the therapist is tracking the play through observation and reflection, and is not actually involved in interactive play with the child. At the high end, the therapist has entered the play as a co-facilitator, and is actively taking part in elaborating and extending the play.

In Figure 3.3, a therapist working on the far-left side of the diagram would be least immersed in the play, and the child would be observed as fully directing the play. Many play therapists have been trained in non-directive approaches. For example, play therapy pioneers such as Axline (1969) followed a Rogerian approach to play therapy (Rogers, 1951). Axline described the principles of the relationship between the child and therapist, which emphasized the *child's* role in making decisions and eliciting change. In reviewing this non-directive approach:

> The therapist does not attempt to direct the child's actions or conversation in any manner. The therapist does not attempt to hurry the therapy along, and the therapist establishes only those limitations that are necessary to anchor the therapy to the world of reality and to make the children aware of their responsibility in the relationship. (Cattanach, 2003, p.50)

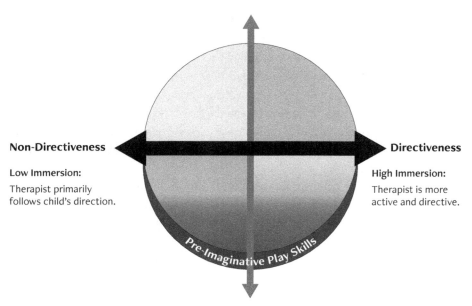

FIGURE 3.3: DIRECTIVENESS DIMENSION

Other practitioners such as Landreth and Sweeney (1999) further emphasize Axline's non-directive work when describing the child-centered approach to play therapy. They focus on the person of the child, the non-diagnostic, non-prescriptive involvement of the therapist, and highlight the innate capacity of children to direct their own growth and healing. Child-Centered Play Therapy is philosophically based, and the therapist works to understand the *child's* perception of their reality, rather than to directly inject the therapist's view of the child's reality. As with Axline (1969), Landreth (2002) follows the Rogerian personality constructs of: 1) the person, 2) the phenomenal field, and 3) the self. These theorists, among others, describe the hallmarks of the non-directive end of the directiveness dimension.

On the far-right side of Figure 3.3, the therapist would be viewed as being fully immersed as evidenced by the child *and* therapist's involvement in a play activity structured by the therapist. Although defined as less "directive" and more "active" by Kottman (2003a, 2020), Adlerian Play Therapy demonstrates the directiveness dimension in that as therapy progresses, the Adlerian play therapist may initially work with the child non-directively, and over time work more directively by modeling and teaching prosocial skills to aid the child in connecting with others. Adler (1937, 1954, 1958) believed that people are socially embedded, goal-directed, subjective, and creative. Therapeutic activities may include family drawing techniques, asking the child questions about early recollections, helping the child gain personal insight, and the use of metacommunication (where the therapist makes a direct interpretation about an observed interactional pattern). Structured phases highlight this play therapy approach, differentiating these activities from the non-structured, non-directive approaches of the Rogerian-influenced play therapists.

Other theoretical approaches to play therapy, such as Gestalt Play Therapy (Oaklander, 2003), Theraplay (Munns, 2000), Ecosystemic Play Therapy (O'Connor, 1997), Cognitive-Behavioral Play Therapy, (Knell, 1999, 2003), and Prescriptive Play Therapy (Schaefer, 2003), may be represented by the far-right end of the directiveness dimension. Of course, as the play therapist makes decisions throughout the play process, the degree of directiveness and therapist immersion in the play may shift in either direction.

Relationships are two way, as is demonstrated by the directiveness dimension. Structuring a portion of the play interaction does not necessarily undermine the entire play therapy process. There are times when the child needs to choose and direct the play activity. However, there are also times when children become immobilized and look for the therapist to provide structure or direction. The freedom to view directiveness on a continuum allows the play therapist to quickly weave in and out of play roles and activities, providing movement along the directiveness dimension. When the therapist works in a purposeful or strategic manner, the child may be able to integrate or utilize the therapeutic intervention in a helpful way through tension relief, problem-solving, or new ways of seeing the self. This exemplifies the power of the interactive nature of human relationships in the play therapy setting.

THE FOUR QUADRANTS

The following briefly describes the four quadrants of the Play Therapy Dimensions Model displayed in Figures 1.1 and 3.1. The quadrants provide an organizing structure for play therapists. No matter what theoretical orientation therapists primarily work within, they will be able to identify the levels of their directiveness, immersion, and the degree to which they facilitate the child's conscious awareness of emerging play themes and activities. At first glance, one may interpret the four quadrants as a means to identify different ways to practice as a play therapist. Although this is achieved, the four quadrants also provide a window into the possibility of using many play therapy models and interventions during a session or series of sessions. The same therapist may work in all four quadrants depending on the style of the child, the presenting need, the capacity for play, and the child's developmental stage. The four quadrants signify a model of possible movement. The therapy process could begin in any quadrant depending on the decision-making variables. There is no prescribed order.

Quadrant I: Active Utilization (Conscious/Non-Directive)

In the upper left corner of Figure 1.1, Quadrant I, *Active Utilization* is identified. In this quadrant, the child initiates the play using their own metaphors, symbols, and/or concrete verbalizations. This quadrant is placed in a more non-directive yet conscious position on the diagram. It is different to working in Quadrant III (which is also on the left side of the diagram) due to the intermittent interpretive comments initiated by the therapist that trigger conscious responses from the child. The therapist at various points enters the play with the child and expands the play into the realm of conscious awareness. *Active Utilization* is typically entered into in a brief, time-sensitive way. It is in this quadrant that a model of interpretation is valuable to have. Those therapists who value conscious awareness, believe in the importance of interpretive comments, and think they have a purposeful role in helping children to reorganize dissociated affect, behaviors, and thoughts will find themselves periodically working in this quadrant.

Quadrant II: Open Discussion and Exploration (Conscious/Directive)

Quadrant II, located in the upper right corner of Figure 1.1, is *Open Discussion and Exploration*. A therapist working in this quadrant would be observed as initiating and structuring a play activity relative to a child's presenting problem. A child may have been referred for a particular issue such as self-control, anxiety, depression, sexual abuse, or aggression, and the therapist will introduce the child to concrete, highly conscious interventions. When working in this quadrant, the therapist is primarily utilizing a developmentally sensitive, cognitive play therapy approach, and will engage in conscious processing of the child's presenting issue. Structured play-based activities may include therapeutic board games, drawing exercises, externalizing activities, role-playing, sandplay re-enactment, feeling card games, etc. The therapist may choose to work in this quadrant when a child needs more structure or feeling language, or if the child has been unable to reorganize a traumatic event through the normal course of play. Quadrant II is considered the place where therapists are observed as introducing the highest degree of consciousness and directiveness to the child. Some play therapists were trained to provide direction and structured activities as a means of intervening with children and may primarily work in this quadrant.

Quadrant III: Non-Intrusive Responding (Unconscious/Non-Directive)

Non-Intrusive Responding is situated in Quadrant III of Figure 1.1. A therapist is working in this quadrant when the child is observed initiating and completely directing the play. If a play therapist works primarily in this quadrant, the play is viewed as having intrinsic value and is process oriented. The therapist generally facilitates the play by following the child's lead. The therapist may engage in tracking responses, such as "now the baby is getting fed," or make reflective statements about a character or a feeling state. The therapist does not attempt to interpret, talk about what is happening, or bring issues or themes up in a conscious way with the child. Depending on the orientation of the therapist, they may or may not join the play when requested to do so by the child. If the therapist joins the play because of an invitation from the child, they take all direction from the child as to how to play their character, including what the character should say. Much emphasis is placed on the inner abilities of the child to process traumatic or stressful matters through the play without the *structured* intervention of the therapist. The therapist remains fully present and observant and tracks the sequences and themes in the child's play for reflection and analysis outside of the session.

It would appear that the number of therapists who have been primarily trained in Directive Play Therapy is roughly equal to those who have been trained in Non-Directive Play Therapy approaches. The Play Therapy Dimensions Model views both directive and Non-Directive Therapy approaches as important and useful and, depending on the child and therapist, they are sometimes utilized by the same therapist in a given session.

Quadrant IV: Co-Facilitation (Unconscious/Directive)

Quadrant IV, *Co-Facilitation*, can be viewed in the lower right corner of Figure 1.1. Initially the child is observed as directing the play. Therapist activity in this quadrant differentiates this quadrant from all of the others. It is here that the therapist has either entered the play at the invitation of the child or entered a character to assist in elaborating the play. The therapist has observed and tracked several themes and patterns and makes the decision to test a hypothesis or elaborate the play by inserting comments, actions, and soft interpretations in the context of the play. *Staying in the play* and elaborating the play to aid the child to interrupt looping (circular, incomplete segments of play) or compulsive repetition is what differentiates this quadrant from the others. Therapist activities are more directive than Quadrant III, but the therapist never attempts to directly discuss or interpret the play with the child in a conscious manner. Therapists may test their hypotheses about what they believe a child may be trying to portray or potentially disclose through their play characters or actions. The therapist may introduce new characters (not directed for use by the child) as helper figures or helpless figures, or they may use more than one character to demonstrate a child's inner conflict. The goal of working in this quadrant is to become a co-facilitator of the play in order to open new avenues for the child to express, process, and internally differentiate emotions and experiences. When observing children playing with one another, this occurs naturally. Each child adds to and elaborates the other's play. They weave a story and project into it new ideas, themes, conflicts, and resolutions. It is the interactive relational nature of play that appears to make it fun. Activity in this quadrant is most closely associated with staying in the fantasy and symbolism of children's play.

FACTORS RELATED TO MOVEMENT BETWEEN QUADRANTS

The Play Therapy Dimensions Model helps therapists to consider movement from their original point of intervention or approach to other intervention possibilities. Many therapists approach therapy from a specific play therapy orientation and, therefore, begin their therapy in a particular quadrant. Some play therapists, such as Child-Centered play therapists (Landreth, 2002, 2012; Landreth and Sweeney, 1999) would remain working in that quadrant due to strong philosophical underpinnings that direct them to do so. The model does not *presume* that movement has to occur; rather, the Play Therapy Dimensions Model views all theoretical orientations as important and valid and is therefore meant to help therapists identify and evaluate their activities with children. For instance, if a therapist were practicing Child-Centered Play Therapy and therefore worked solely in Quadrant III, this would be considered a conscious use of self in the realm of therapeutic possibilities.

The Play Therapy Dimensions Model, rather than intending to suggest that therapists must identify the self as primarily working in one of the four quadrants, invites them to view their therapeutic activities as dynamic and based on a number of factors such as the stage of the therapeutic process, responses of the child to the therapist, the child's play skills, the child's drive and direction in therapy, the context of the presenting issue, and timelines and system parameters. The model suggests that therapists can but do not have to restrict themselves to a single approach to practice; rather, they may view their roles and use of self in the play sessions as continual and evolving, session to session, moment to moment. The model allows for therapists to use a number of styles of interventions with children and elaborates ideas presented in Prescriptive Play Therapy (Schaefer, 2003). Schaefer refers to the idea of incorporating the theories and techniques of a variety of schools of play therapy theory and practice. Prescriptive play therapists are encouraged to utilize diverse play therapy models and related interventions in order to address a spectrum of presenting issues and problems. The therapist would then draw on their broad knowledge, as well as on evidence-based research, to construct an individualized treatment plan. Activities related to case conceptualization are then chosen.

The Play Therapy Dimensions Model takes into consideration the arguments put forth by Prescriptive Play Therapy and provides a view of the play therapy *process* if a therapist were to make use of the self along a continuum of possibilities. It is a way for therapists to identify the *who, what, when, why,* and *how* of the play therapy process on a continual basis. A clinician viewing herself on video would be able to track the use of self and identify what quadrant she was working in at any given point in a session and why. The clinician would also be able to examine her own movement between quadrants by evaluating such things as the degree to which she is directive or interpretive.

DEGREE OF REORGANIZATION: THE CHILD'S PROCESS

How does the therapist know when a child is progressing in play therapy? Most practitioners working with children would say they may never know the exact variables contributing to a child's reintegration, reorganization, or processing, and in fact, it may not be possible or necessary to know. Of necessity is to know the indicators of *movement* toward reorganization in play therapy. A common goal in play therapy appears to be to help children reorganize and reassimilate (or assimilate for the first time) various thoughts, feelings, and behaviors toward the end of personal empowerment and optimal growth and development. Goldfried (1998) in his survey of 12 different therapeutic approaches claimed the corrective experience was viewed similarly as essential, crucial, basic, and critical to the change process. The Play Therapy Dimensions Model can provide a framework for observing and tracking the child's reorganizing and integration process.

Each of the four quadrants is identified by the therapist's activities and the child's direction and level of consciousness during the play therapy session. Even when a therapist more highly identifies with one of the four quadrants, a continuum of directiveness and consciousness exists within that quadrant. The Play Therapy Dimensions Model provides a road map for observing and identifying the child's goals and drives. There is an intersection between the dimensions of directiveness and non-directiveness and consciousness and unconsciousness. It is this intersection that provides the therapist with a way to categorize what is occurring and respond accordingly during the session. It is possible to optimize the flow of reorganization when considering the activities typically utilized in another quadrant. Take, for instance, the child who has been directing a highly metaphorical play scene (Quadrant III, *Non-Intrusive Responding*) and suddenly exits the metaphorical play and begins to talk to the therapist directly about her life and some specific circumstances. The therapist may choose to move from Quadrant III to Quadrant II, *Open Discussion and Exploration*. The Play Therapy Dimensions Model supports movement between quadrants during sessions if the therapist has a sound therapeutic reason to do so and if the client's needs, capacity, and development are considered. Play therapists cannot typically prescribe therapeutic movement prior to a session; rather, it is during a session that the therapist must remain flexible and available to meet the client's needs. For example, a child may suddenly disclose abuse that was never reported at the intake interview. In most jurisdictions there will be little choice but to move to Quadrant II to assist the child to express what they can about their circumstances. Within the same session, the therapist may move back to Quadrant III, *Non-Intrusive Responding*, or Quadrant IV, *Co-Facilitation*.

Whatever direction is chosen, the therapist has a role in assisting in the reorganization process. Rigidly remaining in one quadrant or in one style of therapy may not aid the client in optimizing their flow of reorganization. Frances, Clarkin, and Perry

(1984) describe the concept of differential therapeutics and point out that clients are unique and that one therapeutic approach or intervention may not be effective for everyone. Access to a variety of ways of working with an array of presenting problems will increase efficacy.

The child will inform the therapist of their integration process in both direct and indirect ways. Some children, as in the example above, present with a need to directly approach their issues or concerns and look for direct feedback from the therapist. They may be demonstrating a capacity and need for conscious awareness. Others will demonstrate a level of fragility or defensiveness that requires time and a child-directed approach to reach the same end. Reorganization can happen in many ways and does not always require direct discussion or for matters to be brought to conscious awareness and generalized in some way. Some therapists, however, believe that changes must also occur at the verbal and cognitive levels (in addition to the symbolic play experience), and this is partly achieved by encouragement of insight and a variety of levels of problem-solving (O'Connor, 2000). Children generally process and integrate new learning and meaning through play experiences. Some have more difficulty than others in gaining all that they need through child-directed play due to a variance in the level of their play skills. Other factors to consider when assessing for reorganization include tracking repetitive themes, tracking incomplete play segments, and identifying repetitive loops that lack resolution or closure. If these factors are observed, the therapist may choose to work in another quadrant, either momentarily or for an entire session or series of sessions. These are the decisions of play therapists, regardless of their original training.

The therapists' use of self is often reflected by the nature of their involvement in the play. There are different degrees of therapist immersion as represented by what is outwardly observed regarding the therapist's activities and behaviors during a play session. During a given therapy session, is the therapist *in* the interactive play experience? Or is the therapist reflectively present and not actually engaged in the play itself? There is no "correct" version of immersion; rather the practitioner must be able to decide when, how, and to what degree to immerse the self in order to facilitate client growth and change. The Degree of Immersion: Therapist Use of Self Scale (Appendix B) identifies five categories of immersion and is described in Chapter 13.

Each approach to play therapy describes the *role* of the play therapist. Inherent in these role descriptions are indications and contraindications for the degree of therapist immersion in the therapeutic process. O'Connor (2000), in describing the role of the play therapist in Ecosystemic Play Therapy, indicates a high level of therapist immersion in the therapy process. Right from the outset, an overt establishing of a specific treatment contract with the child (and, if possible, with the caregiver) is addressed. *Open Discussion and Exploration* as exemplified in Quadrant II is part of the Ecosystemic play therapist's approach. The Ecosystemic play therapist will be actively making decisions about the play objects and purpose of the objects as they relate to the developmentally sequenced goals identified in the contract. The therapist will be highly immersed during various points in the play sessions as they either overtly or covertly aid the child to problem-solve. Landreth (2002) describes the therapist role as facilitative and a way of being with children. Child-Centered play therapists would therefore not be directive, not enter into problem-solving, and not ask the child questions or provide explanations. The Child-Centered therapist would be less immersed in an overt way and would primarily be process focused and follow the child's direction. On the lower end of the immersion scale, the therapist would be involved through their emotional and physical presence and facilitative responding. This way of being in the therapy session is exemplified by Quadrant III, *Non-Intrusive Responding*.

The Jungian Analytical play therapist's *use of self* can also be viewed on an immersion continuum (Peery, 2003). Primarily child directed, the Jungian Analytical play therapist is judicious about how actively they participate in the child's play. Sensitive to the archetypal and symbolic themes, the Jungian Analytical play therapist checks out soft hypotheses and at times may make interpretations, but the interpretations stay within the play metaphor. The therapist may enter the play with the child if invited but will try to match and mirror the child's intensity—regardless of the play content. A safe and protected play environment and adherence to the child's unconscious and to transference and countertransference issues are all important considerations. The Jungian Analytical play therapist will likely move between Quadrant I, *Active Utilization*, Quadrant III, *Non-Intrusive Responding*, and Quadrant IV, *Co-Facilitation*. The degree of immersion will be based on what behavioral activities the therapist chooses to engage in at any given time during a play therapy session.

Ericksonian play therapists refrain from using diagnostic labels, focus on the unique makeup of each child, and pay attention to present versus past problems/ issues (Mills, 2001). The therapist's use of self is based on looking for and identifying patterns of belief, behavior, and motivation in each individual. Interventions are often presented in metaphorical ways such as storytelling (Mills, 2001, 2015), art (Mills and Crowley, 1986, 2014), rituals and ceremonies (Mills, 1989; Gilligan, 1987), and living metaphors (Mills and Crowley, 1986, 1988; Mills, 1999). The Ericksonian play therapist is generally non-interpretive, and meaning is derived from the child's point of view. Meaning unfolds in the safety of the relationship and can only be understood when the therapist has truly entered the world of the child. Ericksonians make use of interspersed suggestions that are woven into client discussions and activities. The intent of providing suggestions is to make an impact on clients at an unconscious level (Erickson, 1966/1980; Erickson and Rossi, 1980).

Since Ericksonian play therapists highly value the power of the unconscious in relation to client change, they would likely identify with both Quadrant III,

Non-Intrusive Responding, and Quadrant IV, *Co-Facilitation*. On the lower half of the Play Therapy Dimensions Model, therapists working in Quadrants III and IV spend more time working with the child's unconscious processes than when working in Quadrants I and II, where the focus is to bring matters to conscious awareness. Ericksonian play therapists would therefore likely be moderately immersed and less directive in play therapy sessions, depending on client need.

Gestalt play therapists (Oaklander, 2003) may be viewed as highly immersed and active in the play therapy or not, depending on who is leading the play. Interaction with the child is highly valued, so each session should be viewed individually to identify how immersed the therapist becomes and why. Cognitive-Behavioral play therapists (Knell, 2003, 2015) may be viewed as moderately to highly immersed in the play. By either staying in the play metaphor (utilizing play objects) or by directly introducing a cognitive written exercise, or by modeling activity, the play therapist is highly involved and immersed. The Prescriptive play therapist is trained in a variety of play therapy approaches and makes decisions about how to work with a particular child based on the child's condition or disorder (Schaefer, 2003). In this case, a therapist's degree of immersion in the play would depend on the presenting problem and the makeup of the child. Therapist immersion could move from very low to very high. The Adlerian play therapist would, at times, be highly immersed in the play. The use of self for Adlerians is to be that of a teacher, play partner, inquisitor, and interpreter (Kottman, 2003b, 2011, 2020). During the first phase of therapy, the Adlerian play therapist would be less immersed in the play due to the non-directive use of self as related to relationship building, while during the second and third phases, the therapist would be highly immersed based on direct exploration, discussion, and the use of interpretive strategies.

There are many approaches to play therapy, and these are but a few examples of therapists' use of self and the varying degrees of immersion for each. There are many ways to "use" the self in play therapy. How immersed is the therapist and for what reason? This is a question to be answered if one is to be consciously and thoughtfully intervening with children and families.

LEVEL OF THERAPIST INTERPRETATION

How interpretive is the therapist? This question is related to the *degree* of therapist immersion. Each play therapy approach directs the therapist to consider the context and value of interpretation. Some approaches are relatively non-interpretive, while others are highly interpretive. Global interpretations are often made as a part of case conceptualization, while interpretive comments/verbalizations are made as a part of the direct treatment. Interpretations can be made and kept within the play metaphor, within the therapist–child relationship, or generalized to matters related to the child's outer world. The use of interpretation by therapists is viewed as one form of the therapeutic change mechanism.

KEY POINTS

- The Play Therapy Dimensions Model is a decision-making tool that guides the therapist to identify the critical elements of the play therapy process. The goal of the model is to aid play therapists to answer the *who*, *what*, *when*, *why*, and *how* of the play therapy process.
- The Play Therapy Dimensions Model has been expanded to include a model of thinking that is bottom up. Pre-imaginative play skills, represented in the bottom of Figure 3.1, are the foundation for all play. To fully "play" using metaphor, children need to have mastered a series of early play skills such as sensory play, exploratory play, manipulative play, construction play, relational play, cause and effect play, and imitative play. Children with limitations in their play skills will require a play therapist who will assess what may be missing and then purposefully intervene.
- Play therapists are encouraged to view their therapeutic activities as dynamic and based on several factors such as the stage of the therapeutic process, responses of the child to the therapist, the child's play skills, the child's drive and direction in therapy, the context of the presenting issue, and timelines and system parameters.
- The quadrants provide an organizing structure for play therapists and help identify the levels of their directiveness, immersion, and the degree to which they facilitate the child's conscious awareness of emerging play themes and activities. The therapy process could begin in any quadrant depending on the decision-making variables. There is no prescribed order.
- The four quadrants provide a window into the possibility of using various play therapy models and interventions during a session or series of sessions. The same therapist may work in all four quadrants depending on the style of the child, the presenting need, the capacity for play, and the child's developmental stage. An understanding of indicators of *movement* toward reorganization is critical and is also a common goal in play therapy. The Play Therapy Dimensions Model can provide a framework for observing and tracking the child's reorganizing and integration process.

◎ **Chapter 4** ◎

THE CONSCIOUSNESS DIMENSION IN PLAY THERAPY

Knowing brings one closer to understanding the paths to take.

WHAT'S SO MYSTERIOUS ABOUT CONSCIOUSNESS? HISTORICAL AND CURRENT PERSPECTIVES

For most of written human history, people have been fascinated by the study of consciousness. Over 100 years ago, psychology started as a science of consciousness (Chalmers, 2005). As noted by Damasio (1999), "If elucidating the mind is the last frontier of the life sciences, consciousness seems like the last mystery in the elucidation of the mind" (p.4).

Ginsburg and Jablonka (2019) examined the concept of consciousness from an evolutionary standpoint and hypothesized that a transitional marker present in most vertebrates, called Unlimited Associative Learning (UAL), led to a transition from non-conscious to conscious beings. In essence, UAL is the capacity for associative learning, allowing for open-ended accumulation of long chains of associative links during the lifespan of an animal. As such, it helps animals to bridge temporal gaps to learn about conditional stimuli that are no longer present. Interestingly, Ginsburg and Jablonka hypothesize that associative learning was a driving force behind the explosion of life during the Cambrian period as it is a form of developmental plasticity with a potential for generating adaptive novelty that enables organisms to develop novel behaviors within a single lifetime (Birch, Ginsburg, and Jablonka, 2020).

One of the problems with understanding and exploring this dimension in humans is that the essence of consciousness is subjectivity, and to have a subjective experience there must be a self. The notion of self, in turn, leads to several complex questions such as, what sort of thing could be the experiencer of experiences (Blackmore, 2005)?

Damasio (1999) asserts that consciousness is an entirely private, first-person phenomenon that occurs as part of the private, first-person process we call mind. Consciousness and mind are closely linked to external behaviors that can be observed by third persons, and because of our natural propensity to analyze others, and ourselves, there is a strong link between mind and behavior. Over the last few decades, advances in the cognitive neurosciences have forged links between mind, behavior, and brain (Crick, 2005; Damasio, 1999). New techniques to observe the brain in terms of its structure and function permit researchers to link a certain observed behavior to a presumed mental counterpart, as well as to specific indices of brain structure or brain activity (Damasio, 1999).

A metaphor that is often used for understanding consciousness is the theater metaphor, which in western culture goes back in time to individuals such as Plato. The theater metaphor simply states that what is conscious is like the bright spot cast by a spotlight on the stage of a theater. What is unconscious is everything else, including the people sitting in the audience. However, there are always individuals sitting behind the scenes, such as the playwright and director, who tell the actor in the spotlight what to do or say, and in so doing shape the contents of consciousness (Baars, 2005).

Damasio (1999) notes that research has evolved to a point where we now know there is no homunculus creature in charge of "knowing," and there is no one location for consciousness in the brain. Thus, as useful as the spotlight metaphor seems, neuroscientists largely refute the idea of sitting in the Cartesian theater as an audience of one while waiting for objects to step into the light. Research has progressed to the point where we can now separate consciousness and wakefulness, as well as consciousness and low-level attention. At the same time, Damasio (1999) argues that consciousness and emotions are not separable, as it is usually the case that when consciousness is impaired so is emotion. It seems that we can know none of our personal states without consciousness. As such, consciousness is a critical biological function that allows us to know emotions such as sorrow and joy. Emphasizing this point, Damasio (1999) states, "At its most complex and elaborate level, consciousness helps us develop a concern for other selves and improve the art of life" (p.5).

In the last decades of the 19th century, the philosophical concept of the unconscious, as taught by Schopenhauer and Von Hartmann, was very popular (Ellenberger, 1970). Psychologists were seeking scientific evidence regarding the assumption that part of psychic life escapes humanity's conscious knowledge, which had been held for many centuries. As noted by Ellenberger (1970), it was Gottfried Leibniz who proposed the first theory of the unconscious mind supported by purely psychological arguments. Leibniz thought there were "small perceptions" that remain below the threshold of perception, which play a great part in our mental life. Leibniz took the concept of small perceptions, and threshold, and introduced a dynamic point of view. Leibniz thought of the threshold as a surface where an ever-changing multitude of perceptions or representations constantly fight against one another. The stronger ones push the weaker ones down under the threshold, and the repressed representations strive to re-emerge, and for that reason associate themselves with the other representations. In essence, lying below the threshold was thought to be a compact organized bundle of unconscious representations (Ellenberger, 1970).

The dynamic psychiatry systems espoused by Janet, Freud, Adler, and Jung evolved as a science from earlier approaches to the unconscious that moved from primitive healing to magnetism, magnetism to hypnotism, and hypnotism to psychoanalysis. The basic features of the first dynamic psychiatry approaches were the concept of a dual model of the mind with a conscious and unconscious ego, and the use of hypnosis as an approach to working with the unconscious mind (Ellenberger, 1970). Jean-Martin Charcot spoke of the existence of unconscious fixed ideas as nuclei of certain neuroses, a concept that was further developed by Pierre Janet and Sigmund Freud. Janet wrote about subconscious fixed ideas and their pathogenic role. Janet asserted that bringing these ideas into consciousness was not enough to cure the patient. Instead, one needed to re-educate the patient and transform their ideas. Building on these constructs, depth psychology claimed to have a way to explore the unconscious mind, and Freud's idea of analyzing resistance and transference emerged as a basic tool of psychotherapy (Ellenberger, 1970).

Friedrich Nietzsche, in rebelling against accepted values of contemporary society, such as the principle of the will to power, conceived of the unconscious as an area of confused thoughts, emotions, and instincts. At the same time, he thought of it as an area of re-enactment of past stages of the individual and/or the species. Under the name of inhibition, Nietzsche described what today is called repression. He also spoke of sublimation of sexual and aggressive instincts (Ellenberger, 1970).

Both Nietzsche and Freud were part of what Ellenberger (1970) refers to as an unmasking trend in the search for hidden unconscious motivations, to the extent that words and deeds are seen as manifestations of unconscious motivations, mainly instincts and conflicts of instincts. Jung's theories were also greatly influenced by Nietzsche. Jung even gave an interpretation of Nietzsche's personality in ten unpublished typewritten volumes.

It is essential that integrative play therapists grasp the historical contributions of philosophy and science to the understanding of the self and consciousness, as well as the impact of current research in the cognitive neurosciences, as reflected by the work of Damasio (1999) and Pankseep (1998). As O'Connor and Braverman (2009) highlight, we now have a neurological understanding of the basic emotional operating systems of the mammalian brain, as well as of the conscious and unconscious states which they generate.

Based on neurological evidence, Damasio (1999) asserts that there are different types of consciousness. Core consciousness provides us with a sense of self in the here and now. Core consciousness is seen as a simple biological phenomenon. Returning to the metaphor of the spotlight, core consciousness is the first step into the light but does not illuminate the whole being. Damasio refers to a complex type of consciousness, of which there are many levels, as extended consciousness. This type of consciousness provides us with an elaborate sense of self—an identity and a personhood that includes past and anticipated future experiences. Extended consciousness requires memory and working memory and is enhanced by language.

According to Damasio (1999), the two kinds of consciousness correspond to two kinds of self, the core self and the autobiographical self. Play therapists working from a developmental template will be familiar with the term "autobiographical memory"—an organized record of one's experiences across time and space. Autobiographical memory grows continuously with life experience but can be partly changed or remodeled to reflect new experiences. The emotional milestones identified in child development are possibly the result of the uneven expansion of autobiographical memory and the uneven deployment of the autobiographical self (Damasio, 1999). The autobiographical self is based on autobiographical memory that is constituted by implicit memories of multiple instances of individual experience of the past and anticipated future. Whereas the core self undergoes minimal changes across a lifetime, the contents of the autobiographical self can only be known when there is a fresh or new construction of the core self (Damasio, 1999).

> Sets of memories which describe identity and person can be reactivated as a neural pattern and made explicit as images whenever needed. Each reactivated memory operates as a 'something-to-be-known' and generates its own pulse of core consciousness. The result is the autobiographical self of which we are conscious. (Damasio, 1999, p.174)

Damasio (1999) asserts that consciousness has a survival value and is activated the moment that our internal representation devices exhibit a specific kind of wordless knowledge—the knowledge that our own state has been impacted upon or changed by an object. The sense of self that occurs in the act of knowing an object is an infusion of new knowledge that is continuously created within the brain. The simplest form in which wordless knowledge emerges mentally is what Damasio calls the "feeling of knowing." This term refers to the feeling of what happens when the organism is engaged in the processing of an object; only after this point can we make inferences and interpretations regarding the feeling of knowing. Damasio (1999) states, "In a curious way, consciousness begins as the feeling of what happens when we see or hear or touch" (p.26). Taken from this perspective, consciousness is knowledge, or what Damasio refers to as knowledge consciousness.

Not unlike the earlier, dynamic approaches to consciousness, Damasio (1999) states that the human mind is constantly being split between the part that stands for the known and the part that stands for the knower. However, he proposes that there is a proto-self that is an, "interconnected and temporarily coherent collection of neural patterns which represent the state of the organism, moment-by-moment, at multiple levels of the brain. We are not conscious of the proto-self" (Damasio, 1999, p.174). The proto-self participates in the process of knowing and is a reference point rather than a storehouse of knowledge. When viewed from this perspective, consciousness is the part of the mind concerned with the apparent sense of self and knowing.

Damasio (1999) emphasizes that consciousness must be present if feelings are to influence the subject having them, beyond the immediate here and now. This entails that *having* a feeling is different than *knowing* a feeling or having a conscious understanding of it. While emotions automatically provide the organism with survival-oriented behaviors, in humans our emotions also have an impact on our mind, and because we are equipped with consciousness—or the ability to know we are having a feeling—another level of regulation is reached.

> Consciousness allows feelings to be known and thus promotes the impact of emotion internally, [and] allows emotion to permeate the thought process through the agency of feeling. Eventually, consciousness allows any object to be known—the "object" emotion and any other object—and, in so doing, enhances the organism's ability to respond adaptively, mindful of the needs of the organism in question. (Damasio, 1999, p.56)

Damasio (1999) suspects that consciousness prevailed in evolution because knowing the feelings caused by emotions was indispensable to the art of life.

ARE WE PLAYING A GAME OF HIDE-AND-SEEK?

For the integrative play therapist who wishes to explore the dimension of consciousness in relation to theoretical models or approaches to play therapy, it can seem as though there is a game of hide-and-seek going on. At times, the impact and importance of this dimension is clearly acknowledged, while at other times, it seems as though this dimension has been hidden, forgotten, or possibly repressed from our collective awareness as play therapists. This is indeed surprising given the long history of scientific, psychological, and therapeutic curiosity regarding our conscious mind. However, for the integrative play therapist who strives to understand the unique needs of each child, there is great value in understanding how to conceptualize the impact of both client and therapist moderating factors in relation to the dimension of consciousness. Not only must the therapist be concerned with their use of self, but also they must consider the timing and deployment of reflective and interpretive statements, as these have the potential of unmasking symbols or bringing the child's play activities to higher levels of awareness. Additionally the therapist must consider child moderating factors, such as the nature and strength of the child's defenses, to support the child's ability to process or work through issues.

There are of course specific approaches to play therapy, such as Jungian Analytical Play Therapy, that are directly concerned with the manner in which the child plays out conflicts stored in their unconscious (Peery, 2003; Green, 2009). Within this approach to play therapy, a therapist often works to strengthen connections between the unconscious and conscious mind. Jung thought that when there is an extremely poor connection with the unconscious, due to an erosion of the transitional space between the outer and inner worlds, there is an increased chance of some type of psychopathology. Accordingly, Jungian play therapists believe that work should be directed at helping the child recover the tenuous transitional space by enhancing the connection between the unconscious and conscious (Green, 2009). At times, the therapist will even amplify symbols contained in the play to make them more conscious, both verbally and non-verbally, through play interventions (Green, 2009). In so doing, the therapist helps restore the child's creative capacities.

Continuing with our analogy of a hide-and-seek game, the reader may be surprised to find that certain approaches to Filial Therapy incorporate from psychodynamic theory the importance of the unconscious and defense mechanisms (VanFleet, 2005). Not only does this framework emphasize the need for insight and self-understanding in order for growth to occur, but also it emphasizes that the play process can provide the catharsis needed to release the affect that has been repressed. In essence, emphasis is given to working through issues and reducing defenses to support psychological growth, both in the child as well as the parent. While these are two out of dozens of models of play therapy currently published, they exemplify the complexities faced by an integrative play therapist when trying to understand the value of working with the consciousness dimension.

Why Should Integrative Play Therapists Be Concerned about the Dimension of Consciousness? The Importance of Considering Child Moderating Factors

As integrative play therapists, our initial focus, or "seeking" strategy, when playing this game of hide-and-seek, should begin with the simple appreciation of how consciousness and play are linked. In play there is a centering of attention (O'Connor, 2000); the moment the child begins to play, they are involved in a journey that shines a light on the core self. The cognitive, affective, and interpersonal processes in play that lead to adaptive abilities such as creative thinking and problem-solving (Russ, 2004) inevitably move the child to extended levels of consciousness and tap into the child's autobiographical self (Damasio, 1999).

What the integrative play therapist should take from research in the cognitive neurosciences is that consciousness implies knowledge, such that when a child uses toys or objects, and activates the processes of symbolization and externalization, they are working with a certain level of consciousness. Through the therapeutic process, and the power of play, the child gains a sense of power and control that has an impact on their conscious knowledge base and ultimately their sense of self. Working from a developmental template, the integrative play therapist must consider that as the child grows and develops, they move from an external locus of control to an internal locus of control, or toward what might also be termed as conscience or superego (Davies, 2004). It is important to note that consciousness and conscience are distinguishable. Damasio (1999) states that consciousness pertains to knowing of any object or action attributed to a self, while conscience pertains to the good or evil to be found in actions or objects.

Between three and four years of age, the child becomes more aware, both consciously and unconsciously, of similarities between themselves and their parents, as well as other important persons in their life. While the child might consciously strive to be like their parents, they also unconsciously assimilate certain parental characteristics because of their growing awareness of the adult's power and competence (Davies, 2004).

As noted by Harter (1999, 2015), school-age children have a much stronger capacity for self-observation than do younger children. For example, the older child is more capable and at ease in answering the question, "What are you good at?" because they can take and hold on to an outside perspective of themselves. Toward the end of the school-age period, children begin to reflect on psychological reasons for their strengths or problems, which has implications for intervention planning as they can more meaningfully participate in setting goals. Self-knowledge increases considerably across middle childhood and there have been several interesting studies that examine the child's understanding of where this knowledge resides—in one's parents or oneself? For example, Burton and Mitchell (2003) asked children questions such as, "Who knows best what you are thinking?" and, "Who knows best when you are hungry?" At age six, over 70 percent of children said that an adult (most often a parent but sometimes a teacher) knew what they were feeling. By age ten, ideas about the locus of self-knowledge shifted dramatically, with 75 percent of ten-year-olds stating that they knew best what they were thinking or feeling.

As the child's capacity for self-observation grows, they become more aware of their strengths and weaknesses. The child's views of self, and world view, are of course significantly influenced by early relational experiences. These views are often communicated symbolically in play, but with the older child, they might also be communicated outwardly, through verbalizations. Accordingly, the integrative play therapist is frequently confronted with decision-making about bringing the child's views of self, relationships, and world view to higher levels of consciousness, or allowing the child to work in a less conscious manner using symbols and metaphors.

When working with a traumatized child, play therapists often observe that the child will choose a perpetrator symbol as well as self-objects to represent the self (Goodyear-Brown, 2010, 2019). To assist the child in reorganizing certain aspects of the trauma that have been dissociated or carefully suppressed, the therapist must first establish safety in the relationship and then gradually employ a variety of strategies to assist the child in developing, and holding in their consciousness, a more coherent trauma narrative. The evolving trauma narrative is a part of the child's autobiographical memory and autobiographical self, and the play therapist should have some decision-making parameters for examining the child's readiness and capacity to bring aspects of the trauma to higher levels of consciousness.

Goodyear-Brown's (2010) Flexibly Sequential Play Therapy (FSPT), now referred as Trauma Play™ (2019), is identified as an integrative, prescriptive approach that requires knowledge of a variety of specific play-based techniques, an understanding of the powers of play, and an understanding of how the curative factors of play operate (Drewes, 2011). The model emphasizes a "Continuum of Disclosure" whereby the child is supported to be in control of opening and exploring trauma content. Goodyear-Brown (2010, 2019) emphasizes that a great deal of finesse and expertise are required in applying this model, as the goal is to meet the unique needs of each traumatized child. Based on discussions of the consciousness dimension, decision-making concerning how fast or slow the therapist introduces traumatic material for processing, in an attempt to guide the child along the continuum of disclosure, would be based on an understanding of the psychological mechanisms underlying the consciousness continuum.

When working with the Trauma Play™ model, once safety is established in the therapeutic relationship there are several expressive and cognitive-behavioral strategies at the therapist's disposal to help the child reorganize certain aspects of the trauma. The child's play creations are thought to represent various emotional or sensory aspects of the trauma, or what Goodyear-Brown (2010, 2019) refers to as nonsequential moments within a trauma history. In experiential mastery play, children use symbols and create scenarios that allow them to safely gain a mastery experience in relation to some type of traumatic or disturbing subject matter. Goodyear-Brown describes this type of play as a prop-based gradual exposure process, whereby the therapist helps the child move through their immobilizing fears and works to desensitize their trauma content. Shelby (1997) also describes a specific directive intervention, similar to the approach taken by Goodyear-Brown, which she refers to as the experiential mastery technique. In this technique, the child is encouraged to draw a picture of the scary content, talk about the emotions connected to the content, and then choose a way to manipulate the drawing that assists the child in feeling empowered in relation to the content.

While identified as strategies that lead to symptom reduction, based on gradual exposure and desensitization, decision-making regarding when to introduce these techniques should be based on an understanding of how certain child moderating factors interface with the dimension of consciousness, such as the child's defense mechanisms, developmental stage, and emotional capacity. More specifically, the therapist would need to consider the child's ego strength and ability to tolerate material coming closer to conscious awareness, the types of defenses activated (or needed) by the child, as well as the child's developmental capacities to work through this material in a verbal, more conscious manner. It would also be important for the integrative play therapist to realize that these are not just directive techniques based on principles of desensitization, but that underlying psychological processes related to autobiographical memory and autobiographical self are invoked through these techniques. To create a coherent story or trauma narrative, the child must work with a certain level of consciousness and be capable of accessing part of their implicit and explicit memory structures. The challenge here is that to cope with the traumatic material, the child may have split off affective and sensory impressions related to the trauma and, in so doing, compartmentalized them from the verbal story. Even after a new trauma narrative has been formed through the therapy process, the child may be left with a range of cognitive distortions, particularly false attributions related to the cause of the traumatic event (Goodyear-Brown, 2010, 2019). These distortions engender anxiety and low self-esteem and must thoughtfully be challenged and restructured. Although there are a variety of play-based, cognitive-behavioral strategies available to the play therapist which encourage the child to externalize specific thoughts and kinesthetically manipulate them until they experience a sense of control, it is imperative that the therapist recognizes that the child is working at a certain level of consciousness and the child's readiness and capacity to manage higher levels of conscious self-knowledge will depend on a number of factors, including their need to maintain certain defenses to protect their sense of self.

Crenshaw and Mordock (2005) note that one of the therapeutic tasks in working with aggressive children is to help them develop, or access, more mature defense mechanisms. These authors note that play therapists are often tempted to use play materials to, "occupy the defensive child" (p.5) while efforts are made to increase the child's verbalizations. However, by latency age, children often use masking symbols to assist in maintaining a state of calmness and to provide distance from unacceptable thoughts, impulses, and actions (Crenshaw and Mordock, 2005). In the therapeutic context, the use of fantasy drawings helps children to develop masking symbols to work through specific feelings or emotions while maintaining distance from them.

Paradoxically, the power behind techniques such as drawing an anger volcano is that they make use of the symbolization process, but by inviting the child to come closer to explore their masking symbols, the child also comes closer to exploring their needs and impulses. Fortunately, the child does not need to hold all of their feelings in full conscious awareness. However, to make use of the symbolization process, the child needs to have access to abstract thinking skills and defenses such as repression (Crenshaw and Mordock, 2005). The latter construct denotes that the child selectively forgets or pushes from higher levels of conscious awareness a specific event, unacceptable feeling, thought, or impulse (Davies, 2004). For adults and children alike, this type of ego defense can be viewed as adaptive as it supports our ability to cope in stressful circumstances. Although defenses such as denial and blaming may also contain anxiety, they can contribute to maladaptive behaviors such as aggression, particularly when others confront these defenses. At the more extreme level, the ego defense of splitting refers to the anxiety-arousing part of what is repressed becoming split off from the child's conscious image of self. Splitting is a more primitive defense that when taken to an extreme is linked to dissociation (Crenshaw and Mordock, 2005). An integrative play therapist, working with an understanding of defenses and the child's need to protect the self, will recognize that certain needs, impulses, and wishes should not be met "head on" by the therapist. Instead, these defenses should be welcomed and, in some cases, gradually uncovered. To this end, the therapist often works to assist the child in developing more mature or adaptive defenses and, in so doing, makes use of interpretations.

This now brings the integrative play therapist involved in the hide-and-seek game of consciousness to consider the role of therapist moderating factors, such as the use of interpretations. Recognizing that consciousness implies self-knowledge, the integrative play therapist should not shy away from considering the role of interpretations. As noted by O'Connor (2000), one of the primary, curative aspects of Psychoanalytical Play Therapy is the interpretation offered by the play therapist, as interpretations help make the child's conflicts conscious and allow for change. At the most basic level, the integrative play therapist needs to decide whether it is helpful to provide interpretive comments, with the intent to raise the awareness of the child client, or whether it is of greater benefit to the child to remain below a certain level of consciousness by tracking or reflecting what is occurring in the child's metaphorical play. In the traditional approach to psychoanalysis, ego defenses are usually interpreted before internal drives (e.g., need for power or affiliation), and surface material before deeper, unconscious material (O'Connor, 2000). Crenshaw and Mordock (2005) subdivide interpretations into two major categories. One category, empathic interpretations, are interpretations that help the child understand universal feelings, individual feelings, feelings about conflicts, and others' behaviors.

Empathic interpretations are used to help the child understand their feelings better, such as when a therapist attempts to normalize the feelings of a child who is entering a new therapeutic relationship. As stated by Crenshaw and Mordock (2005), "Interpretations of universal feelings are efforts to help the child realize that many children have similar feelings, to facilitate discussion of how things really are, and to correct the child's self-defeating misconceptions" (p.143).

The second category of interpretations referred to by Crenshaw and Mordock (2005), which deals strictly with unconscious material, is dynamic interpretations. This type involves the interpretation of defenses, transference, and drives or wishes. O'Connor (2000) and Crenshaw and Mordock (2005) each emphasize that the therapist needs to do some preparatory work in the use of interpretations, particularly when working with children who have fragile defenses.

> Dynamic interpretations transcend the clinical data and are preceded by a prolonged preparatory process during which the child's misconceptions have been clarified through empathic interpretations. Conflict always blurs reality, and anxiety distorts it. Clarifying comments change the nature of the child's play as the child integrates new knowledge. The play becomes more elaborate, less disguised, and more interpretable. (Crenshaw and Mordock, 2005, p.144)

There are times when the child needs distance from troublesome thoughts and feelings, but there are also times when brief interpretations can be facilitative and provide insight to the child that may otherwise have gone unsaid in language. A well-timed interpretation framed to apply to the characters or objects in the child's play, rather than directly to the child, can bring awareness to an issue or feeling that is entering the child's pre-consciousness. In as much as the integrative play therapist is viewed as a participant observer, the selective and thoughtful use of interpretations may support the child to deepen or extend their symbolic play, taking it in a direction they need based on a growing awareness of their feelings or experiences—or self-knowledge.

LEARNING TO EMBRACE THE GAME OF HIDE-AND-SEEK

The integrative play therapist must find ways to understand and embrace the power embedded in the consciousness dimension. By becoming more fluent within certain decision-making parameters, which in the Play Therapy Dimensions Model relates to an understanding of the four quadrants as well as the child and therapist moderating factors, the therapist will have a better appreciation for the *who, what, when, why,* and *how* of the play therapy process. To briefly illustrate this point, when the therapist makes interpretations within the metaphor, they honor the child's primary need to contain some of their unconscious material and conceal their perceptions of the world within the fantasy of the play. When the therapist reaches too far or pushes too quickly, and abruptly raises material into conscious awareness by interpreting the meaning of symbols, they are in effect describing the unconscious to the child. In so doing, the therapist either invites the activation of certain other defenses or psychologically disarms the child to the point where they might feel vulnerable and unsafe (Yasenik and Gardner, 2014).

The therapist must also work from a developmental template. For instance, later school-age children are more capable of understanding direct interpretations that are phrased in concrete terms and presented with empathy (Davies, 2004). However, the school-age child often works hard to repress and compartmentalize painful affects. Defenses such as repression parallel the child's general tendencies to be present-oriented rather than think about the past. In essence, the child uses defenses, along with their own capacities for conscious suppression and self-distraction, to keep certain feelings at a distance (Crenshaw and Mordock, 2005; Davies, 2004).

As previously discussed, in supporting the child to develop a trauma narrative, the therapist may need to help structure the chaotic play into a narrative that clarifies what happened, establish a sequence of cause and effect, and be prepared to describe the child's affective reactions (Gil, 1991, 2006). This type of work entails that we move from symbolic play expressions to creating a verbal narrative that is more available, in consciousness, to the child. In many cases, we reach the point in therapy where the child gains relief by talking about their experiences from a coherent perspective. This therapeutic process involves finesse and expertise on the therapist's part, particularly the ability to weave up and down the dimension of consciousness according to the rules for hide-and-seek!

KEY POINTS

- According to Damasio (1999) there are different types of consciousness. Core consciousness provides us with a sense of self in the here and now. Extended consciousness provides us with an elaborate sense of self.
- Research in the cognitive neurosciences helps the play therapist understand that when a child accesses symbolic play they are working with a certain level of consciousness. Through the play process, and access to the therapeutic powers of play, there is the possibility of impacting conscious knowledge and ultimately the sense of self.
- Consciousness implies self-knowledge; self-knowledge and capacity for self-observation should be understood from a developmental perspective.

- Interpretations offered by the play therapist help make the child's conflicts conscious and therefore more accessible and understandable.
- Play therapists need to decide whether it is helpful to provide interpretive comments with an intent to raise awareness or whether it is of greater benefit to the child to remain at lower levels of consciousness by tracking and reflecting what is occurring in play.

◎ Chapter 5 ◎

THE DIRECTIVENESS DIMENSION IN PLAY THERAPY

The trajectory of the arrow depends on the skill of the archer.

SO, WHAT KIND OF THERAPIST ARE YOU?

It has been our experience that when asking play therapy practitioners to describe their practice model, many begin by identifying a preference for a specific model or approach to play therapy, such as Adlerian, Child-Centered, or Gestalt. As the discussion unfolds, we hear more about preferences for working in either a directive or non-directive manner. Interestingly, this discussion is often quite polarizing, with therapists taking one side in opposition to the other side. As the discussion continues, heated debates occur about the pros and cons of asking children to help clean up at the end of the session, when to set limits, and whether or not it is a directive stance to pre-select certain materials for inclusion in the play therapy room. Clearly, play therapists are a passionate bunch! However, debate concerning the "correctness" of a directive versus a non-directive approach remains at the forefront of the practitioners' minds, particularly when asked to describe their practice model. From our viewpoint, these discussions are healthy and help move the therapist from a theoretical model or orientation to one that is much more personal and demanding of reflection on the complexities of the play therapy process.

The primary model or orientation of the therapist tends to provide explicit direction concerning where to position oneself on the directiveness dimension. One's positioning follows from the primary theoretical constructs of the model or approach taken, the underlying principles or goals of the model, the emphasis placed on specific change mechanisms, and most importantly, the preferred (or prescribed) role of the therapist. While these practical and theoretical constructs guide the therapist to assume a certain therapeutic role and take a position or therapeutic stance along the directiveness dimension, they do not ensure effective decision-making about when or how to move, even slightly, along this dimension. The non-directive side of the continuum (see Figure 3.3) is most clearly evidenced in the child-centered approach to play therapy. However, close inspection of the child-centered approach suggests there are variations in the way contemporary experts such as Landreth (2002, 2012), Guerney (2001), Guerney and Ryan, (2013), VanFleet, Sywulak, and Sniscak (2010), and Wilson and Ryan (2005) think about certain strategies and non-directive skills. There are also important differences in the manner in which certain approaches to Child-Centered Play Therapy conceptualize the stages of play therapy, with some following the stages first outlined by Moustakas (1955), while others either adhere to or elaborate on the stage view first outlined by Guerney (1983, as cited in Cochran *et al.*, 2010a; Cochran, Nordling, and Cochran, 2010b). To complicate matters, Guerney (2010) cautions that Axline's (1947) eight basic principles, which serve as the foundation for Child-Centered Play Therapy models, are overlapping and interdependent, leaving this approach open to misapplications.

This does not mean that the Child-Centered practitioner is left directionless, as there are a number of current publications that explicitly spell out core child-centered, non-directive skills (Cochran *et al.*, 2010b; Landreth, 2002, 2012; Ray, 2011). Furthermore, Axline's principles, by speaking to the importance of facilitating versus directing change (Guerney, 2010; Sweeney and Landreth, 2009), provide the practitioner with a compass for establishing and examining their role and direction in the therapy process. Even so, Guerney (2010) and Cochran *et al.* (2010b) believe that simply referring to one's model of practice as non-directive is insufficient, emphasizing that the term "non-directive" is actually a misnomer. In discussing this matter, Cochran *et al.* (2010b) highlight the fact that, by stating that one is taking a non-directive approach, one fails to indicate the power of this approach, as others assume being non-directive is tantamount to being passive or inactive. To the contrary, the Child-Centered play therapist is seen as taking an active role in facilitating self-expression, helping the child to self-direct, and facilitating growth in self-responsibility. One of the key points made by Cochran *et al.* (2010b) is that when one speaks of facilitation from a child-centered perspective, one is really speaking about change that comes from within the child, and therefore belongs to the child. Kottman (2011) aptly summarizes this point in discussing the role of the Child-Centered play therapist:

> Child-Centered play therapists fulfill this role by using nondirective skills— tracking, restating content, reflecting feelings, returning responsibility to the child, and setting necessary limits. They do not use skills that would involve leading the child in any way, so they avoid interpreting, designing therapeutic metaphors, and using bibliotherapy and other techniques that take the child somewhere the child would not naturally go. (p.50)

In discussing the model of Child-Centered Play Therapy taught through the National

Institute of Relationship Enhancement, Cochran *et al.* (2010a) clearly state that they do not see their model as non-directive, even though it is child-centered. Returning to the notion of non-directiveness being somewhat of a misnomer, they note that the therapist is always active. They state too that the playroom is also a source of direction, as it is full of carefully selected toys that help direct the child to self-express. To this end, one of the primary focuses of the Child-Centered play therapist is, instead, how to remove the impediments to self-expression for the child.

This brief discussion highlights the fact that when a therapist is working in Quadrant III, *Non-Intrusive Responding*, they are likely moving, even in a slight manner, back and forth along the *directiveness* dimension. To make the point more transparent, the continuum is called the "directiveness dimension," not the "binary choice of Non-Directive/Directive Play Therapy."

Kottman (2011, 2020) notes that Adlerians assume either a non-directive or directive approach depending on the phase of the therapy process, as well as the lifestyle of the child. As a result, Kottman emphasizes that the decision to be directive or non-directive is both, "fluid and systematic" (p.47). To illustrate this further, one might examine the differences in perspective taken by Child-Centered and Adlerian play therapists in terms of cleaning the room at the end of the therapy session. Kottman (2011) states that, in contrast to Axline's belief that having a child help clean up the room is equivalent to asking an adult to (metaphorically) "clean up" their own words in a session, working or collaborating together in clean-up is potentially supportive of the therapeutic relationship. Flexibility is, however, paramount to the Adlerian's decision-making. For instance, Kottman (2011) notes that there are situations where a shared approach to clean-up might be contraindicated, such as with children who are over-anxious or over-responsible.

What would an integrative play therapist say about the non-directive versus directive debate? The simple answer, as outlined by Gil (2006), is that the integrative play therapist adjusts their approach to each child. Of course, experienced clinicians such as Gil (2006) and Drewes (2011) further emphasize that the integrative therapist must be knowledgeable about various therapy approaches and be armed with an array of therapeutic skills. Additionally, the therapist must work hard to understand the child's needs and direction. For instance, in working with traumatized children, Gil (2006) emphasizes the importance of understanding the role of two competing and instinctive drives for children—mastery and suppression. As stated by Gil (2006):

> Children seem to negotiate their emotional injuries by utilizing two basic drives that can guide their behaviors. The first drive is to master what is painful or confusing, restoring a sense of control and mastery; the second drive is to avoid painful emotions, thereby eluding attempts to engage in therapeutic work. (p.8)

When working with children who exhibit posttraumatic play, there is a need to help the child integrate some of the traumatic material (Gil, 2006; Goodyear-Brown, 2010). Integrative play therapists will often choose to first observe the child and follow the child's lead to gain an understanding of the child's needs and possible drive to suppress or gain mastery over their experiences. Gil (2006) refers to this type of therapy situation as non-directive, low stress, and low demand. Gil notes that the decision to begin therapy in this manner must be made on a case-by-case basis, "Intervening too quickly may interfere with the play's inherent capacity to produce positive results; waiting too long may cause the child further revictimization, which...can reinforce feelings of helplessness and vulnerability" (Gil, 2006, p.161). After establishing safety in the relationship, Gil might consider moving toward low-challenge/low-intrusion interventions, such as asking the child to make physical movements to warm up their body, or providing a verbal, non-interpretive narration of the child's play. High-challenge/high-intrusion interventions might eventually follow, such as directing the child to one segment of the play, and in so doing, disrupting its sequential rigidity (Gil, 2006).

In considering how one might move along the directiveness dimension, from an integrative perspective, or even from the perspective of a specific model of practice, the play therapy practitioner must simultaneously consider a number of constructs, not least of which are the individual child's needs and the therapeutic powers of play. Unfortunately, there is little in the professional literature that provides us with an in-depth understanding of decision-making for this dimension, which is very surprising given that the directive/non-directive approaches represent long-standing, traditional means of conceptualizing the play therapy process (Kottman, 2011).

THE COMPASS AND THE GAUGE

As stated in Chapter 3, the freedom to view directiveness on a continuum allows the play therapist to weave in and out of play roles and activities, providing movement along the directiveness dimension. While the theoretical model or approach taken by the practitioner serves as a compass, pointing them along the directiveness dimension, during the course of therapy the practitioner needs a gauge to tell them which direction to move, how much to move, and most importantly, the timing of when to move.

Surprisingly, the gauge is the child! At times, it is rather obvious what the child needs as they communicate this both verbally and non-verbally. For instance, when a child is highly anxious and is immobilized when entering the playroom for the first time, they show this non-verbally by standing in the middle of the room and staring at the floor, versus exploring the play environment. At this point, the child is likely looking to the play therapist to provide some structure and direction. Although the therapist may choose to initially track what is occurring and make reflective statements, if the child continues to stand and stare, the simple act of walking over to the toy shelves and briefly picking up a noise-making toy in a curious, exploratory fashion may provide some tension relief and communicate to the child that the therapist is an adult who is playful.

Tracking skills are viewed as a basic or essential skill for play therapists and are used in numerous play therapy approaches, such as Adlerian, Jungian, Child-Centered, and Narrative. Tracking is used to let the child know that the therapist is attending to the child, and what is being communicated in play is important to the therapist (Kottman, 2011; Landreth, 2012; Sweeney and Landreth, 2009). Practitioners working from different theoretical approaches would concur that this is a non-directive skill, as it is delivered in a descriptive, non-interpretive manner, by either stating what the child is doing or describing what is occurring with the play objects. However, Kottman (2011) notes that some therapists will choose to use more tracking statements of play objects in early sessions and gradually move toward using more tracking statements of the child's behavior in later sessions. Skilled therapists know that how frequently or actively we track, and what we choose to track in play, is largely based on the responses of the child. At times, the child may sense that the therapist is moving too fast in the relationship and respond defensively or be resistant to tracking comments. This response can be communicated verbally by refuting what was just stated by the therapist or correcting all or part of what was stated by the therapist. The child may also communicate a response non-verbally such as pivoting away from the therapist or spending more time actively exploring the object. The response of the child does not necessarily mean that the tracking statement was a therapeutic "hit" or "miss," but it certainly functions as a gauge of where the child is at in the relationship and provides further direction to the therapist in terms of where to go next.

Kottman (2011) surveyed 17 contemporary experts in play therapy theory and noted that six of them stated that they do not use tracking in the way they apply their theoretical approach to play therapy. Those therapists who adopt more of a non-directive approach, such as Child-Centered and Jungian therapists, indicated that they usually track throughout the play therapy process and see tracking as an essential tool for interacting with the child. In other approaches, such as Adlerian, narrative, and prescriptive, tracking is used more frequently in the early phases of treatment, when emphasis is placed on establishing a relationship with the client. With passing time, the frequency of tracking statements decreases, and other tools or strategies come to the forefront. Interestingly, Kottman (2011) found that the use of tracking varied from individual to individual, and even among those practitioners sharing the same theoretical orientation. In discussing this trend, Kottman (2011) states:

This variance may be due to a combination of individual therapeutic styles and comfort with tracking as an intervention, the individual personalities of each of the experts, differing interpretations of theory, or personal philosophies about modifying the theoretical approach to individual clients. (p.116)

As integrative play therapists, we are not surprised by the diversity of responses found by Kottman and feel it exemplifies the complexities of the play therapy process. We are also not surprised that in her examination of other core or basic skills, such as restating content and reflecting feelings, there was a similar trend in terms of non-directive approaches generally using more of these skills, as well as some variation of use according to the stage of therapy. In deciding what to reflect, the therapist must again look to the child, and their responses, as being the primary gauge. For example, the way a child verbalizes a feeling suggests whether they "own" the feeling (e.g., "I am angry at my brother"). In such cases, the therapist would likely provide a brief, clear, and succinct reflection that directly mirrors the feelings back to the child (e.g., "You are mad at your brother"). In contrast, subtle indirect expressions of the child, where emotions are implicit in what the child says (e.g., "My brother was at home when I got back from school") require a reflection that is more tentative and less definitive (e.g., "When you got back home, you noticed your brother was there"). The emotional tone embedded in the therapist's response is of paramount importance. The child might experience a therapist who responds with little expressed emotion (e.g., a "flat sounding" response) as missing the emotional significance of this event.

The play therapist must also decide whether they are focusing on here-and-now feelings, or looking for affective patterns within or across sessions, or some combination of the two. Once again, the therapist's theoretical orientation, the referral issues and goals, and the therapist's personal style are thought to interact in the decision-making process (Kottman, 2011, 2020).

As discussed in Chapter 3, therapists working on the left side of the directiveness dimension (Figure 1.1) primarily follow the child's lead or direction, but at any point in the therapy process, there may be subtle and important shifts in the level of therapist immersion. The term "immersion" is meant to describe the various ways and degree to which the therapist engages in specific behaviors, language (verbal and non-verbal), and emotions during the play therapy session. The nature and level of therapist immersion can be taken to represent a certain position on the directiveness continuum; as the therapist becomes more immersed, they move toward the right side of the continuum. When working in Quadrant III, *Non-Intrusive Responding*, a shift in immersion can be very subtle, as evidenced in slight, purposeful changes or increases in the emotional tone of a reflective statement. We will see this in action as we review the cases of Ellis and Haley in the following chapters. Subtle changes in therapist immersion are necessary if we are reading and responding to the child's verbal and non-verbal presentations.

The Degree of Immersion: Therapist Use of Self Scale (Appendix B) discussed in Chapter 13 is one way for play therapists to become more aware of their "use of self" during play therapy sessions. Five scales including verbal discussion, reflective statements, emotionality, physical self, and interpretations are provided to assist the therapist to manage and evaluate the degree of immersion in a given play therapy session.

From an integrative perspective, all forms of immersion can be exactly right depending on the presenting needs of the child. Acting as a gauge, the child will tell the therapist, verbally and non-verbally, if the degree and form of immersion are helpful or intrusive. "Immersion" as a term for the description of use of self in play therapy is useful to help therapists identify when and if they should continue their way of responding in a given session.

When thinking about the directiveness dimension, the integrative play therapist must question not only *what* skills are primarily used but also *how* to use their skills and *how* to monitor the child's response.

Examining the far-right side of the directiveness dimension, Paris Goodyear-Brown (2010, 2019) notes that she uses a series of interventions during the termination stage of therapy to help abused children integrate the trauma content into a more positive sense of self. For example, in a structured therapeutic drawing activity referred to as the "before, during and after technique," the therapist helps the child explore transformations of their initial images, and through guided discussion and exploration, there is a focus on narrative building. In discussing the case of a child named Andy, Goodyear-Brown (2010) states:

> For Andy to integrate the trauma of the loss of his mother into a positive sense of self, he needed markers in the sand, moments of meaningful leave-taking. He also needed accurate information about how she died and what had been done with her body. In this case, the therapist plays multiple roles of providing information, structuring the goodbye, building coherent narrative, and supporting the child in his grief. (p.339)

Not only does this technique denote a high level of structure and direction, but also the way the therapist is immersed in the activity and joins with the child plays a significant role in the outcome. The therapist is actively involved by asking questions, providing information, and making empathic responses. Even with a highly structured activity, subtle shifts along the directiveness continuum have a significant impact, therapeutically. Accordingly, the directive play therapist must also constantly monitor their use of self during moment-to-moment interactions with the child.

THE OBSERVER-PARTICIPANT ROLE

Moustakas (1997), in delineating his "Relationship Play Therapy" model or approach, focused on the use of a secure therapeutic relationship as the basis for the child's exploration of interpersonal interactions and movement toward individuation. At the same time, Moustakas asserted that the therapist must be an active participant in the play if invited to join the play by the child. Although working in Quadrant III, *Non-Intrusive Responding*, and allowing the child to remain in the lead, the moment the therapist enters the play there is a shift in the level of immersion, and movement along the directiveness dimension.

This discussion brings to mind the concept of the "observer-participant," as applied to the therapist's role. As discussed in Chapter 3, for the Jungian play therapist, this term signifies that the therapist is simultaneously attached and detached, which allows the therapist to think analytically about what is going on, verbally, non-verbally, and symbolically (Allan, 1997). While other therapy approaches may not share the analytical stance taken in Jungian Play Therapy, they think of the therapist role as an observer-participant, to the extent that they enlist the therapist to take on both non-directive and more directive activities or roles to engage the child or to bring forward certain material (Kottman, 2011). When the therapist moves from a *Non-Intrusive Responding* stance (utilizing mostly non-directive skills) to being an active observer-participant (utilizing a diverse range of techniques or skills, including interpretations), there is a marked shift in therapist use of self and movement on the directiveness dimension.

TAPPING THE THERAPEUTIC POWERS OF PLAY

The integrative play therapist needs to be conversant with change mechanisms and the curative powers of play and, most importantly, be skilled in applying the curative powers to meet the unique needs of their child client (Drewes, 2009, 2011). Schaefer (1993) and Schaefer and Drewes (2009, 2014) have generated an extensive list of therapeutic powers, which should be carefully reviewed by all integrative play therapists. Although a thorough discussion of each factor is beyond the scope of this discussion, it is important to note that each factor has a specific, potentially beneficial outcome for child clients. Some factors have been alluded to already, such as self-control, access to the unconscious, and mastering fears and counterconditioning. Drewes (2009) notes that the curative or therapeutic powers of play become the change mechanisms within play that help alleviate problems and foster change. In speaking of an integrative perspective, Drewes (2009) comments, "This approach is based on the individualized, differential and focused matching of curative powers to the specific causative forces underlying the client's problem" (p.1).

While it is acknowledged that further research is required to understand which specific therapeutic powers are most effective with specific presenting problems (Drewes, 2009), the therapist's understanding of when, how, and why to access these powers is critically important (Prendiville and Parson, 2021). Once again, the practitioner's theoretical model or approach will provide some guidance in these matters, but ultimately it will come down to the role the therapist assumes and how skilled they are at examining factors related to use of self.

Play is now recognized as a powerful means of communicating (Landreth, 2002; Sweeney and Landreth, 2009), and through play the child can express their conscious and unconscious thoughts and feelings (Schaefer and Drewes, 2009; Kottman, 2011). To tap into a therapeutic power, such as self-expression, the therapist must consider the child's ability to self-express, the modality or means of self-expression (e.g., direct or indirect), and what is being conveyed through the child's expressions. Returning once more to the use of tracking and reflecting statements, the therapist must be skilled in the way they phrase their statements, the emotional tone conveyed, and the timing or pacing of the statements. The child's response, verbally or non-verbally, will act as a gauge as to whether the statement was a "hit" or a "miss." A well-timed and appropriate, emotionally matched statement may serve as a therapeutic "hit" because it tapped one of the therapeutic powers of play, such as self-expression, not because it was a non-directive-based skill that the therapist routinely employs.

So, what kind of play therapist are you? When approaches or models of play therapy seem to collide, as is often the case when play therapists begin to explore an integrative perspective (Yasenik and Gardner, 2004, 2012, 2014, 2019; Gardner and Yasenik, 2008), there is a heightened need for awareness of therapist use of self. The next time someone asks you about your model of practice, we hope that your response goes well beyond the non-directive/directive debate and focuses more on your use of self as the practitioner. After all, this is really what the question asks.

KEY POINTS

- Therapists working on the left side of the directiveness dimension primarily follow the child's lead or direction, but at any point in the therapy process, subtle and important shifts in the level of therapist immersion might occur, which create movement along this dimension.
- The term "immersion" is used to describe the various ways and degree to which the therapist engages in specific behaviors, language (verbal and non-verbal), and emotions during the play session (including embodiment and emotional self).
- One's theoretical model may serve as a compass, pointing the therapist

along the directiveness dimension. However, the child is the gauge, as their responses inform us as at to what their underlying needs are in terms of movement along this dimension and whether our responses are a "hit" or a "miss."

- Play therapists should work to understand the specific underlying change mechanisms operating and be familiar with the therapeutic powers of play conceptualized by Schaefer and Drewes (2014).

◎ Chapter 6 ◎

NON-INTRUSIVE RESPONDING

Quadrant III

Practice in the art of "being with" rather than "doing for."

We begin in Quadrant III and not Quadrant I (as might be expected), because Quadrant III is where a play therapist trained in non-directive work would be situated. Non-Directive Play Therapy approaches are the most broadly taught and utilized methods of play therapy intervention in the world. Beginning here allows us to enter a common space to begin our exploration. Quadrant III, *Non-Intrusive Responding*, falls within the lower left corner of Figure 3.1. This chapter examines the unique demands placed on a therapist when working in this quadrant and explores the *who*, *what*, *when*, *why*, and *how* of effective practice.

THE *WHAT*: THE DEFINING FEATURES OF QUADRANT III

Quadrant III occurs within the intersection of the unconscious and non-directive areas of the Play Therapy Dimensions Model, indicating that the child initiates and directs the play while the therapist acts as a *non-intrusive* responder who follows the child's lead. Consistent with a non-directive approach, a therapist working in Quadrant III typically joins the play only when requested to do so by the child. This follows from a fundamental belief in children's natural strivings for growth and their capacity for self-direction.

In Quadrant III the child is encouraged to accept responsibility and essentially chooses the theme, content, and process of the play. As children use play to organize their experiences, one of the therapist's primary tasks in this quadrant is to maintain a stance of non-evaluative acceptance, thereby establishing a relationship that honors the child's ability to use the symbolic language of play for self-expression. Accordingly, the therapist does not attempt to interpret what is happening in the play or to bring up issues in a conscious way with the child, as it is through the use of symbolic materials that a child can distance themselves from traumatic experiences, while retaining a sense of control (Landreth, 2001).

◎ 86 ◎

The terms *Non-Intrusive Responding* and Non-Directive Play Therapy are not one and the same. *Non-Intrusive Responding* describes therapeutic activities and roles, whereas *Non-Directive Play Therapy* denotes a play therapy model based on the philosophical beliefs of client-centered or Rogerian psychotherapy. To complicate matters, Non-Directive Play Therapy has been implemented in various ways and, as a result, has been subject to misinterpretation (Wilson *et al.*, 1992). Although it describes a reflective style of therapist response, some have taken this to mean that the therapist does little else but parrot statements of the child. Non-directive approaches have also been mistaken to imply therapist "inactivity." However, Rogers' descriptions of therapy sessions clearly indicate that person-centered therapists provide direction and set limits. In fact, certain activities and conversations are discouraged as the therapist works to have the client focus on specific feelings and behaviors.

In reviewing the commonalities and differences amongst approaches to play therapy Wilson *et al.* (1992) highlight that there is a central philosophic difference between Non-Directive Play Therapy and other approaches; Non-Directive Play Therapy sees the child directing their own activities and the therapist as a facilitator of therapy rather than "director of events." In summarizing the meaning of non-directive, from a person-centered philosophical perspective, Wilson *et al.* (1992) note the following:

> In other words, the term "non-directive" is used to describe one essential part of the process, the encouragement to the client to identify and bring to that session what he or she wishes; and to try and distinguish this style from other approaches where the therapist may direct the client to the subject matter, and, through interpretive comment, to a particular understanding of this meaning. It is not an attempt to encapsulate the whole orientation. (p.20)

Axline is widely regarded as introducing a non-directive approach to play therapy, by incorporating Rogerian principles into eight guidelines for practice. However, those who review the play therapy literature commonly acknowledge that Axline's descriptive accounts of a non-directive approach, as influential as they were, failed to develop into a comprehensive therapeutic model. For instance, Axline (1976) suggests that the process of Non-Directive Therapy is interwoven, with each principle overlapping and interdependent on the other. Fortunately, Axline's principles have been placed within clear models of practice that help guide therapeutic contact with children, such as Child-Centered Play Therapy (Landreth, 2002) and Non-Directive Play Therapy (Wilson *et al.*, 1992).

Broadly speaking, non-directive approaches are based on the tenet that children have within themselves a basic drive toward health and are able to solve their problems if offered the opportunity. Accordingly, the goal of Non-Directive Play Therapy approaches is to allow the child to become more self-actualized (Landreth, 2002; Wilson *et al.*, 1992).

This occurs by providing a therapeutic environment that helps reduce the conflict the child is experiencing between themselves and the environment. As noted by Landreth (2002, 2012) there are three important therapist-related factors that influence and support the child–therapist relationship, and ultimately the child's movement toward self-actualization: 1) the therapist being "real," which comes from the therapist's self-understanding, self-acceptance, and ability to engage in a genuine relationship with the child; 2) the therapist's ability to convey warmth, care, and acceptance; 3) the therapist's ability to convey sensitive understanding, which essentially means the therapist's ability to connect to the child's phenomenal world. The nature and importance of the therapeutic relationship is clearly articulated by Landreth (2002, 2012):

> Child-Centered Play Therapy is an immediate and present experience for children in which the therapeutic process emerges from a shared living relationship developed on the basis of the therapist's consistently conveyed acceptance of children and confidence in their ability to be of help to themselves, thus freeing children to risk using their own strengths. Experiencing of this acceptance of themselves, children begin to value themselves and come to perceive and accept themselves as unique and separate. (p.83)

THE *HOW:* THERAPEUTIC ROLES AND ACTIVITIES

Therapists trained in non-directive approaches to play therapy readily identify with the therapeutic roles and activities of Quadrant III. However, just as there has been confusion over non-directive approaches, there is likely to be confusion over what constitutes *Non-Intrusive Responding*. The term "non-intrusive" is not synonymous with "non-emotional" or a detached style of relating. As previously indicated, a therapist working at the non-directive end of the directiveness dimension remains fully present and observant of the child's emotional states and play sequences. This is accomplished, in part, through "tracking comments" such as, "Now the girl is going up the slide." Kottman (2003a) notes that tracking comments convey to the child that their behavior is important enough for the play therapist to take notice.

In discussing their approach to play therapy Wilson *et al.* (1992) suggest that Non-Directive therapists do not have the patent on the core therapeutic roles and characteristics outlined by Rogers, such as genuineness, authenticity, and non-possessive warmth. Nonetheless, Non-Directive therapists identify that an essential feature of non-directive work is accurate empathy, through responding to the deeper content of what is being communicated by the child. This occurs through the process of *reflection*.

> The reflection is in a strict sense non-interpretive, in that it remains in the present, uses on the whole the material that the client has used, and avoids what has been

described as the "now and then" kind of interpretation, that is, one that links current material to past events. (Wilson *et al.*, 1992, p.23)

Axline (1969) referred to reflection as the mirroring of feeling and affect. Depending on the stage of therapy, a therapist working non-intrusively might choose to communicate their involvement by using reflective statements about a character representing the child's feeling states. Reflective statements such as, "That tiger sounds mad," are often interspersed with tracking comments and convey understanding or acceptance of what is occurring in the play. The reflective statement, "It seems like you're still not too sure about this place," looks beyond the child's actions and play activities, toward their intentions or feeling states. The process of reflection signals that the therapist is responsive to what the child is doing, saying, or experiencing. It often requires considerable experience to match a child's affective state. A minimized affective response runs the risk of communicating to the child that the emotion expressed is not appropriate. In contrast, a reflective statement that exceeds the affective expressions of the child may be misleading, as it sends the message that the child should have the same levels of emotional response as the therapist. However, whether explicitly or implicitly communicated, when feelings are accurately reflected, they serve to establish an affective connection and may help the child to express their emotions (Kottman, 2003a).

Non-intrusive responses, represented in the form of tracking and reflective statements, are essential in establishing a therapeutic relationship as they communicate to the child that the therapist is accompanying the child on their journey of self-exploration. So as not to impose meaning, a therapist who is working in a strict non-intrusive manner avoids labeling the child's toys or play actions. They also avoid suggesting or structuring play activities. There are many practitioners who work non-intrusively and yet occasionally label play actions or use structured exercises. However, objects are named or labeled *after* the *child* has provided some reference point or description, and structured activities or games are likely to be introduced in a tentative manner, and only then if the child clearly expresses a need or interest in such activities (Wilson *et al.*, 1992).

Therapists in the process of consolidating their practice model for play therapy frequently express comfort when working in Quadrant III. However, this is sometimes based on the wrong reasons. For instance, therapists might state that working in a non-directive manner provides a "fail-safe" approach as they assume that by following the child's lead they will "do no harm." This is tantamount to saying, "The more non-directive I am, the better." This is an oversimplified view. A therapist must be prepared to assume various roles within Quadrant III, such as gently reflecting feelings or engaging directly with the child in various play scenarios.

Another risky assumption for the beginning therapist is that relationship formation skills are readily transferable between client age groups. As will be seen in the case illustrations that follow, there is a unique set of skills required when working with children in Quadrant III. Unfortunately, therapists sometimes believe that skills previously utilized with teens or adults readily generalize to children; this is simply not the case. Therapists operating from this perspective are often surprised when an invitation for a child to join them in play is met with passivity, confusion, or anger. Further discussion with a supervisor often reveals that they assumed that if they maintained the essential therapeutic roles of communicating warmth, acceptance, and sensitive understanding of the child, they would be able to make full emotional contact with the child. While these are essential ingredients, in many cases, making emotional contact with children is a challenging task that requires a broad skill set.

As noted by Irwin (1983), play allows the child to put overwhelming experiences and conflicts into a symbolic arena. In Quadrant III the child is often deeply immersed in the symbolic nature of play and chooses objects, activities, and dramatic scenarios with little overt awareness as to how these images or symbols relate to their interpersonal or intrapersonal dynamics. Further, the energy and psychological resources that the child brings to bear are very telling in terms of the child's experiences and emotional needs. Therapists must remain mindful of the importance of staying with the symbolic representations embodied in the child's play. In supervision sessions we frequently discuss this as the need to be "in the play" while also observing it from "above." This phrase refers to the ability to remain emotionally connected with the child, while "hovering" above the play and making use of various tools in our skill set, such as accessing our intuition and generating therapeutic hypotheses. While generating hypotheses through tracking the sequences of themes in play, therapists working in Quadrant III would hold their hypothesis for reflection outside of the session. In the latter context, they may use their new insights and understanding to consult with members of the child's support system.

The intricacies of maintaining a non-intrusive style of responding are highlighted in the following case illustration.

ILLUSTRATIVE CASE STUDY:
VIDEO QUADRANT III SEGMENT—ELLIS

Download the case examples video and transcript from https://library.jkp.com/redeem using the code RTECPZF.

In the accompanying video, Lynde, the therapist working with Ellis, begins the therapy process by working in Quadrant III. For many children, entering the play therapy room for the first time can be exciting, anxiety provoking, and even threatening. In the case of Ellis, Lynde would have spent a few minutes initially orienting him to the playroom. This simply means that Lynde would have briefly pointed out various areas of the room so that Ellis knew where things were in the room. Most importantly, the goal of this brief introduction was to communicate permission for Ellis to fully explore his environment.

This segment opens with Ellis posing the question, "Why am I here?" This suggests that despite an initial attempt to support Ellis's entry to the playroom, strong feelings and reservations remain. Lynde responds by briefly informing Ellis that in the playroom he is free to do what he wants. Without saying anything, Ellis picks out two puppets: a bird, and an alligator. Ellis throws the bird puppet toward Lynde, signaling that it is for her. Following Ellis's lead, Lynde places the puppet on her hand, communicating a willingness to join him in play. Although this is a subtle response, it signals several important dimensions of the relationship. First, by maintaining proximity to Ellis in the playroom, but without hovering around his every move, Lynde is communicating a willingness to establish emotional contact with Ellis's perceptual and experiential world of reality. Second, by waiting for Ellis to initiate the play activity, Lynde is maintaining a stance consistent with her earlier communication in which she indicated that in the playroom Ellis can decide which activities to use. Third, Lynde is "in the play," and yet from "above," she is trying to sense Ellis's reactions and experiences in that moment and use this information to guide her in accessing intuitive empathic responses. Although Lynde's role is to begin to develop an understanding of Ellis's world view, this does not necessarily mean that she is trying to analyze Ellis's play or *think ahead* by anticipating his actions, as this may pull her out of contact with Ellis and place her in the role of subtly directing the play.

Through his alligator puppet Ellis asks the question, "Why are you here?" This is a noteworthy opening as it signals Ellis's tensions and uncertainties about the relationship. Lynde seeks direction from Ellis by asking, in a whispering voice, what her puppet should say. Lynde's response is one that maintains contact with Ellis while seeking direction from him. By following Ellis's direction and having her puppet restate Ellis's response of, "To help you," Lynde remains in the play. Lynde's return of the decision-making power to Ellis proves to be an important response as it allows Ellis to express strong emotions through his alligator puppet. Immediately after the alligator remarks, "I don't need any help!" it attacks Lynde's puppet. To maintain a flow in the play exchange, Lynde chooses to give voice to her puppet's distressed and hurt feelings, which briefly intensifies the alligator's aggressiveness.

In tracking Ellis's affective reactions, Lynde sees that Ellis is smiling. When Ellis's puppet pauses and takes several deep breaths, Lynde asks (in a whispering voice) what her puppet should say now. Ellis indicates that the puppet should say, "Stop it." After the bird makes this statement, there is an abrupt ending as Ellis moves off to a corner remarking, "I don't want to do this anymore." Noticing that Ellis is unable to complete this play segment, and has pivoted away from the play, Lynde's puppet states, "Oh...he doesn't want to do this anymore." This reflective statement is a critical response, particularly at this early stage in the therapeutic process, as it communicates an understanding that in the playroom Ellis can decide to terminate a play scenario, without judgment or evaluation. Additionally, Lynde maintains emotional contact with Ellis, through her puppet's acknowledgment of his decision. As a result, shortly after this segment, Ellis decides to set up a play scenario with miniature cars and invites Lynde to join him.

There are numerous observations and hypotheses generated by this brief play segment. First, Ellis's characterization of both puppets is noteworthy: Ellis assumed control of an aggressive-style puppet while providing Lynde with a puppet character that was directed to act in a passive manner and which was eventually hurt. Given the referral issues, this may represent times in the past when Ellis has been overpowered, hurt, or victimized. Second, although Ellis's alligator puppet assumed an aggressive role, which sometimes provides children with a sense of mastery over past troublesome experiences, the abruptness of the ending suggests that Ellis felt overwhelmed and unable to contain or reorganize his feelings. Ultimately, it would seem that he was unable to bring resolution or closure to the play scenario. This does not mean that this play segment had little therapeutic value. In fact, Ellis had the opportunity to safely try on a role that had certain levels of power and control. In her non-intrusive responses, Lynde briefly reflected what it feels like to be hurt and victimized, which is an important step in the process of helping Ellis reorganize his feelings and experiences. However, to shift his world view, Ellis will likely need to revisit these themes at various points in future sessions.

Interestingly, Ellis quickly moved to a different play scenario with miniature cars where he once again represented themes of aggression and control. During this brief play segment, Ellis set up a small car track and tossed Lynde a small car, directing that she should follow him. Ellis then ran over this car with his own and began to smash into all the other objects. This may not have occurred unless Lynde had provided a voice to the hurt and troublesome feelings in the previous play segment and conveyed a sense of permission for Ellis to direct and choose play activities. Most importantly, Lynde's unqualified acceptance of Ellis's self-expressions is a primary support for Ellis to generate his own pathway of change and growth.

As illustrated by this play segment, things happen very quickly in the playroom! In Quadrant III a therapist must respond quickly, in the play, while also giving careful consideration to the pacing, tone, and style of their *Non-Intrusive Responding*.

THE *WHEN*: CONSIDERATIONS FOR
THE PLAY THERAPY PROCESS

The term "process" refers to the movement or change that occurs during treatment. Axline (1982) described a process of change or movement in the patterns of children's self-expression through play, noting that as sessions progressed, many of the children's feelings came to be expressed symbolically, moving from toy to toy, toy to invisible person, child to imaginary person, child as real person, and child to the object of their feelings. Thus, through a process of self-expression, children were seen as gradually bringing their feelings to the surface and learning to either control or discard them.

To facilitate movement, therapists need to understand when and how to respond. One of the primary questions that needs to be addressed in Quadrant III is, "How do I respond non-intrusively?" Another important question is, "When should I say something?" These are process-related questions which usually surface during supervision meetings in the form of, "Wouldn't it be better if I just remained an observer?" and, "Why isn't there movement in the play, especially since I have been careful not to intrude on the child's play?"

To answer the first question, "How do I respond non-intrusively?" think back to the play segment where Ellis is setting up a scenario with miniature cars. Lynde's tracking statement, "It looks like you're picking some of those things," contains non-specific descriptors that are non-intrusive. Furthermore, Lynde refrains from *over-narrating* Ellis's play activities; she does not issue tracking comments for each movement or activity that Ellis does. However, to ensure that Ellis knows that she is actively engaged, Lynde provides reflective statements. These are more than a restatement of the content of Ellis's verbalizations. For example, when Lynde responds to Ellis's one-word request to "follow" him with her miniature car, Lynde responds, "You want me to follow you now." This is an accurate reflective response; Lynde carefully uses her intonation and chooses additional words to communicate that she is listening and understands the immediacy and directness of Ellis's message.

Questions concerning the *when* of *Non-Intrusive Responding* are best addressed through considering factors that relate to the effectiveness of certain therapeutic activities. In supervision meetings, these translate into a discussion of the therapeutic "hits" and "misses." For example, the effectiveness of a reflective statement is often gauged by whether it is congruent with the child's phenomenal field and signals to the child that the therapist empathically understands their experiences. A reflective statement that is a "hit" may be observed by a child intensifying the play; this is indicated when the symbolic nature of the play intensifies and moves toward lower levels on the consciousness dimension. At other times, a therapist might feel they are accurately tracking the play and issuing timely reflective statements; however, they may present as "misses" in the context of the play. This may be noticed when fragmentations or disruptions occur in play sequences, which is often the child's way of signaling that they need more psychological distance. This does not necessarily mean that the reflection was totally off base. Instead, it may have been too close to the child's experiences or it may be that the child is not yet ready to integrate the feelings associated with these experiences. It serves little purpose to make reflections that push through a child's defenses, particularly when they are unable to absorb certain feelings, information, or insights.

The question, "Wouldn't it be better if I just remained an observer?" is critical to understanding therapeutic processes in Quadrant III. As opposed to *non-responding*, which places activities outside of the Play Therapy Dimensions Model altogether, *Non-Intrusive Responding* emphasizes that there is a dynamic, interpersonal relationship operating at all times. *Non-Intrusive Responding* does not exclude the possibility of the therapist entering the play when invited by the child. However, for some therapists, entering the child's space appears as though it may increase the risk of directing or taking over the play. While this is a possibility, there are numerous ways to safeguard the therapeutic relationship. For instance, a therapist might alter voice tone or whisper when asking the child to tell them what a character might say or do, emphasizing the therapist's need for direction from the child. Lynde did this several times with her puppet character. A therapist might also signal a willingness to enter the play, non-verbally, by moving closer to the child's field of play. Additionally the therapist might subtly animate or give voice to play actions, which not only signals to the child that the therapist is tracking the play but also indicates a certain degree of playfulness and interest. This was observed during the car crash scene when Lynde made several brief animated comments such as "whoa" and "wow."

"Why isn't there movement in the play, especially since I have been careful not to intrude on the child's play?" This question is best addressed through considering the underlying mechanisms of change in play therapy. Most play therapy approaches recognize that timely therapeutic communications that offer safety, acknowledgment, empathic understanding, and acceptance of potentially disowned feeling states and experiences are curative in nature (Landreth, 2002; O'Connor, 2000). Unless sufficient energy has been put forth in establishing a climate of trust during the initial stages of therapy, the child will likely withhold their self-expressions. The question of movement must also be considered from the viewpoint of *what* we are looking for or tracking in the child's play and *how* we come to understand the meaning in children's play. Frank (1982) suggested that it is useful to think of play as figurative language; a child's play will reveal equivalents of most familiar forms of speech, metaphor, hyperbole, etc. While this provides a framework for thinking about symbolic expressions in play, it must also be recognized that the play activity of children represents a complex mixture of conscious and unconscious expressions (Amster, 1982). Furthermore, understanding of what is occurring in play must occur within a developmental perspective. This requires knowledge of what is typical of children at certain stages of development. As noted by Landreth (2001):

In assessing play behavior the observer, then, is constantly comparing what an individual child is doing, saying and feeling, to what is normal for that child's age, level of development, and environment. These comparisons can then provide some clues to what the unique meaning may be. (p.11)

Typically, play therapists look to understand the child's inner emotional experiences through themes represented in the play. Themes are simply the recurrence of certain events or topics in the child's play. They may surface during a single play therapy session or across several sessions. Although themes may not be easily recognized, as they may be represented through different play objects, activities, or modalities (art or dress-up play), the repetition of play behaviors and sequences signals that the child is playing out certain emotional issues.

When a theme is no longer observable, it may indicate that the child has been able to move forward emotionally, as the child has reorganized some part, or all, of a troublesome thought, feeling, or experience. At times, a theme may occur repetitively, leading the therapist to believe that the process has become "stuck." This is when it is important to recognize that the change process can be slow, particularly for children who have experienced multiple traumas or disruptions in their lives. Further, the repetition may signify that the child is in the process of working through certain feelings, which for the play therapist should raise questions concerning the type or form of facilitative response that may be most helpful to the child. In Quadrant III, this may imply that the child needs more reflective comments to get in touch with disowned feelings.

An understanding of where the child is in terms of the overall therapy process is also critical to conceptualizing whether movement is occurring. There are numerous conceptualizations about the play therapy process, emphasizing various stages, such as the beginning stage, working stage, and termination stage. Moustakas (1982) described a five-stage process for emotionally disturbed children. In the first stage, they present with diffuse negative feelings and then move into the second stage of ambivalent feelings that retain elements of anger and hostility. In the third stage, they progress to negative feelings directly focused on specific relationships or individuals in their lives. In the fourth stage, they present ambivalent feelings with a mixture of negative and positive feelings. By the fifth stage, they develop clear, distinct, and usually realistic feeling and attitudes. Moustakas concluded that as children move through these stages, they gradually achieve greater insight and understanding of reality.

Therapists working in Quadrant III may find the model of stages conceptualized by Wilson *et al.* (1992) helpful as it is also based on a non-directive approach to play therapy. However, caution is required when using a stage model for understanding the play therapy process, as underlying emotional processes do not occur in a step-by-step fashion, and the stages are not readily identifiable. Caution is also required when relating or overlaying stages to specific children as there are limitless variations in children's health or adjustment and the nature of their familial, cultural, and external support systems. Keeping these considerations in mind, movement in the play therapy process is generally indicated by the child's ability to express feelings with greater focus and intensity. In many cases, children move from exploratory, non-committal play toward symbolic play that is representative of their view of self, families, and experiences. As this work continues, the relationship that was initially formed with the therapist becomes critically important to the child's ability to bring focus and specificity to these feelings and experiences.

Process questions related to the *when* of play therapy may be answered through re-examining the primary tenets of non-directive work. The belief is that the child has an innate internal drive to lead the play which supports a self-actualization process. Accordingly, therapists need to exercise patience with the change process. It is easy for therapists to forget this basic principle and try to push the child faster than they are able or ready to go. Alternatively, therapists may think they need to abandon this quadrant altogether because they assume that the child is incapable of bringing forward and working through important themes. For many children who have experienced trauma, we find repetitiveness, fragmentation, and looping in their play scenarios (White, Draper, and Pittard Jones, 2001). The play therapist must be careful not to misjudge these important elements of the play process, as they are essential to the child's reorganizing of past traumatic experiences. Quite simply, it takes time and repetition for the reorganization process to occur.

A final consideration for the play therapy process is the therapist's use of self. Most would agree that in a therapy process that is as highly relational as play therapy, we are certain to bump into ourselves at some point. In some cases, this can be as simple as becoming bored with a play activity and failing to track the child's activities because we have lost all contact with the child. At other times, we may pull away from the child because our emotions have been triggered by something the child says or does. McInnes (2019) asserts that playfulness is at the heart of the relationship, rather than the act of play. Thus, the therapist's capacity to tap into their playful self is critically important. As noted by Chown (2015), where there is playfulness there is attunement, affection, and affirmation. These factors are so critical to the play therapy process that Chapter 13 is devoted to the topic.

THE *WHO*: CLINICAL APPLICATIONS

Quadrant III has great appeal to practitioners as it has broad clinical applications with respect to addressing a range of presenting issues. In their review of studies concerning the effectiveness of Child-Centered Play Therapy, Sweeney and Landreth (2003) note that this approach has demonstrated effectiveness with hearing-impaired children, grieving children, children with emotional or physical challenges, and even a child with trichotillomania.

Quadrant III is also well suited to working with children from diverse cultural backgrounds. As noted by Landreth and Sweeney (1997), in child-centered approaches the child is free to communicate in a manner that is comfortable and typical for the child, including cultural adaptations of play expression.

It has been the experience of practitioners at the Rocky Mountain Play Therapy Institute™ that Quadrant III is particularly helpful to the *highly directive* child. Many practitioners have worked with children who readily engage in play. Upon entering the playroom, they quickly choose play objects or activities. They also provide clear directions to therapists, concerning when or how to enter the play and which roles they are to assume. The highly directive child is able to do this, and more! At times, the degree of direction may seem so high that a therapist may feel that there is little room left for any spontaneous contributions or responses. Further, should the therapist attempt to partially structure or direct a play activity to focus energy on specific material, the child verbally protests or suddenly stops the play.

The highly directive child is ideally suited to therapeutic techniques and processes associated with Quadrant III. Rather than working against the child's presentation style, which may feel "controlling," the therapist can convey a clear sense of permissiveness, empowering the child to lead the play from the beginning stages of therapy. Through initial responses that reflect feelings and provide recognition that the child knows what they want to do, the child is provided with an immediate sense of acknowledgment and acceptance. Over time, the child often softens their approach, recognizing the unique nature of the therapeutic relationship. As trust continues to develop, the highly directive child may start to explore other aspects of the therapeutic relationship, including the dynamic, reciprocal, and responsive nature of the relationship.

Play interactions with a highly directive child help remind the therapist that the play environment is fundamentally one in which the child can exert control. The sense of feeling in control, versus having control, is an important element in emotional development and mental health (Landreth, 2001, 2012). In the safety of play, the child can confront frightening experiences and be in charge of the outcome. By expressing themselves in play, children also experience self-direction and, ultimately, may come to understand that their choices are valued. This indicates that the therapeutic activities and processes associated with Quadrant III are extremely important to most children. However, as the play therapy process unfolds, some children may benefit from experiences associated with the other quadrants.

SHOULD I STAY OR SHOULD I GO? INDICATIONS FOR WORKING IN QUADRANT III

Critical decisions must be made by all play therapists about their therapeutic effectiveness, regardless of their orientation. The Play Therapy Dimensions Model suggests that therapists view their therapy activities as dynamic and flexible, but this means there are several indications for *staying* or *going* from each of the four quadrants. Let us consider Quadrant III, *Non-Intrusive Responding*, and use the following six indicators to evaluate potential movement between quadrants.

Indicator 1: Therapeutic Process

Is the child in the beginning, middle, or end phase of the therapeutic process? If the therapeutic activity is identified as *Non-Intrusive Responding*, it is possible to be working non-intrusively in any phase. Many therapists will begin therapeutic work in Quadrant III because they do not know the child or there are vague referral issues. If the child appears to be effectively processing their issues while working in Quadrant III (during any stage of the process), the therapist should *stay* working in Quadrant III, unless there is evidence that the child could and would gain from more direction and structure.

Indicator 2: Responses of the Child

There are many types of responses made by children during play therapy sessions that indicate a therapist should stay working in Quadrant III. As previously discussed, some children have a high need for power and control and immediately take over the session. Their need to direct the play themes, character identification and use, and their therapist provides the therapist with information that Quadrant III, *Non-Intrusive Responding* would be the place to begin and possibly *stay*. Additionally, therapists working with children who do not appear able to raise issues on their own directly (or be interested in this) would likely begin working in Quadrant III. If children are not responding (ignoring) soft hypothesis testing, they may not be ready or able to enter more directive forms of play therapy; therefore, staying in Quadrant III would be indicated.

Some children are more capable than others regarding voicing their hurts or pain directly or relating an issue through concrete symbols. These young people need the opportunity to work in more directive or facilitative ways with their therapists. These therapists would therefore not necessarily stay working in Quadrant III; rather, they would go and work in Quadrant IV, *Co-Facilitation*, or Quadrant II, *Open Discussion and Exploration*.

Indicator 3: Child's Play Skills

Consideration is given to the child's play skills when deciding whether to begin in, stay in, or go from Quadrant III. Children who are highly constricted, or those who display a highly disorganized approach to planning and goal selection, or have difficulty with inhibiting behavioral impulses, may have better success working with therapists who provide more structure and direction. Some children demonstrate limited play ability because of past trauma or delays in their play development. Staying in Quadrant III, *Non-Intrusive Responding*, may not provide these young people with the most effective therapeutic experiences. Children who present with moderate to high play skills may need the opportunity to direct the play, therefore therapists working with these children would likely *stay* working in Quadrant III.

If a child presents in play therapy with significant cognitive and/or neurological difficulties, *staying* in Quadrant III would be less effective and may, in fact, trigger undue anxiety for the child. Instead, Quadrant II, *Open Discussion and Exploration*, may be a better choice, as therapeutic activities are chosen (and structured) in accordance with the child's needs and developmental capabilities.

Indicator 4: Child's Drive and Direction in Therapy

Some children engage in highly "driven" play, while others engage in moderate, adaptive play. Still others present as chaotic and disorganized, disengaged, or directed in their play. Quadrant III, *Non-Intrusive Responding*, is a good quadrant to work in to identify the child's drive and direction without imposing a predetermined therapeutic agenda. Children tell us what they need. They may disclose or directly state issues they need to talk about, in which case movement to Quadrants I or II may be indicated. Alternatively, the child may be providing a fully emerging thematic presentation of their issues and worries, and Quadrant III is the most appropriate and non-disruptive place to be working with the child.

Indicator 5: Context of the Presenting Issue

Some children come to therapy to address matters related to specific adjustment issues, while others are in therapy due to long-term abuse and loss or pervasive developmental difficulties. The more specific the issue (with an accompanying support system), the more likely it is the therapist would choose to move from Quadrant III, *Non-Intrusive Responding*, and engage in Quadrant IV, *Co-Facilitation*, or Quadrant II, *Open Discussion and Exploration*.

There is a stark difference between working with children whose core self-identity and world view have been negatively affected, and those whose worries are specific to, for instance, a problem in getting along with a friend. Children with early disruptions related to loss or abuse or developmental interruptions often need the opportunity to process their experiences through child-directed play. Many of these children will lead their therapists back to earlier stages of development in an attempt to re-experience and recover from early losses. Therapists working with these children will likely spend a considerable amount of time in Quadrant III and, when appropriate, move to Quadrant IV. Indications for movement from Quadrant III to Quadrant IV typically include such things as the children's need to have their feelings validated, the need to have a voice for their pain, the need for elaboration of self-concept, the need to be challenged regarding their views of the world, the need to learn about problem-solving, etc. Work on these issues becomes apparent to therapists when the child is cycling around in therapy, and repeating play segments that are incomplete and/or unresolved.

Indicator 6: Timelines and System Parameters

Non-Intrusive Responding appears to be more broadly utilized by those providing medium- to long-term therapy. Therapists working in managed care with limited time to see children may wish to move to Quadrant IV, *Co-Facilitation*, or Quadrant II, *Open Discussion and Exploration*. Due to time restraints, the child could be helped to experience relief more directly. If this is not ethical considering the referral issue, it is the therapist's responsibility to refer the child to another service or alert the parents about the difficulty of beginning a process that will be interrupted.

ILLUSTRATIVE CASE STUDY—HALEY

Download the case examples video and transcript from https://library.jkp.com/redeem using the code RTECPZF.

As illustrated on the video, there are several points where Susan, Haley's therapist, weaves in and out of Quadrant III. Susan's style and approach might be referred to as *responsive* as she adjusts the degree of direction and levels of therapist immersion in response to Haley's expressed needs and play skills. These adjustments are not made blindly or without careful consideration. It is unlikely that a child will tolerate adjustments such as these unless a trusting therapeutic relationship has first been established.

As mentioned on the video, there have already been several sessions with Haley where the therapist has primarily adopted a non-intrusive style of responding. Susan's judgment was that the session should once again begin in Quadrant III. Susan's conceptualization of the therapeutic goals and activities for Quadrant III included the following objectives.

- To help Haley develop a more positive self-concept.
- To assist Haley in assuming greater levels of self-responsibility.

- To foster higher levels of self-direction.
- To bring forward positive experiences and feelings of control.
- To foster greater coping resources and become more trusting of herself.

In the beginning moments of this session, Haley takes a few moments to decide what to play, and she eventually chooses the dollhouse. Considerable time is spent selecting characters for the house and assigning roles. Even though Haley has been working with her therapist for several sessions, she timidly asks permission when choosing activities and objects. You will notice that Susan carefully tracks Haley's activities and selection of characters without assigning additional meaning to them.

Haley's play scenario begins with a scene of family characters waking up in the morning. Recognizing that in previous sessions Haley has repetitively played out similar scenes and appears to be somewhat stuck as she is engaging in safe or non-committal play, Susan decides to shift toward Quadrant IV, *Co-Facilitation*. At this point, Susan introduces two new characters and shifts the play theme toward peer acceptance issues. Susan's introduction of this issue, and her immersion in the play, appears to open new directions and possibilities for Haley to explore the nature and impact of peer interactions. In fact, Haley takes direction of the play and extends it beyond previous points by having her character suggest that the three characters she chose to represent "friends" go to the playground. At this point, Susan moves back to Quadrant III, *Non-Intrusive Responding*, and follows Haley's lead. As seen through this case example, *Non-Intrusive Responding* is ideally suited for esteem-building and empowerment. When a therapist carefully paces their comments and carefully tracks the play, the child incrementally moves toward greater degrees of personal empowerment, health, and well-being.

MOVEMENT WITHIN THIS QUADRANT

A circumplex model helps the practitioner understand that even subtle movement along a dimension impacts variables associated with that dimension. As integrative play therapists, we are constantly examining the client–therapist–treatment interactions, and part of this examination is to consider shifts in directiveness or consciousness, accompanied or supported by shifts in therapist use of self.

Within Quadrant III the therapist is deciding what to track and when to leave space by not providing a tracking comment. The therapist must also decide whether to make a reflective statement that primarily relates to content, affect, or both elements. Additionally, the degree to which the therapist is immersed in the play and makes use of their physical or emotional self impacts the direction of the play and the child's subsequent response. Combined, the degree of immersion and type of tracking or reflective statements influence movement within this quadrant in subtle or pronounced ways.

For example, when a therapist working with a traumatized child in the early stages of treatment notices that the child's metaphorical play reflects diffuse negative affect, such as pushing or banging characters and objects without clear or connected storylines, the therapist might choose to track the actions but not immerse themselves emotionally in the play to any great degree. This decision, in part, is based on the understanding that the child has begun to communicate symbolically and likely needs distance or space from the experiences they are trying to gain mastery of. At this moment, the therapist is positioned toward the far-left side of the quadrant, represented by point A in Figure 6.1. Although the therapist is actively tracking play actions, they are choosing not to add emotional tones to their comments. Furthermore, as the child's play represents lower levels of consciousness, the therapist also chooses not to make reflective comments that connect affect and intent, such as a character feeling hurt or confused by what happened.

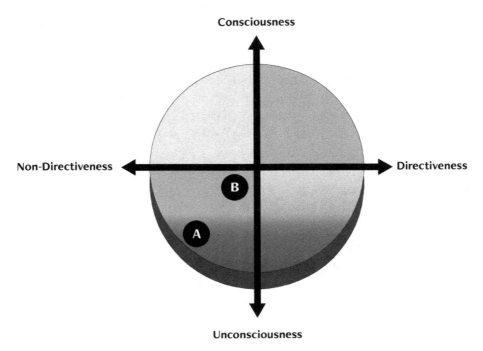

FIGURE 6.1: THERAPIST MOVEMENT IN QUADRANT III

After several sessions, the therapist notices that the child's play continues to show themes of hurting and anger, but there is a clear relational context to these interactions, such as an older sibling in an animal family portrayed as hurting a younger one. Noticing this shift, the therapist chooses to increase the emotionality of their tracking statements while also reflecting that the young one keeps getting hurt and, despite calling out, no one responds. The therapist's immersion is of course in response to what is represented symbolically, but it is also aimed at supporting the child's communication. Understanding that the child is now working at a higher level of consciousness, the therapist makes greater use of their self, with movement toward the far-right upper portion of this quadrant, as represented by point B in Figure 6.1.

As noted earlier, in therapy there is seldom static positioning on either dimension. It is more likely that movement or weaving occurs along each dimension in relation to specific therapist–child–treatment interaction factors. Practitioners can take advantage of this circumplex representation to articulate *when*, *why*, or *how* movement occurred, and conceptualize *where* the play therapy process might go next.

KEY POINTS

- The term *Non-Intrusive Responding* is not synonymous with Non-Directive Play Therapy. It describes a dynamic range of therapeutic activities and roles, not a model of play therapy.
- A play therapist working in Quadrant III, *Non-Intrusive Responding*, is very active in conceptualizing issues and formulating hypotheses, while also remaining in the field of play.
- Non-intrusive responses, such as tracking and reflective statements, are essential in establishing a therapeutic relationship, as they communicate to the child that the therapist is present and attuned to what is being communicated in play.
- To remain "non-intrusive," a therapist may seek direction from the child, such as when using the whispering technique to ask for direction, or carefully pace their tracking comments based on the moment-to-moment response of the child.
- Indications for staying or leaving this quadrant include the stage of therapy, the child's play skills, and the child's need to direct the play or gain mastery. Generally, a "do no harm" perspective is not a sufficient reason for remaining in this quadrant.

◉ **Chapter 7** ◉

CO-FACILITATION

Quadrant IV

Show me your world and I will enter it with you.

Quadrant IV, *Co-Facilitation*, as depicted in Figure 3.1, occupies a notable space within the Play Therapy Dimensions Model. While falling on the right-hand side of the *directiveness* dimension, it remains clearly within the lower portion of the *consciousness* dimension. This intersection suggests, above all else, that therapeutic activities, including interpretations, "stay in the play."

THE *WHAT:* THE DEFINING FEATURES OF QUADRANT IV

Although therapeutic activities are directive in Quadrant IV, as compared to Quadrant III, *being directive* is not the primary characteristic of the therapist's role nor is it meant to be the defining feature of the therapeutic relationship. Instead, the goal of working in this quadrant is to become a co-facilitator of the play to open new avenues for the child to express, process, and reorganize feelings or experiences.

The term *Co-Facilitation* speaks to therapeutic activities and processes based on a shared or egalitarian relationship. As Kottman (2020) notes, to have an egalitarian relationship, there must be a sense of shared power and responsibility. To maintain an egalitarian relationship, the therapist usually enters the play at the invitation of the child and only after the therapist has tracked a number of themes and patterns in the child's play will the therapist make the decision to test a hypothesis about what the child may be trying to portray or potentially disclose through play characters or actions. This process is represented by the Jungian Analytical play therapists' approach to soft hypothesis testing.

> For example, when the patient picks up the toy sword the therapist might have a soft hypothesis that the patient desires to feel more powerful and in charge. The therapist could respond with the validating comment, "You have a sword now." Acting in a more

participating/amplifying role the therapist might test her soft hypothesis about the patient's desire to feel empowered and say, "That is a very large and powerful looking sword." If the therapist's comments and nonverbal participation are resonant with the archetypal and symbolic theme in which the patient is engaged, even her more active interpretive words and reactions will blend in, almost unnoticed, to the ongoing play activity. (Peery, 2003, p.40)

From the Jungian perspective, hypotheses are either borne out or dropped as the play unfolds. However, a therapist working in Quadrant IV only tests hypotheses within the play. Similarly, therapist-generated insertions *stay in the play*, safeguarding the child's sense of ownership. For example, in the swordplay scenario described above, the therapist might elaborate the play by introducing new characters as helper figures, or use one character to demonstrate the child's inner conflict. Staying in the fantasy and symbolism of a child's play allows the therapist to elaborate the play, potentially creating new pathways for self-expression.

The degree of therapist immersion increases considerably in Quadrant IV, compared with Quadrant III. This signifies that the therapist's role shifts from a non-intrusive responder to that of an *observer-participant*. Allan (1997) defines this as being simultaneously attached and detached, allowing the therapist to think analytically about what is happening, verbally, non-verbally, and symbolically. In this role, the therapist is more than a witness to the child's play; the therapist must assume the challenging task of making tracking or reflecting statements while also co-facilitating the play process through soft interpretations. These can only occur if the therapist has attempted to think about and understand, in depth, the child and the meaning of the child's play activities.

THE *HOW:* THERAPEUTIC ROLES AND ACTIVITIES

Numerous models of play therapy acknowledge applications of a directive approach to working therapeutically with children, including Cognitive-Behavioral Play Therapy (Knell, 2003), Psychoanalytic Play Therapy (Bromfield, 2003), Adlerian Play Therapy (Kottman, 2003a, 2020), Ecosystemic Play Therapy (O'Connor and New, 2003), Gestalt Play Therapy (Oaklander, 2003), and Object Relations/Thematic Play Therapy (Benedict, 2003). These models may also be applied in a manner that moves toward the lower, unconscious end of the consciousness dimension. While this implies that various models potentially fall within Quadrant IV, it is the therapist's use of self, or degree of immersion, that usually determines whether therapeutic activities fall within Quadrant IV.

As noted in Chapters 3 and 13, the therapist's use of self is reflected by the nature of their involvement in the play. There are different degrees of therapist immersion.

High levels of immersion are outwardly represented by the therapist's active involvement in interactive play sequences. However, use of self may be viewed across several categories: verbal, emotional, physical, self-system, and cultural use of self, and type and frequency of interpretations. These dimensions are discussed in greater detail in Chapter 13, along with a Therapist Use of Self Scale (Appendix B) that assists play therapists to increase their awareness of the potential impact they have on child clients. For the moment, it is important to emphasize that a therapist working in Quadrant IV is often highly immersed in the play but never attempts to directly discuss or interpret the play with the child in a conscious manner.

Use of self, from an Ericksonian perspective, is based on looking for and identifying patterns of belief, behavior, and motivation in each individual. Ericksonian play therapists highly value the power of the unconscious in relation to client movement or change. As noted by Mills (2001; Mills and Crowley, 2014), rather than imposing interpretations, an Ericksonian therapist first allows meaning to "unfold" as it relates to the child. Mills further emphasizes that it is the child who gives meaning to an object, not the therapist. Therefore, when a child is engaged in a dramatic play sequence, the child's present self-expressions are appreciated by the therapist and utilized to help the child access other inner resources.

Similar to other play therapy approaches, the Jungian approach emphasizes the expression and transformation of emotions. From a Jungian perspective, children use sandworlds and miniature figures to externalize their inner struggles. The child projects different emotions or feeling tones onto the figures, resulting in change or growth in the feeling tone. Although primarily child directed, there are times when the Jungian Analytical play therapist becomes immersed in the play.

> The Jungian approach is to "stay at the level of the feeling of the child" and to follow the child's dramas and plays as they unfold. The therapist witnesses the child's play, reflects feelings, and comments on them. The therapist takes his or her lead from the child. The therapist is essentially developing a feeling-toned relationship with the child, while mirroring and being attuned, and giving words to the range of feelings and thoughts that are being expressed or enacted. (Allan, 1997, p.116)

Through the amplification process (which may involve immersions of a verbal and emotional nature), emotions that were previously trapped become free and may be experienced in the child's consciousness and integrated into the child's personality structure (Allan, 1997).

The phenomenological approach to play therapy emphasizes that the therapist is mainly responsible for understanding and interpreting the child's play (Mook, 2003). While the therapist plays an active, encouraging role to facilitate the child's expression through play or verbal dialogue, they operate from the basic realization that the child is also involved in trying to understand their play scenarios and may require distance in this process.

> On a child's request, they may be asked to play the role of some play figures or play an active role themselves. In doing so, they become playfully and imaginatively involved. Therapists dialogue with children through the play figures and their feelings, thoughts, and actions. They join them in their rhythm and use their voice intonations to selectively verbalize play actions and discretely reflect feelings of expectation or surprise or other enacted feelings that the child expresses but does not yet verbalize. When children meet obstacles in their play worlds, therapists attempt to help them overcome it by raising questions or suggesting possible help, and thus facilitate the continuation of the play story. At all times, therapists respect the anonymity of the play figures in the play world and do not expose their possible real identity. This is of central importance because it enables children to project and express strong and threatening conflicts and feelings, which may lie at the heart of their problems and which they could express only in the relative safety of their play worlds. (Mook, 2003, p.271)

When therapists are first introduced to Quadrant IV, they often express concern about overwhelming the child by moving too fast with verbal insertions. This is an important consideration, as we have seen examples in supervision where the therapist has played "overtop" of the child. This signals the need for the therapist to increase self-awareness and heighten self-understanding, which is addressed in greater depth in Chapter 14. With increasing awareness and practice opportunities, the well-attuned therapist will recognize that they must go about the process of elaborating the play in a careful and gradual manner, using their clinical intuition as well as case formulations to guide them. Bearing in mind that the therapist is a *co-facilitator* in this quadrant, they must primarily take direction from the child. This occurs by tracking the child's affective and physical expressions, as these markers inform us about the pacing and intensity of therapeutic activities, such as insertions.

Therapists also voice the concern that working in a co-facilitative manner, utilizing soft hypothesis testing or interpretations, disrupts and potentially contaminates the therapeutic relationship. There is certainly the potential for interpretations to become intrusive, particularly when a child demonstrates the capacity to make meaning from their play activities. On this matter, the phenomenological approach to play therapy is very informative as it emphasizes the hermeneutic circle of understanding, interpretation, and validation. Essentially, an interpretation is never abstract but a concrete application of understanding to specific circumstances of the child. As noted by Mook (2003):

> Thus, if we seek to understand and interpret an imaginative play in play therapy, we

need to listen to it as a whole and first ask what the play is telling us and, secondarily, what it reveals about the child's life world. (p.266)

Following from this, Mook asserts that there is no interpretation without first understanding and no understanding without some level of interpretation. In most cases, it would be ill-advised to move toward interpretive comments without careful consideration of various contextual factors, including the nature of the therapeutic relationship and the stage of the therapeutic process.

Recognizing that therapeutic processes such as transference and countertransference will be activated in Quadrant IV, as the use of self is heightened, therapists must be prepared to differentiate emotions that are related to the child's issues (transference) from those related to unresolved issues in themselves (countertransference). As noted by Allan (1997), the therapist should be prepared to use their ego to assess internal feeling states, to analyze the play, and to use these insights to understand the less conscious processes of the child.

Transference and countertransference processes should not be ignored or shut down. When therapists are properly attuned, these processes help guide the selection and pacing of therapeutic activities. Allan (1997) suggests that awareness of these issues may point us in various directions: to continue to observe, to reflect feelings and thoughts, to ask for clarification or amplification of the symbol, and to use interpretations to link feelings and thoughts to past and present. Guidelines for exploring transference and countertransference issues during supervision are discussed in Chapters 11 and 12.

ILLUSTRATIVE CASE STUDY:
VIDEO QUADRANT IV SEGMENT—ELLIS

Download the case examples video and transcript from https://library.jkp.com/redeem using the code RTECPZF.

Several sessions after beginning her work with Ellis, Lynde shifts her therapeutic activities as well as her use of self, moving toward the right side of the directiveness continuum. This is a *responsive* shift based on Lynde's understanding of Ellis's view of the world. As Ellis has consistently portrayed themes of aggression and vulnerability in his play scenarios, Lynde adopts a co-facilitative role to create additional opportunities to strengthen Ellis's coping resources.

Although Lynde begins to direct and elaborate the play, it is important to note that Ellis retains ownership of the play space. Not only does he initiate sandplay, but also he is the one to decide on the number of army figures allotted to each side. Additionally, Ellis moves, adds, and animates these figures as the play develops.

Lynde continues to track the play and makes reflective comments, just as we observed in her work in Quadrant III, *Non-Intrusive Responding*. For example, after Ellis offers a few army figures to her, Lynde remarks, "So you want me to have these guys." Following immediately, Ellis's characters begin firing. We quickly see that Ellis is setting up a one-sided battle scene; the army figures on his side outnumber the other side and have more weapons, including a tank and airplane.

Lynde might have decided to remain in Quadrant III as Ellis is certainly active in his play initiations. Also, the themes he portrays are central to the referral issues, as Lynde has come to understand them. However, Lynde has decided to explore Ellis's world view through elaborating the play and by using soft hypothesis testing. This is not to say that therapists never formulate hypotheses in Quadrant III, as they are constantly gauging and altering reflective statements based on an understanding of the child. Further, while interpretations are not offered directly to the child in Quadrant III, this doesn't mean that a hypothesis isn't generated and held in mind about the child's phenomenal field.

In Quadrant IV, hypotheses are activated and gradually tested through play-based elaborations and verbal insertions in the play. For example, Lynde begins to pursue the hypothesis that Ellis may see or experience the world as a vulnerable place and likely does not feel that external help or assistance is available. This seems to be a reasonable hypothesis, based on previous sessions as well as the fact that Ellis sets up a battle scene where one side is significantly under-resourced. Going with this hypothesis, Lynde incrementally inserts comments and elaborates activities in the play. For instance, when her side is being shot at, Lynde inserts the comment, "There's so many of them...they keep shooting at us...there's not many of us and so many of them!" As her side continues to be fired upon, Lynde moves this further along by stating, "I wonder if we can get some help?" Lynde's wording selection is critical; her "wondering" leaves Ellis with choices about where to go with the play but also opens to him the *possibility* of accessing help. Immediately following this, Ellis provides a few additional soldiers for Lynde's side, although he continues with the attack. Astutely, Lynde moves this a bit further along by inserting the comment "Boy, it's hard when you are all alone...you just can't do very much." This insertion is certainly a notch or two above what we have been referring to as reflective statements; it is a soft hypothesis designed to elaborate the play and resonate with Ellis's feeling states.

Next, Lynde elaborates the play by introducing a commander, symbolizing the potential of accessing external or internal resources. Ellis immediately picks up on this and develops a leader or decision-maker position on his side. Lynde's actions stimulate further *elaboration* of the play. However, keeping with the spirit of her co-facilitative role, her actions are embedded within the context of Ellis's play and, most importantly, are consistent with her initial hypothesis. Notice that Lynde also *immerses* herself more deeply in the play by giving voice to a number of feelings and experiences. For instance, characters on her side begin to tell the commander that they are scared and feel alone. This offers a strong reflection or amplification of feelings of vulnerability and isolation that Ellis has previously represented in his play scenarios. Lynde's use of self, represented in her verbal and emotional immersions in the play, appears to mobilize Ellis; he provides more helpers to Lynde's side and then launches an attack with a secret weapon—an airplane. A question that might be posed at this juncture is whether Ellis's provision of extra characters is representative of an emerging sense of self-awareness. In support of this, rather than annihilating Lynde's side, which has occurred in earlier sessions, the airplane crashes. At minimum, this response can be flagged as a change in the aggressive sequencing in Ellis's play.

Maintaining her co-facilitative role, Lynde's side constructs a barrier, elaborating on the hypotheses that Lynde has already formulated and brought into the field of play. Symbolizing the need for self-protection, the barrier prompts curiosity and action from Ellis. Initially, Ellis's side attempts to push through the barrier with a tank. This maneuver is aborted but Ellis has gained sufficient ego strength to persevere; this is represented when a single army character wipes out the barrier. The scenario briefly resolves with Ellis's side capturing and burying all of the characters on Lynde's side. In the past, Ellis has somewhat aggressively "pushed through" barriers or boundaries in play, such as when he attacked Lynde's puppet in the opening session. Ellis is now more self-contained and self-regulating. Although this shift in Ellis's imaginative play has the potential to bring forward new understanding of Ellis's real life, the meaning of this one-time occurrence must be seen in the context of previous play scenarios as well as the broader context of Ellis's life experiences. Thus, Lynde is careful not to over-ascribe meaning to it; yet it is something that she will track in future sessions.

As the scene fades, Lynde remarks, "There's just no escaping now!" Lynde's comment, while in keeping with the play events, is recognized as more than a reflective statement; it is a planned verbal insertion delivered in sync with ongoing play activities. The intent of this insertion is to help Ellis make meaning out of his current play in relation to his past experiences. Although Lynde does not expect that Ellis will suddenly gain new understanding or insight, or be able to use this information to problem-solve, by observing Ellis's response, Lynde will be able to modify and pace future insertions and interpretive reflections. Importantly, Lynde did not directly impose her thoughts on Ellis. Instead, her insertions were delivered in the context of the play, providing Ellis with emotional space to absorb or deflect the comment.

Prior to her next supervision meeting, Lynde will complete the Degree of Immersion: Therapist Use of Self Scale (Appendix B) to monitor her use of self and the degree of immersion in the play. This tool asks therapists to examine five areas of immersion: verbal use of self, emotional use of self, physical use of self, self-system, and cultural use of self. As observed in this play segment, Lynde's verbal insertions are carefully paced and always remain in the play, allowing Ellis time to respond how he chooses to in play.

It is important to remember that therapists can vary the directness and literalness of their play-based elaborations and verbal insertions. As Winnicott (1971) stated, children enter a magical world in play, one where they get to suspend reality if they wish. If a therapist makes their elaborations or insertions too transparent, they run the risk of pulling the child out of the play just when the child needs the play context to enact feelings or experiences. In the play segments just reviewed, Lynde utilized a commander character to give voice to feelings of vulnerability. This was accomplished in a less transparent manner, in the form of a soliloquy. In this example, comments directed toward the commander give words to experiences that Ellis may be unable to verbalize because they are too painful or confusing. Possibly, these insertions increased Ellis's awareness of certain feelings, although this is not necessarily the objective or goal. It is perhaps enough that Lynde has given words to certain feelings as this helps Ellis extend his play, taking it in directions that are important to him.

Finally, in this play segment, Lynde's use of self and the ensuing therapeutic activities occur midway along the directiveness dimension in Quadrant IV. Through her elaborations and insertions, Lynde periodically provides direction. However, she does not structure the choice of play activities, nor does she constantly direct the play. Thus, we see that an egalitarian, co-facilitative relationship is evolving.

THE *WHEN:* CONSIDERATIONS FOR THE PLAY THERAPY PROCESS

While a therapist may favor certain quadrants or choose to adhere to one throughout all stages of therapy, it is often helpful to adopt a "weaving" process, particularly when working from an integrative perspective. After viewing countless videos where *Co-Facilitation* was a central and organizing component of the therapy process, several important trends related to the "rhythm" of play therapy were discovered. This term, coined by Allan (1997), refers to the rhythm and flow of the play therapy process as children move from the introductory to working and termination phases of therapy.

The term "rhythm" is well suited to the process of play therapy as it equates to the synchrony that musicians search for when they are engaged in the art of playing music together. There is a pulse and rhythm that unifies members of a jazz quartet; it forms the underlying stream of consciousness from which they improvise and work together. This analogy holds well when thinking about the therapist's use of self and immersions in the play. If the therapist has done their job of observing and tracking the child's involvement in the play, and has fostered an egalitarian relationship, the therapist will be attuned to the child's rhythms and pulses. Accordingly, play-based elaborations and insertions will "keep time" with the cadence or pace established by the child, as well as the child's musical key (thematic content).

One of the trends observed with *Co-Facilitation* is that it sometimes requires a progressive crescendo. This implies that we gradually immerse ourselves in the play, slowly increasing the intensity or frequency of our insertions while checking for the child's ability to tolerate or integrate these changes. Similar to movement through the levels of interpretation, as discussed in Chapter 3, therapist immersions and co-facilitative responses need to be carefully paced.

Therapists working in this quadrant need to constantly monitor and reflect on their use of self, particularly the degree of immersion in the play, as co-facilitative responses bring therapists into direct contact with their own emotional, physical, and spiritual parts of self. To illustrate the importance of monitoring and evaluating therapist immersions, let's eavesdrop on one small segment of a supervision session. A therapist had been working with a six-year-old girl who was heavily invested in doll play. For this child, the dolls were symbolic of her life experiences; she had been placed in numerous foster care situations and was struggling with pronounced issues of loss and abandonment. The therapist quickly recognized these issues in the drawings the child completed during a previous session. However, when activities shifted to dramatic play, something also shifted for the therapist. The therapist kept remarking that she was having a hard time tracking what was occurring in the play. During a review of session videos, the therapist kept pushing the fast-forward button, moving beyond the spot where the child was setting the stage for her play by selecting dolls and dressing them. Realizing that there might be something important to examine about this portion of the sessions (particularly as the therapist reported that set-up could take up to three-quarters of the entire session), the supervisor asked to review these segments.

Within a few minutes of watching, the therapist jumped up and exclaimed, "I can't believe I missed that; she's already in the play and talking through her characters. I just thought it was boring, so I didn't pay much attention." This is a talented therapist who quickly processed this issue, coming to the realization that in her own play history, doll play always seemed tedious, as so much time went into dressing the dolls that it seemed to take away from the fun. During portions of the session where the therapist entered the play, it was also revealed that she did so on a verbal level, but not on an emotional level. That is, she essentially sidetracked herself into talking to, and about, the child, placing these conversations outside of the context of the play, rather than immersing herself *in the play*, which appeared to be what the child was inviting her to do. In the sessions that followed, the therapist, armed with this new understanding, joined in doll play and was able to immerse herself emotionally. Her doll character became animated and exhibited feelings that accurately mirrored the child's experiences. The therapist also elaborated certain portions of the play, and the child began to move with this, demonstrating stronger abilities to disclose hurt feelings in the context of the play. This was not a child with low play skills; she was capable and ready to deepen the play once her therapist realized the importance of immersion and found a comfortable way to enter the play.

THE *WHO:* CLINICAL APPLICATIONS

Therapeutic activities within Quadrant IV, *Co-Facilitation*, are applicable to children with a wide range of presenting issues. Because of its unique positioning along the directiveness and consciousness dimensions, it is well suited for children who have experienced relational, traumatic, or abusive experiences, particularly those who appear to have become stuck when engaged in non-directive activities. Quadrant IV is also indicated for children who are emotionally constricted, those who experience difficulties with emotional self-regulation, and those with reduced play skills.

Children who have been abused may appear "stuck" in play and engage in looping (circular, incomplete segments of play) or compulsive repetition of fragments of their traumatic experiences. Often, it is not that the child lacks the cognitive skills or general play skills to continue the play, but they are blocked emotionally, to the extent that the play process cannot evolve. Therapists need to carefully track these occurrences and work to understand their significance. The Tracking and Observation Form (Appendix C) is a tool developed for this purpose. It is unnecessary, often ill-advised, to rescue children from these temporary play states. Simply put, there is much to be gained in the working-through process, as it is part of self-healing. At the same time, therapist-generated insertions, such as a helper character, may provide momentum.

Many therapists have encountered children who struggle to maintain a flow in their play sequences and are constantly stopping or switching play activities because they have little experience or capacity to move the play along. For these children, a co-facilitative approach may be extremely helpful. This does not imply that the therapist should carry the burden of the play. Instead, brief and timely insertions and elaborations may be all that is required to avert fragmentations or disruptions in the play.

Some children present as emotionally constricted, evidenced by a limited range of expressiveness when engaged in play activities. More commonly, these children may be seen as showing neurotic tendencies, in the sense that they are defensive and tend to close themselves off emotionally from those around them. These children are also in need of a facilitative therapeutic process that gently coaches them to become involved in imaginative play.

There are also those children who experience significant difficulties with self-regulation. We recall a session with a seven-year-old boy who decided to put on a puppet play. The therapist was directed to sit down and pretend that he was in the front row of the audience. As the play began, the child coordinated two puppets that began to fight with each other. Suddenly, the child burst through the puppet theater, and his puppets attacked the therapist. After a video review of this segment, it became clear that the child did not intend to damage the puppet theater or attack his therapist. However, he had such difficulties regulating himself that when strong emotions were experienced, he was unable to contain himself and remain in the play. As puppet plays were a favored medium for this child, additional thought went into how to support his needs for self-expression, while also assisting him with the task of self-regulation. One idea was to have a puppet character join the therapist in the audience. The puppet would make tracking observations and reflective comments, to signal to the child that the therapist was present. Additionally, the puppet would give voice to certain actions and emotions conveyed in the play, offering an external vantage point to assist in the regulation and modulation of emotions. Ultimately, it was also decided that if the child's puppet still needed to attack, the therapist's puppet would be a safe target for discharging feelings. As it turned out, this co-facilitative approach worked extremely well! The child was able to elaborate his puppet play, with the support of tracking comments and insertions by the puppet commentator in the audience.

SHOULD I STAY OR SHOULD I GO? INDICATIONS FOR WORKING IN QUADRANT IV

Supervision sessions, based on the Play Therapy Dimensions Model, often reach what we call the ultimate question, "Should I stay in this quadrant or should I go?" On the surface, this question is misleading as it presumes there is a "right" place. It also risks the possibility of making false starts into certain quadrants without reflecting on the overall therapy process. Therapists simply don't weave between quadrants because they can; they move along the two play therapy dimensions because there are sound clinical reasons for staying or going. Let us consider Quadrant IV, *Co-Facilitation*, by using the following six indicators to evaluate potential movement to or from this quadrant.

Indicator 1: Therapeutic Process

Quadrant IV is usually accessed after a therapeutic relationship has been formed. Thus, it is more likely to occur during the middle or working phase of therapy, as this quadrant is well suited to helping children move through the reorganization process. A therapist would likely stay in this quadrant if there were synchrony between the therapist's insertions and elaborations and the child's responses. When movement becomes stagnated and the child either appears to need more structure and direction or shows a need to direct the process, it may signal that it is time to go to Quadrants II or III. During the termination phase of therapy, where a child is seeking more conscious closure and is beginning to talk openly about issues, it may be time to consider shifting to Quadrant II, *Open Discussion and Exploration*. In Adlerian Play Therapy, the final phase of therapy is reorienting/re-educating the client, and activities such as direct conversations and structured play experiences are used to assist the client in generating strategies to capitalize on their personal assets or to strengthen needed skills (Kottman, 2019).

Indicator 2: Responses of the Child

The types of responses made by children during play therapy sessions that indicate a therapist should stay working in Quadrant IV are: the child responds to soft hypothesis testing and begins to elaborate the play; the child introduces new themes; the child makes use of play objects and characters in new ways; and the child integrates old play themes with new ones which, in turn, represent newly emerging understandings and reorganization. These responses may represent what we have conceptualized as a turning point in play therapy, of which there are four types: a change in thought, behavior, affect, or understanding about something; the emergence of a level of awareness not previously available to the child; a moment in time where the child makes use of themselves or play objects in a way not previously observed; and a change in what is illuminated or seen in play—a change in the way of viewing self or others (Yasenik and Gardner, 2019). A therapist should *go* to Quadrant III, *Non-Intrusive Responding*, if therapist facilitations are shut down and ignored by the child or if hypothesis testing indicates that the insertions are not consistent with the direction that the child needs to move toward.

Indicator 3: Child's Play Skills

Consideration must be given to the child's play skills when deciding whether to begin in, stay in, or go from Quadrant IV. *Stay* if the child has very high play skills and is moving toward *Co-Facilitation* on their own. Alternatively, a child with diminished levels of play skills requires greater levels of structuring or facilitation. With this child, a therapist should consider *staying* but prepare to become more immersed in the play, demonstrating to the child other possibilities for self-expression. A therapist may choose to *go* to Quadrant II, *Open Discussion and Exploration*, when working with a child who has high verbal abilities and shows a need to talk about their experiences. Similarly, children with high levels of problem-solving ability may be driven toward Quadrant II (see Chapter 9).

Indicator 4: Child's Drive and Direction in Therapy

Some children engage in highly "driven" play, while others engage in moderate, adaptive play. Still others present as chaotic and disorganized, disengaged, or directed in their play. *Co-Facilitation* is indicated when there is a clear sense of the therapeutic agenda, and the therapist has established a strong case conceptualization based on the context of the child's issues. *Stay* in Quadrant IV when the drive and direction of the child are on a pathway consistent with the context of identified issues. *Go* back to Quadrant III, *Non-Intrusive Responding*, when the drive and direction are inconsistent with what was previously identified. This may signal that the child has additional issues or concerns not yet identified by the therapist. A therapist might also *go* to Quadrant I, *Active Utilization*, because interpretive comments may foster an increase in the child's drive and direction by accessing new insights. Movement to Quadrant II, *Open Discussion and Exploration*, is indicated when the child drives the therapeutic agenda to be more consciously addressed.

Indicator 5: Context of the Presenting Issue

Although some children come to therapy with specific adjustment issues, others have experienced long-term abuse or face developmental challenges. A therapist should consider *staying* in Quadrant IV if a child would benefit from exposure to therapist-led demonstrations that provide opportunities to practice emotional response sets, modulate feeling states, and, through characters and play objects, rehearse intrapersonal or interpersonal exchanges. When working from these perspectives, a therapist would typically *stay* unless the child requires more structure and direction to consciously organize these experiences or is unable to tolerate the intensity of certain issues and requires greater emotional distance. As discussed earlier, therapists must be careful not to disarm a child's defenses; often the play therapy process cannot move faster than the child is able to manage because the child has rudimentary structures set up to hold or contain matters that still need to be sorted out. With these factors in mind, those children with low levels of resiliency or inner core strength may benefit more from activities in Quadrant III; children with greater levels may accommodate, and possibly seek, open verbal discussions, and may be prone to engaging in activities associated with Quadrants I or II.

Indicator 6: Timelines and System Parameters

Inherent in Quadrant IV is the therapeutic processing of the child's symbols and metaphors, rather than a direct discussion of the presenting issues. This is often of great value as it allows a therapist to quickly gain a deeper understanding of the child's experiences and world view. Once a therapist has gained a new understanding, they may consider *staying* in Quadrant IV if it appears that the child has the internal resources necessary to resolve issues and exhibits the drive or need to do so in a timely fashion. At times, activities such as reflective interpretations stimulate talking and problem-solving on the part of the child; this may represent that the child is ready to

MOVEMENT WITHIN THIS QUADRANT: ILLUSTRATIVE CASE STUDY—HALEY

Musically speaking, where there are crescendos there usually are decrescendos. In play therapy, progress is often cyclical. A child in the working stage of play therapy will sometimes engage in repetitive, looping play themes; they may gain mastery of certain feelings or issues but need to go back and organize other experiences. Co-facilitative interactions play a key role in this process.

In the segment representing Quadrant IV, Haley begins to construct a family scene at the dollhouse. Susan's interactions initially represent *Non-Intrusive Responding*. However, Susan notices that Haley returns to a safe play scenario that occurred in previous sessions. Susan decides to build a *crescendo* by moving in a co-facilitative direction. First, Susan introduces two girls that call at the house. This is a thera-pist-generated elaboration, but one that Haley tolerates and accepts as likely because it is well timed and fits within the context of her play scenario. Next, Susan's char-acters have a brief discussion amongst themselves about what they would like to do. Notice how they also include Haley's character in a discussion about jumping off the Jones's garage roof. One of Susan's characters, in conversation with the other, indicates a worry about this activity. Here, Susan accomplishes more than a verbal insertion: to reflect disowned feelings of Haley's, one of Susan's characters begins to react emotionally to this idea. We then notice that Haley's character takes the lead by asking if the girls would like to come inside her house to pet her cats. Initiations such as this were not observed in previous sessions with Haley; therefore, it signals that something is shifting in Haley's play sequences. Not only does Haley demonstrate the ability to elaborate the play, but she also shows greater tolerance for taking risks in the play. This moment, where there is a sharing of the lead in play, is represented by point A in Figure 7.1. Briefly, the therapist has introduced a friendship scenario which is closer to Haley's issues and experiences, yet not at a level of consciousness where she is reflecting on direct or recent experiences with her peers.

Susan immediately responds to this shift by testing a soft hypothesis. One of Susan's characters states that it would be "boring" to go up and look at the cats. This insertion and Haley's responses are noteworthy. The insertion reflects the rejection that Haley has experienced at school. Haley's resolve in sticking with her initial invitation, and her direction that Susan's characters should agree to go upstairs with her, suggest that the insertion was a hit. This is evidenced when Susan asks how a character should respond to the question, "Do you like my cats?" Haley directs that the character should say, "Yes, they do like the cats!" As this segment progresses,

Haley's play becomes more literal, offering a glimpse of experiences such as teasing which is portrayed in a hide-and-seek play scenario. This is a noteworthy shift in Haley's play, as she appears to tolerate greater levels of emotionality and, to some extent, higher levels of consciousness. Interestingly, although Haley directs Susan's character to become angry and make accusations of cheating, Haley abruptly ends the play. This raises the question of whether Susan's therapeutic responses were a "hit" or a "miss." In one sense, Susan's use of her emotional self is a "hit," when taken from the viewpoint of Haley's movement and elaboration of play themes. Although closure was abruptly reached in this play scenario, it is not necessarily a "miss," as we might hypothesize that for the first time Haley was able to enter her phenomenal world more deeply. Importantly, this segment represents movement toward higher levels of consciousness, as it parallels Haley's friendship experiences. This interactional moment is represented by point B in Figure 7.1.

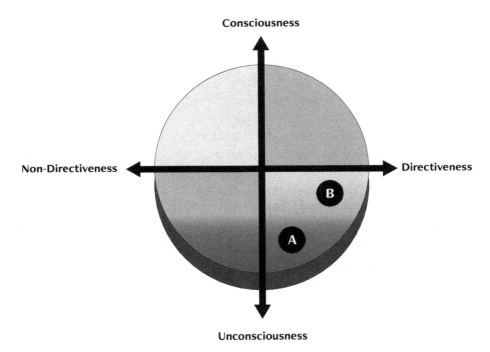

FIGURE 7.1: THERAPIST MOVEMENT IN QUADRANT IV

Naturally, more play experiences are required for Haley to reorganize or gain mastery over these experiences. Nonetheless, Haley has clearly entered the working stage of therapy. Susan's co-facilitative stance creates new play opportunities and vistas for Haley. In this play sequence, Susan honored the rhythm established by Haley but gently shifted the emotional tone. Susan's use of self, represented in her verbal discussions, emotionality, and physical use of self in play, ultimately facilitated and expanded Haley's ability to take risks. Additionally, Haley expressed a broader range of feelings and represented issues that were not previously observed in her play.

KEY POINTS

- A primary goal in becoming a co-facilitator of the play is to help open new avenues for the child to explore, express, process, and reorganize feelings or experiences.
- Typically, the therapist enters the play at the invitation of the child or after tracking play themes and patterns in the child's play.
- Transference and countertransference processes need to be carefully monitored in this quadrant, as the therapist is making great use of self.
- *Co-Facilitation* requires that the therapist remains prepared to take direction from the child. There is a continual weaving process rather than a static anchoring to a role or therapeutic stance.
- The effectiveness of a co-facilitative response should be viewed across time and mapped on to changes and movement in the overall play therapy process.

◉ Chapter 8 ◉

ACTIVE UTILIZATION

Quadrant I

The space where conscious and unconscious meet.

As represented in Figure 3.1, Quadrant I, *Active Utilization*, is in the upper left corner of the Play Therapy Dimensions Model. This quadrant is on the non-directive side of the directiveness dimension, yet within the upper portion of the consciousness dimension, representing that the child initiates the play while the therapist intermittently issues interpretive comments that may elicit conscious responses from the child. *Active Utilization* is usually entered into in a brief, time-sensitive manner. Therapists who emphasize the importance of interpretive comments as part of the healing process for children will likely find themselves periodically working in this quadrant. Additionally, therapists who have observed a particular repetitive theme or representation during the play may choose to purposefully utilize and deepen the exploration of the emerging material.

THE *WHAT:* THE DEFINING FEATURES OF QUADRANT I

Drawing on Ericksonian theory and philosophy, Mills and Crowley (1986) emphasize that the term "utilization" connotes a profound respect for the validity and integrity of the child's presenting behavior. Central to the technique of utilization is the discrete set of skills and abilities to observe, participate in, and reframe what the child presents. As applied to play therapy, the process of *Active Utilization* denotes that the therapist brings forward key elements of the child's play into the realm of conscious awareness by offering a verbal, interpretive context to explore and potentially resolve specific issues.

When working with children, a play therapist is involved with the whole child. This means that therapeutic activities have an impact on the child at various levels: cognitively, affectively, and linguistically. The emergence of language in children brings forward the ability to construct a narrative of their life-story and influences

◉ 120 ◉

the development of an enduring portrait of the self (Harter, 1999, 2012). As noted by O'Connor (2002), there appears to be a strong correlation between children's mental health and their use of language. In part, the child's ability to use language as a bridge from action to symbol to thought, as well as language's central function in emotional self-regulation, suggests that language should play a central role in the treatment process. Accordingly, it is not surprising that certain approaches to play therapy, such as Ericksonian Play Therapy (Mills, 2001, 2015; Mills and Crowley, 2014) emphasize that *story* is the language of play. Correspondingly, in working with children who have been severely traumatized, Terr (1983) suggests that children need to *verbalize* as well as to play.

Quadrants I and II share unique positions in the Play Therapy Dimensions Model as they denote that the child's play and verbalizations occur at a higher level on the consciousness dimension. The verbal interchanges that occur in these quadrants often assist in the organization and mobilization of cognitive and affective schemas that have become stuck, including schemas that support a false self. While many play therapists would consider that the child's symbolic play-based language is sufficient to promote the development of a true, authentic self, this does not readily occur in emotionally troubled children, as their affective schemas do not appear to be very mobile (Wilson *et al.*, 1992). In exploring the mobility and generalizability of affective schemas, Harris (1989) found that both younger and older children with emotional problems express ambivalent and complex emotions without having the ability to be consciously aware of negative and positive emotions together. Harter's (1999) research suggests that it is only as children approach middle childhood that they begin to achieve cognitive insight into complex emotions. These findings have important implications for the verbal approaches used by play therapists when working in Quadrant I, particularly the timing and way interpretive comments are made.

In Quadrant I, decision-making concerning the *what* is partly based on an understanding of the functions and importance of language in children's development. As noted by Harter (1999), language affords the ability to objectify the self and transcend one's immediate experiences. It also promotes heightened levels of relatedness and leads to the development of a personal narrative. However, Harter (1999) cautions that language can "drive a wedge" between interpersonal experiences as they are lived, and as they are verbally represented, leaving children vulnerable to the possibility of incorporating the views and biases of others, including therapists or parents, in ways that lead to the development of a false self. For example, a parent may reject a child's felt self by approving only of the falsely presented self (Crittenden, 1994). In turn, displays of false-self behaviors, where they meet the goals or needs of someone else, increase the possibility of alienating the child from those inner experiences that represent their true self (Stern, 1995).

Children who have experienced abusive treatment by caregivers or have been traumatized are at risk for suppressing their true selves and displaying various forms of false-self behaviors (Harter, 1999, 2012). In such cases, some form of interpretation may be required so that repressed or unconscious material can be accessed, used, and made sense of by the child. In the psychoanalytic literature, the term "interpretation" often refers to labeling statements that provide opportunities for the child to connect current behaviors with past experiences or memories. For play therapists, O'Connor (2002) asserts that interpretations are a specific form of language that is reassuring as it normalizes this process, placing it within a developmental framework. As a verbalization, O'Connor emphasizes that play-based interpretations make active use of an event or emotion conveyed in the child's play to help "make meaning."

> Although much of what a child acquires in therapy will come out of the corrective experiences she has in session, changes will also be produced by the verbal and cognitive work completed during the session. In fact, what most effective therapy has in common is that it gives clients an opportunity to come to a new understanding of their situation and to therefore experience themselves as having response choices. (O'Connor, 2000, p.152)

When used effectively, interpretations flow with the play and support the therapy process. For instance, a therapist working in Quadrant I is careful not to override the child's need to enter imaginative play activities, as these are the fabric of the corrective experience. However, when it seems that the child may be assisted to develop a new understanding, a therapist might bring certain elements of the play to greater conscious awareness of the child, through interpretive comments. This contributes to children's cognitive processing of their in-session experiences. In turn, children may come to the realization that there are other options or choices in managing or changing their circumstances. Upon re-entering imaginative play, children, armed with new insights or understanding, may deepen and intensify their play scenarios, representing movement in their internal schemas (beliefs about the problem).

Bretherton (1987) identifies a process of "defensive exclusion" where negative information about the self is not incorporated, since it is too psychologically threatening. This process allows the child to select, edit, or change the "facts" in service of personal needs and wishes. In play therapy the child, as author of the self, can access this process along with defense mechanisms such as fantasy. The latter mechanism permits children to play out and share their experiences with others or, alternatively, to withhold, change, or modify these experiences. It is essential that therapists working in Quadrant I recognize the importance of such mechanisms, particularly the role they play in regulating the impact of in-session experiences for the child. A therapist who is trained to understand these processes and who has conceptualized where the child is developmentally, psychologically, and contextually may use interpretations to modulate the impact of in-session experiences or to foster a new understanding of these experiences.

With young children whose ability to verbally process and transcend experiences through language is limited, play becomes the corrective or reparative experience as the playing-out and modification process brings forward feelings of containment or mastery (O'Connor, 2000). While younger children may not be as capable of processing interpretive comments, language may still act as a vehicle for self-expression and understanding. For instance, with young children, certain feelings, actions, and objects might be labeled. In turn, these verbalizations may form a corrective experience. O'Connor (2002) provides an excellent rule of thumb by emphasizing that the lower the child's developmental level, the more therapy relies on experiential, corrective events. In contrast, interpretive approaches are more readily applicable to children at more developmentally advanced levels.

Interpretive comments need to be appropriately sequenced and modulated otherwise they may be ineffective or, in some cases, psychologically disarming to the child. O'Connor (2002) notes that the impact of interpretations can be modulated by adjusting the *distance* between the child and the form and content of the interpretations. Having stated this, interpretations offered directly to the child, in the context of real-life experiences, are sometimes necessary for gains in therapy to generalize to other areas of the child's life. At the same time, unless "softer" and more distant levels of interpretation have previously occurred, the child will likely feel overwhelmed by direct interpretations. Those interpretations made within the field of play, such as when interpretive material is projected to characters in the child's play, provide distance. Yet, they may need to be repeated and eventually bridged to other facets of the child's life. As Mills (2001) notes, the provision of opportunities for children and adolescents to expand their awareness is often essential to their healing process.

Before launching into the complexities of the therapeutic roles and activities associated with *Active Utilization*, let's examine Quadrant I through the case of Ellis.

ILLUSTRATIVE CASE STUDY: VIDEO QUADRANT I SEGMENT—ELLIS

Download the case examples video and transcript from https://library.jkp.com/redeem using the code RTECPZF.

Ellis begins this play segment by setting up a fort, complete with guards or lookouts. He comments to Lynde, "You can have these guys," as he throws three characters in her direction. Ellis's exclamation, "This is my fort," indicates that he is in the lead and ready to launch into play.

As the play evolves, one of Ellis's characters takes a character from Lynde's side, placing this figure inside the fort. There is a sense of power and control portrayed when Ellis's character laughs. Since Lynde has already examined Ellis's capacity to tolerate stronger reflections, she chooses to move through a brief sequence of insertions that raises the emotional intensity of the play. This begins when Lynde comments, "That guy's locked up in there...he's locked up and he can't get out!" Ellis's character replies, "You're locked up, and you can't get out." Although Lynde does not have physical control of her miniature character at this moment, she intensifies the play by talking through the character, "Just locked up in there...and there's no way out." Ellis immediately states, "Exactly!" This response suggests that Lynde's insertion was a hit, as it was consistent with the evolving theme.

So far it looks as though Lynde might be moving toward Quadrant IV, *Co-Facilitation*. She is tracking Ellis's responses and carefully pacing her reflections. However, Lynde decides to bring underlying themes to conscious awareness by commenting that what just occurred appears to be like what Ellis has told her about the happenings at his school and on the playground. It is at this point that Lynde has moved into Quadrant I, *Active Utilization*. She has brought a theme, represented in Ellis's play, out in the open. While remaining in her character voice, Lynde states, "They trap kids, and they are mean, and don't let them out." Recalling that in the referral it was reported that Ellis had been teased and harassed in a washroom as well as on the playground, Lynde's statement is interpretive but remains in the field of play. Further, her selection of the words "trap" and "mean" are purposeful, as they raise Ellis's awareness of underlying feelings and motives of the children he encountered, as well as those represented in his characters. By highlighting these elements Lynde essentially gives meaning to one of Ellis's troublesome experiences.

As will be discussed in this chapter, Lynde's interpretation embodies some of Ellis's experiences through language and is delivered in a manner that supports the play process, versus interrupting Ellis's play. This is evidenced when Ellis briefly pauses, as if absorbing Lynde's comments, and then returns to his character voice stating, "Friend...you can escape, but don't get too comfortable!" Ellis then throws the character over the top of the fort, releasing it from imprisonment (for the moment).

At this point, Lynde is holding certain hypotheses in mind. She senses that Ellis's characters are showing trickery, not unlike the bullies that have been described by Ellis and his parents. Lynde also recognizes that Ellis's pause may signal his readiness to integrate interpretive comments, if they are appropriately paced and sequenced. With this information in mind, Lynde re-enters the play.

In the next play segment, one of Ellis's characters notices that someone escaped and orders that he be put back. Through her character, Lynde responds, "Oh no, here comes another bully!" The insertion of the word "bully" is again purposeful and is based on the hypothesis that Ellis's play continues to revolve around themes of power and aggression. Staying with the affective tone of the play, Lynde's character reacts to being guarded, commenting, "That mean bully—he's watching there." Interestingly, the guard turns and walks away, and one of the prisoners escapes. This also seems to have been a trick, as the guard notices that the prisoner is gone and decides to steal two more characters. With a new guard in place, who is laughing, Lynde then makes another interpretive statement, "That mean bully, he's just watching those small ones." Lynde's interpretation once more points out the power imbalance. This signals to Ellis the significance embodied in the play metaphors and symbols. Specifically, the words "small ones" highlight specific attributes of this relationship, particularly the powerlessness and vulnerability of certain characters. We might hypothesize that this portion of the play *stories* or mirrors Ellis's experiences. The purpose of providing this interpretation is to create movement in Ellis's cognitive and emotional schemas; this occurs as one of Ellis's characters announces that the prisoners will be given a "second chance." At this point, there is a noteworthy shift in the play sequence; instead of characters escaping, they are given an opportunity to leave. It may be hypothesized that Ellis's view of the world, and empathy and understanding of self, briefly shift here, allowing movement and reorganization.

In the closing stage of this segment, the leader discovers that more characters have escaped. Announcing that he is going to guard all three prisoners, the leader remarks, "...and you cannot escape." Lynde underscores the emotional intensity embedded in the statement by Ellis's character by reflecting, "No more second chances." Ellis responds, "Bullies don't give second chances!" This is the first time in the play that Ellis uses the word "bullies." Lynde utilizes this and brings it to Ellis's attention by saying that what happened sounded just like what happened to Ellis on the play-ground. This launches the beginning of a sequence of interpretations that directly link what happened in the play to Ellis's life experiences. Ellis's readiness to integrate this is evidenced in his response, "Yeah, that is...it happened to me." Although the scene fades at this point, in future sessions Lynde might continue to issue interpretive comments, bridging certain elements of Ellis's play to his experiences at school. The intent would be to help Ellis make sense of these experiences. Over time, this may prepare Ellis to openly explore, and problem-solve similar situations, as part of a weaving process between Quadrant I and Quadrant II.

Even though the play shifted toward brief discussions, activated by the therapist's interpretations, the tone of the play never became adversarial, that is, themes of power and control were not about "Ellis versus Lynde." Instead, tensions remained at the level of the play. This would not have occurred unless Lynde had carefully paced her interpretations and delivered them in a non-judgmental manner. Further, Lynde provided *space* for Ellis to project his experiences onto the objects he selected. Finally, Lynde's weaving back and forth between quadrants offered Ellis emotional distance and control. Ellis may not have tolerated this had Lynde not kept her interpretive comments in the field of play, allowing Ellis to choose to respond, deflect, or ignore her interpretive communications. Above all, Lynde never stopped tracking and following Ellis's play initiations.

THE *HOW:* THERAPEUTIC ROLES AND ACTIVITIES

The emphasis placed on interpretations in Quadrant I may leave many play therapists feeling uncomfortable. Play therapists who have not been trained in the use of interpretations may mistakenly think that interpretations are provided in a rapid-fire process, with the purpose of digging out or uncovering meaning for the child. While the child may discover new meaning through interpretive comments, the goal is not necessarily to make certain feelings or thoughts readily conscious. Instead, the goal is often to make them more "available" for exploration and resolution in the context of the play. Therapists should also be reminded of the unfolding process of play therapy; as part of this process, interpretations frequently occur in a progressive sequence, flowing with the stages of the play therapy process.

Depending on the therapist's training and theoretical orientation, it may also seem that interpretations increase the risk of "deciding for the child." However, this is inconsistent with the purposes behind the concept of utilization, particularly as applied to Quadrant I. As illustrated in the play segment with Ellis, Lynde was a keen observer and participant who followed Ellis's play themes; the interpretations that she offered were based on Ellis's initiatives in play.

There are many excellent frameworks for conceptualizing therapeutic interpretations, such as the interpretive levels that O'Connor (2002) derived from the psychoanalytic literature. One of the values of this framework is that it is accompanied by a carefully thought out, six-step sequential process. The Play Therapy Dimensions Model identifies three levels of interpretation, moving from a level where verbalizations are embedded in the field of play to deeper interpretive comments that relate directly to the child or the therapeutic relationship. The levels are described below.

- *Level 1—Reflective interpretations*: These are comments that reflect observed affect, motives, and behavior exhibited in the field of play, through the use of play characters or themes.
- *Level 2—Linking interpretations*: These are comments that directly link current play-based themes to known elements of the child's experiences, past or present.
- *Level 3—Bridging interpretations*: These are comments designed to mobilize internal resources by signaling the similarities between current play-based themes and those represented in previous play sessions, bridging and highlighting the meaning and significance of these themes and experiences to the child's life story.

Reflective interpretations honor and validate the child's thematically represented realities. They occur in the field of play and are often given voice through characters. In the case of Ellis, Lynde gradually moved toward a Level 1, *reflective interpretation*. This occurred when she stated, "They trap kids, and they are mean, and don't let them out." As O'Connor (2002) notes, reflections such as this communicate an awareness of and interest in the thought behind the action.

Later in the play, Lynde offers a Level 2, *linking interpretation*, when she states, "This is a lot like what you told me about kids playing that game on your playground. They trap kids, and they are mean, and don't let them out." Statements such as this expand the child's awareness of certain experiences and accompanying feelings. Like other forms of interpretations, Level 2, linking interpretations, are simply another form of language that provides an opportunity for the child's unconscious/conscious mind to accept or reject certain possibilities. Although the scene fades shortly after Lynde's linking interpretations, in future sessions, she might have offered a Level 3, *bridging interpretation*. At this interpretive level, Lynde would have highlighted the meaning and significance of the power differences between play characters, noting that the "good guys" tried to do the right thing but always got tricked or trapped by the "bad guys," who seemed to enjoy this type of power and control. Next, Lynde would bridge these thematic representations to times when Ellis faced similar powerless experiences. At this point, other therapeutic communications might assist Ellis's understanding or acceptance of certain disowned feelings and experiences. For example, Lynde might comment:

> Sometimes bad things happen to kids, and they get so upset that they must find a way to get their feelings out. This can happen in lots of ways, like getting mad at friends over little things, like taking things from someone in their family, or even by hitting someone because the anger suddenly blasted out.

These comments represent displacement communication strategies. They provide psychological distance because the comments do not presume that the child themselves had this experience. Instead, the emphasis is on feelings or behavioral reactions that happen to *some kids*. Nonetheless, as part of a bridging interpretation, they provide an important therapeutic stepping stone, bringing forward experiences and allowing the child to make sense of internal feelings, processes, and motivations that direct behavior.

THE *WHEN:* CONSIDERATIONS FOR THE PLAY THERAPY PROCESS

As this quadrant presents as one of the most complex and challenging ones in the Play Therapy Dimensions Model, there are *three principles* to guide the practitioner through the therapy process.

The *first principle* is that the three levels of interpretation are typically offered in order of decreasing frequency over time. Level 1, reflective interpretations, usually occur in the early stages of therapy and decrease over time when it is clear that the child requires less "distance" from the interpretive process. If a therapist has made reflective statements and insertions since the early stages of the therapy process and has actively tracked the child's play skills and responsiveness, there will be several obvious indicators of the child's readiness and tolerance for deeper interpretations.

As a child enters the middle or working stage of therapy, there is often greater capacity to tolerate and accept interpretations that are more direct or transparent. Thus, the frequency of Level 2 and Level 3 interpretations gradually increases. However, recalling that affective schemas are not highly mobile, therapists must be careful with the pacing and timing of more direct interpretations. For instance, there may be points at which it appears that an interpretation is not well tolerated by the child, evidenced by the child's negation of the statement or through a pivot or disruption in the play.

The *second principle* is that when interpretations are provided, there must be an attempt to examine the impact of the interpretation. Accordingly, the Play Therapy Dimensions Model has an accompanying Tracking and Observation Form (Appendix C) for examining movement in the play therapy process. This tool, which is discussed in greater detail in Chapters 11 and 12, guides the therapist to carefully explore various components of the play process, including the child's ability to initiate play sequences. It also captures relational and affective components along with thematic representations. By tracking movement or changes in these areas, a therapist might begin to see shifts in the child's world view and underlying cognitive schemas. In turn, this provides guidance for the pacing and timing of interpretations.

The *third principle* is that interpretations, even at the lowest level, should be congruent with the evolving therapeutic relationship. Interpretations are not just thrown out to see if the child "catches" them. Nor are they used as one-time occurrences as part of a fishing expedition. When interpretations occur under these circumstances, it usually signals that the case has not been fully conceptualized, placing the explicit or implicit therapy contract with the child in jeopardy.

While Level 1 interpretations usually occur once the initial relationship-building stage of therapy has passed, there are certainly exceptions to this pattern. A Level 2 or 3 interpretive comment that signals to the child the therapist's recognition of the child's feelings and experiences may initially comfort a child who has a known history of abuse. Essentially, these comments offer validation to the child. When a child who has witnessed domestic violence, for example, covers their ears in response to a loud noise made by a play character, a therapist might comment, "That loud noise might seem scary because of some of the things that have happened at home." In this case, the comment is delivered in a manner that communicates an understanding of the child's life experiences. The therapist would not expect the child to confirm or deny the reality of the comment, even though it hopefully moves the child toward a new conscious understanding of their life experiences.

THE *WHO:* CLINICAL APPLICATIONS

Quadrant I has potential applications for children who have been traumatized as well as those who have transitional adjustment issues, such as children of divorce. Well-adjusted children tend to discuss certain experiences in their world. Children who are facing transitional adjustment issues, such as children of divorce, often have a strong need to "make sense" of their experiences but may not be as talkative. While they may have access to other internal, adaptive coping resources that traumatized children lack, they may be emotionally and verbally constrained by lack of parental interest or even by fear of retaliation. This may lead them to be fearful of discussing their feelings. Whether or not they consciously realize that feelings can or should be shared, they often struggle to understand the experiences of their family and feel overwhelmingly confused about their internal feeling states. A child's limited feeling vocabulary of "happy," "mad," and "sad" cannot begin to speak for the experiences they are attempting to make sense of and reorganize. Whether the child is dealing with the loss of a parent through divorce, or the loss of a sibling through death, a therapist may need briefly to move into Quadrant I, utilizing the child's play-based expressions to expand awareness and to allow the child's unconscious mind to accept or reject other possibilities.

We remember a seven-year-old girl, Vanessa, who repetitively played out a sand-play scene about "Little Piggy." Each time, before constructing her sandworld, Vanessa searched for a tiny character she named Little Piggy on the sandtray shelves, which was quite a chore, because this was the smallest of all the figurines and the one most prone to being misplaced on the shelves. Once she located Little Piggy, Vanessa would cradle this object in her hands for a few moments, remaining speechless. As her sandworld evolved, it initially took the form of a fun, magical world with castles and wizards who appeared as helpers. However, this was not a static sandtray but a dynamic, moving one. Chaos soon erupted and Little Piggy was kidnapped and taken to another castle. No one knew where Little Piggy was, except the two guards who kept fighting over who might rescue Little Piggy. This scene was a literal representation of Vanessa's family life. Her parents were at war with each other and Vanessa was left feeling confused and emotionally vulnerable. Recognizing the literalness and repetitious nature of the sandplay, Vanessa's therapist began to use Level 1, reflective interpretations, gradually moving toward Level 2 and Level 3 interpretations. Over the course of therapy, the flow of interpretations was a non-linear, to-and-fro process, as it appeared that Vanessa needed to replay and reorganize a range of family-based experiences, including the arguing between her parents, her father's move from the family house, and her mother's emotional fragility.

As previously mentioned, the lower the child's developmental level, the less value and/or impact interpretive comments may have. Children at lower stages of development will likely benefit more from experiential play activities that offer corrective, mastery-based experiences. The therapeutic goal is not just symptom reduction but also the developmental advancement of the child. Interpretations for children at this developmental stage serve the purpose of expanding their self-expressions and awareness, allowing their unconscious minds to accept or reject other possibilities. By the latency stage of development, the child's verbal communication skills have usually increased to a point where there is greater reliance on verbalizations, and there is less reliance on symbolic play. At this stage, Quadrant I, *Active Utilization*, may provide new pathways for self-understanding. Trauma has an impact on all levels of the child's development, including their attachment to caregivers, the way they regulate affect, their sense of self, and their use of symbolic and representational thought (Drewes, 2001). Regardless of the chronological age of the child, trauma may have caused a severe impact on their developmental and play capacities. As trauma overwhelms the child's coping abilities, they often engage in repetitive forms of play. As Boyd Webb (1991) notes, just as a mourning adult needs to review over and over the details surrounding the death of a loved one, children who have been traumatized may repeatedly seek to reconstruct a crisis experience symbolically, through play. In its more extreme form, posttraumatic play takes the form of secretive, monotonous, ritualized play that fails to relieve the child (Terr, 1983). For this reason, Terr recommends the use of preset or prearranged play that gives meaning and focus to the child's experiences. Often, a psychotherapeutic reconstruction occurs, utilizing materials suggestive of the experience. As part of the reconstruction, the therapist includes a verbal review of the traumatic experience, using interpretive comments to help the child make sense of these experiences and relieve them from guilt or fear associated with the trauma.

SHOULD I STAY OR SHOULD I GO? INDICATIONS FOR WORKING IN QUADRANT I

Quadrant I, *Active Utilization*, is seldom accessed in isolation of the other quadrants. It should not be viewed as a quick fix but rather as part of an encompassing therapeutic process that facilitates healing. Mills (1989) describes a braiding process in which a child's symptoms or problems are woven together with their inner resources and the "metaphorical task," which broadly speaking is the idea or behavior to be learned. Mills states that all three components are given equal power, resulting in the resolution of the presenting problem through a process of utilization, appreciation, and/or transformation. Within the context of the Play Therapy Dimensions Model, a therapist should conceptualize movement between the quadrants as part of a dynamic braiding process. This requires that therapists continually evaluate movement according to the following six indicators.

Indicator 1: Therapeutic Process

Quadrant I is typically accessed after a therapeutic relationship has been formed; thus, it is more likely to occur during the middle or working phase of therapy. In most cases, a therapist would briefly enter this quadrant and *stay* only as long as it may be required to establish a foundation for lower-level, reflective interpretations. What will be gained from this initial exposure is an understanding of the child's tolerance or readiness for emotional experiences that potentially bring forward higher levels of consciousness and self-understanding. As noted earlier, interpretations that are "too close" to the child or ill-timed may result in the child pivoting away from the play or shutting down the process altogether. If this occurs, a therapist should consider "leaving" until a foundation has been established. This may occur through pairing cognitive processing with known experiences of the child outside of the session. For example, the pairing of a child's moods or feelings, in relation to certain school-based experiences, helps differentiate themselves and may prompt insight into the child's behavior. Although the flow of interpretations is seldom linear, toward the termination phase of therapy, in which a child is seeking more conscious closure and is beginning to openly talk about specific issues, the use of Level 2 and Level 3 interpretations may be timely. Often, these deeper levels prompt children to engage in detailed discussions about their experiences. In turn, this becomes a strong indicator that other, cognitive processing strategies, such as problem-solving, may be helpful to the child. At this point, consider shifting to Quadrant II, *Open Discussion and Exploration*.

Indicator 2: Responses of the Child

The types of responses made by children during play therapy sessions that indicate that a therapist should *stay* working in Quadrant I are: the child responds to Level 1, reflective interpretations, and begins to elaborate the play through the introduction of new themes or characters; the child begins to verbally disclose certain feelings or experiences; the child, in an attempt to differentiate certain feelings or experiences, begins to ask questions; and the child begins to narrate certain portions of the play, which is akin to "storying" the child's experiences in a more conscious manner. A therapist should *go* to Quadrant III, *Non-Intrusive Responding*, if the therapist's interpretive comments are ignored or bypassed by the child, or if it appears that the child's drive and direction in play remain at a less conscious, symbolic level.

Indicator 3: Child's Play Skills

Consideration must be given to the child's play skills when deciding whether to enter or *leave* this quadrant. *Stay* if the child exhibits strong play skills and has already shown tolerance for a co-facilitative play process (sharing in the direction of the play with the therapist). Essentially, children who readily enter fantasy play scenarios, and who tolerate insertions from the therapist, often have the flexibility to move back and forth between Quadrant I and Quadrant IV. With these children, a therapist should consider briefly *staying* in Quadrant I but should anticipate that the child may need to return to less conscious, more symbolic means of processing. Alternatively, a therapist may choose to *go* to Quadrant II, *Open Discussion and Exploration*, when working with children who have high verbal abilities and show a need to talk about their experiences.

Indicator 4: Child's Drive and Direction in Therapy

Some children engage in highly driven play in which intense and repetitive imaginative actions reflect turmoil and distress. An example of this is seen when repeated themes of fighting or destruction surface across sessions. If there is a clear sense that the child has the internal resources to consciously process these issues, *go* to Quadrant I, *Active Utilization*. Under these circumstances the therapeutic agenda becomes one of appreciating and utilizing the predominant themes, through interpretive comments. *Go* back to Quadrant III, *Non-Intrusive Responding*, should the child's reactions indicate the need for greater emotional distance, represented in a strong, continuing drive to play out the child's thoughts and feelings. Alternatively, a therapist might also *go* to Quadrant II, *Open Discussion and Exploration*, because interpretive comments have shifted the child's understanding of certain life events and increased the need to talk or ask questions about certain experiences. Once in Quadrant II, there is an emphasis on supporting the child through helping to build specific coping skills.

Indicator 5: Context of the Presenting Issue

A therapist should consider *staying* in Quadrant I when it appears that the child would benefit from knowing that the therapist is aware of certain types of traumas in the child's life. Often, this strengthens the therapeutic relationship, as it is validating to the child and frees the child up to engage in other forms of self-expression, including talking. Deeper interpretations may follow, lending meaning to the child's in-session experiences. Once this point is reached, the therapist may begin to make linking or bridging interpretations, forming conscious connections between the child's actions, play objects, or characters. This encourages the child to assume an observer stance and helps make meaningful connections between the play and past troublesome life experiences. A therapist would typically *stay* if these connections are forming. Children with low levels of resiliency or ego strength may first require more time in

Quadrant III, or weave back and forth between Quadrants I and III, before they are ready for deeper interpretations.

Indicator 6: Timelines and System Parameters

Although therapists must be careful not to totally disarm a child's defenses, there may be times when the therapy process appears stuck, and there is mounting pressure to restore the child's ability to cope. At this point, transference-based interpretations may help the child recognize the uniqueness of the relationship with the therapist, differentiating the therapist from other individuals in the child's life. This can pave the way for new self-expressions and explorations in play. With the gradual movement toward deeper interpretations, there is often a parallel movement in play-based disclosures. For example, a child may begin to show small fragments of violence and powerlessness that mirror family-based experiences. Indirect disclosures provide a new understanding of the child and may require immediate processing, indicating movement to Quadrant II, *Open Discussion and Exploration*. Alternatively, a therapist might consider the use of gentle, reflective interpretations to support the child.

ILLUSTRATIVE CASE STUDY—HALEY

Download the case examples video and transcript from https://library.jkp.com/redeem using the code RTECPZF.

We return once more to the video case example of Haley. However, this time we will base our discussion on factors identified through the Tracking and Observation Form (Appendix C) and the Child Moderating Factors Scale (Appendix A), as well as the principles previously identified in this chapter.

Turning first to the Tracking and Observation Form, the Quick View (Road Map) tells us that Susan was previously working in Quadrant III, where most of the play had been dramatic/symbolic play. With respect to the play therapy process, we are beginning to see growing abilities and capacities for Haley to direct the play. Interestingly, Haley is the one who suggests the playground and the hide-and-seek scenarios, which are more literally and closely aligned to her experiences at school. This represents movement in the direction of consciousness. Haley's emotional range, when examined on the tracking form, represents increasing levels of expressiveness. As well, there is greater risk-taking in her play. When Haley's character finds the other two girls hiding behind the house and gives a direction to Susan by stating, "They're mad at her and call her cheater," we begin to see thematic representations of rejection and victimization. Recognizing this, and sensing that Haley has the emotional capacity and resilience to have an interpretive comment brought forward, Susan offers a Level 2, linking interpretation, by remarking, "You know, that kind of sounds like or reminds me of what you told me before about how hard it is sometimes at the school when sometimes kids are being mean to you." The timing of this is consistent with one of our principles, as Haley has already given a partial disclosure to Susan about her experiences at school, and Susan has been actively observing and tracking Haley's responses to earlier, reflective statements.

The Child Moderating Factors Scale (Appendix A) encourages us to examine several child moderating factors. For example, we might rate Haley's play skills as a 4, representing that she is using imaginative play and introducing more complex themes. Additionally, this segment affords a glimpse into Haley's world view. While not *pervasively* negative, as we have seen neutral and positive elements of family relationships in Haley's dollhouse play, we now see a context-specific, relational schema exhibited that is hostile.

The first principle, namely, to examine the impact and effectiveness of our intervention, requires us to look closely at the child–therapist relationship and the overall play therapy process. As discussed on the video, Susan notices a pause in Haley's play immediately after her character said, "Hey, that's not fair...you're nothing but a cheater—cheater—cheater—cheater!" At this point, Haley's character identifies that she is going home, and Haley herself states that the play ends there. Although closure in play was reached, it occurred quickly and with tensions. Sensing that certain feelings were brought forward in the play, a linking interpretation is offered over a brief series of verbal interchanges with Haley. Looking carefully at the video transcript (which can be downloaded from https://library.jkp.com/redeem using the code RTECPZF), we see that Susan first links the play to Haley's school life and experiences. Next, she purposefully communicates the understanding that it must be "hard" when kids are being "mean." Haley affirms this by stating, "The kids at my school can get pretty mean." Moving beyond a reflective interpretation, Susan then elaborates her interpretation, remarking, "That must be really hard going to school and then dealing with kids who are being mean to you." Haley signals acknowledgment by nodding her head. Thinking that this sequence of interpretations has not only provided meaning and validation for Haley but also opened the possibility of looking more closely at this specific situation, Susan now prepares Haley for movement to Quadrant II, *Open Discussion and Exploration*, where they jointly discuss and enact other possibilities for coping with what has occurred.

MOVEMENT WITHIN THIS QUADRANT

Experience has taught us time and again that the child is the one who sets the speed limit in therapy. Interpretations can be offered, but unless some of the core conditions are present, including developmental and relational parameters, they may be of little value. Yet, when the core conditions are present, the therapeutic process can certainly be deepened by using interpretations.

It is important to again emphasize that movement is not linear. Correspondingly, movement from a Level 1 to a Level 3 interpretation may not immediately foster higher levels of conscious processing. The Level 1, reflective interpretations, provided by Ellis's therapist, through noticing the bullying behaviors of characters in play, likely fostered movement even though the reflection occurred at a lower level of consciousness in this quadrant, as depicted by point A in Figure 8.1

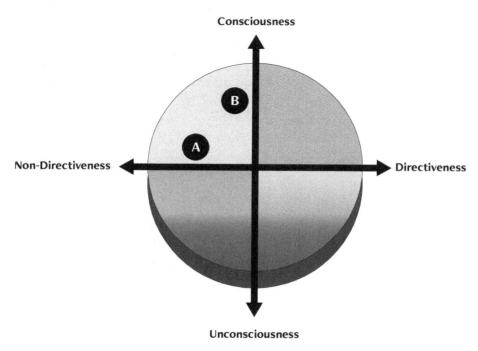

FIGURE 8.1: THERAPIST MOVEMENT IN QUADRANT I

After more time spent in the play metaphor, the therapist offers a Level 2, linking interpretation, connecting Ellis's play to his experiences at school. As illustrated by point B in Figure 8.1, this moment is positioned at a higher level of consciousness as a direct connection is made between Ellis's school experiences and characters' actions depicted in play. Future case planning might explore the possibility of introducing Level 3, bridging interpretations, where there is an invitation to explore the meaning and significance of recurring play themes to the child's life story, moving yet again toward higher levels on the consciousness dimension.

KEY POINTS

- Quadrant I is typically accessed after a therapeutic relationship has been formed and is more likely to occur during the middle or working phase of therapy.
- In most cases, a therapist would briefly enter this quadrant and stay only as long as required to establish a foundation for lower-level, reflective interpretations.
- Three levels of interpretation are identified: reflective, linking, and bridging interpretations.
- Three principles are offered to guide the practitioner in the use of interpretations. Overall, interpretive comments need to be carefully sequenced and modulated, otherwise they may be ineffective or, in some cases, psychologically disarming to the child.

◉ **Chapter 9** ◉

OPEN DISCUSSION AND EXPLORATION

Quadrant II

Explore your world with me so that you may find the words to sing your song.

Quadrant II, *Open Discussion and Exploration*, represents a form of play therapy in which the therapist selects and presents specific activities based on the needs of the child. As depicted in Figure 3.1, this quadrant is positioned on the far-right side of the directiveness dimension. This indicates that the therapist is immersed in the play through offering structure and direction. In this role the therapist openly discusses issues and may provide interpretive comments that focus attention and stimulate conscious awareness and processing of material that previously was less consciously available to the child. The child's play activities, and the interactive context surrounding these activities, also place this quadrant in the upper portion of the consciousness dimension.

THE *WHAT*: THE DEFINING FEATURES OF QUADRANT II

One factor that distinguishes Quadrant II from Quadrant IV, *Co-Facilitation*, is that the therapist brings structure and sequence to the play activities, to the extent that they are a director *and* facilitator of the therapy process. Rather than working solely in a co-facilitative manner, the therapist purposefully chooses play activities that prompt the child to gradually engage in conscious processing of the presenting issues.

Therapists working in settings that require a brief, accelerated approach to child therapy, including schools and private practices, frequently work in Quadrant II, as they rely on structured, prearranged activities to bring symptom relief or to foster open discussion of the presenting issues. As noted by Knell (1995), short-term interventions are increasingly used for preschool populations, as children this age often

◉ 137 ◉

present with transient or mild adjustment issues that do not require extensive or lengthy interventions.

Although there is a high degree of structure and direction in Quadrant II, this does not limit the range of play materials or activities accessible to the child. Materials vary widely, including books and stories, dolls, role-plays, and games. The way these activities are used also varies according to the therapists' underlying theoretical orientation. For example, Richard Gardner's Mutual Storytelling Technique (Gardner, 1971), which is based on a metaphoric counseling approach, has been modified to include a wide range of media such as computers, storytelling, and drawing activities. In some cases, storytelling occurs within a therapy process that incorporates elements of competition to stimulate interest and involvement (Brewer, 1998; Repp, 1998).

Numerous play therapy models, such as Adlerian, Gestalt, Ecosystemic, and Cognitive-Behavioral, use prearranged play activities to focus attention or to stimulate and deepen play activities. While therapists working from these approaches may weave back and forth along the directiveness dimension, certain models, such as Structured Play Therapy (Jones, Casado, and Robinson, 2003), view the therapy process from a strictly directive perspective. However, even when adopting a highly structured approach, careful consideration is given to the sequencing of session topics, along with pacing the intensity of exercises and activities. As noted by Jones *et al.* (2003), therapists working from a structured approach must not overwhelm a child by pressuring them to focus on issues when they are not ready. As will become evident in this chapter, choosing an activity and pacing its introduction and use are a complex process based on numerous factors. Yet, when activities are implemented in a sensitive manner, they have the potential to enhance the therapy process.

Quadrant II emphasizes an open dialogue of thoughts and feelings, often leading to the exploration of "choices" through active problem-solving or the rehearsal of new coping strategies. Accordingly, decision-making concerning the *who*, *what*, *when*, *why*, and *how* for this quadrant is rooted in an understanding of the ways in which affect organizes experience, thinking, and behavior.

While there is a multitude of information-processing models available to guide the practitioner, the view expressed by Greenspan (1997) concerning the emotional architecture of the mind is particularly helpful. Taking a developmental perspective, Greenspan notes that the infant's first sensory experiences occur within the context of relationships that provide additional emotional meaning to these experiences. Each sensory experience or perception is believed to be dual coded. That is, the infant labels the experience by its physical properties as well as by its emotional qualities. For example, a child might dual code or cross-reference the feeding routine as "eating" and "feeling close to Mother." Over time, feeding experiences merge with other experiences to build a more elaborate, subjective description of the child's sensory and emotional worlds (Greenspan, 1997). When viewed from this perspective, we begin to see how emotions organize experiences and behavior, eventually assisting the child in coping with or modulating their emotions.

Greenspan's model also asserts that infants discriminate among choices and situations by carrying their own set of emotional cues from situation to situation, not by learning conscious rules or examples. Essentially, they carry what Greenspan calls a discrimination meter composed of past emotional cues that automatically guide the child in terms of what to say, think, or do. The ability to discriminate becomes the sixth sense that helps the child negotiate social situations. Unfortunately, some children's unique information-processing profile, or negative life experiences, dulls their sixth sense to the point where the ability to make important distinctions is impaired. This leads to diminished levels of problem-solving and emotional regulation.

Greenspan's model has important implications for play therapists working in Quadrant II. While a structured activity might be selected to foster new ideas and strengthen problem-solving abilities, Greenspan stresses that problem-solving follows an emotional pathway, to the extent that it is not until the child arrives at an intuitive, emotionally mediated response or idea that "feels right" that they expose the idea or strategy to logical analysis to see if it might address the problem at hand. Thus, when children are faced with deciding, they need to consult their own catalogue of emotional and physical experiences. The emotions that organize this catalogue help create categories from which children select memories and intuitions that relate to the presenting circumstances. It is at this point that children select among a number of possibilities, subjecting them to the level of analysis or logic that is available to them at their stage of development. As noted by Greenspan (1997), the ability to examine critically emotionally derived ideas, and organize them logically, is ultimately related to the interaction between the maturation of the child's brain as well as their accumulated experiences.

Knell (2003) suggests that young children often have cognitive distortions that fit with their stage of development. Yet these beliefs may become maladaptive as they have a negative impact upon the child's ability to cope with certain situations. For example, young children may associate incidents of misbehavior with parental separation. In other cases, such as a child struggling with the birth of a sibling, a child may not have a specific, maladaptive cognition attached to the event, but instead may lack adaptive self-statements to adequately cope with feelings. Using a Cognitive-Behavioral Play Therapy approach, puppets or stuffed animals might be selected as part of a coping model strategy to illustrate problem-solving and to verbalize coping skills. While the explicit goal of the puppet play is to model problem-solving skills or introduce solutions to problems that parallel the child's life experiences, the therapist should keep in mind the organizing role of emotions. Essentially, when working with a scripted or directed play activity, children often need first to have an emotionally mediated experience, offered through the process of playing out certain options or choices. This allows them to intuitively feel that a certain action or solution is possible, following which they can subject this idea to some form of logical scrutiny or analysis.

Danger (2003) describes an adaptive doll play technique with a five-year-old child experiencing separation anxiety that illustrates some of the primary therapeutic roles and activities involved in Quadrant II. Danger (2003) notes that structured or adaptive doll play is frequently used to dramatize specific, anxiety-provoking events, such as preparing children for invasive medical procedures. In the case example of a five-year-old child, an initial phase of Child-Centered Play Therapy sessions occurred to foster a therapeutic relationship. Next, the therapist scripted a story based on the mother's description of the sequence of events that occurred during the child's school day. Importantly, just prior to the storytelling experience, the child was asked to arrange doll furniture to set the stage for the story. This helped create a concrete representation of the child's world. During the first structured session, the child was reported to experience difficulties relinquishing control of the story. However, by the second session, the child was less insistent on directing the story and contributed small parts that were representative of her life, such as describing what family members were eating. Subsequent to this, the child's ability to focus and accept the story rapidly increased. By the fifth session, the child was able to tell the story on her own.

As discussed by Danger (2003), this intervention included several important elements such as: focusing on one, specific, targeted behavior; using familiar, concrete details from the child's environment; using the child's name directly; including a shared, concrete action at the end of the story; and repeating the story at least three to five times.

Approaches such as Ecosystemic Play Therapy, which assert that play offers children a corrective experience, carefully select and introduce structured activities that allow the child to re-experience or recreate an event or relationship. O'Connor (2002) suggests that corrective experiences, which are defined as one or two types of events that prompt critical shifts in the child's thinking, involve a certain degree of retrospective and prospective problem-solving. To accomplish this, the therapist provides the child with new information or an alternate understanding of past events, or does something in the play that causes a shift in the child's thinking and subsequent behavior. For these experiences to serve a corrective function and carry therapeutic value, the therapist must be able to conceptualize several factors: the types of play activities that will lead to a correction of the child's experiences; the child's world view or assumptions about the workings of the world; the child's patterns of social and behavioral interaction; and the child's level of development. The purpose of introducing and structuring corrective experiences is to allow the child to gain a sense of mastery over past feelings, to support new understandings of the problem, and to foster the knowledge that choices exist.

Within models such as Cognitive-Behavioral Play Therapy and Ecosystemic Play Therapy, problem-solving activities created by the therapist occur experientially or through open discussion. There is also an underlying belief that the problem-solving process represents the consolidation of corrective experiences in therapy, enabling the child to generalize what they learn in therapy to other areas of their life.

The following case example illustrates the use of a structured activity and the therapeutic strategies used for varying the emotional intensity of this experience. It also exemplifies the manner in which a therapist raises issues to consciousness, creating opportunities for the child to discuss and openly explore thoughts, feelings, and alternatives.

THE *HOW:* THERAPEUTIC ROLES AND ACTIVITIES

There are many published resources that play therapists working in this quadrant can draw upon, including therapeutic games, therapeutic stories, and structured psycho-educational worksheets that focus on feeling identification and problem solving. The selection of materials and play modalities is almost limitless, making the selection process challenging.

As always, we should begin with a focus or understanding of the child, by asking questions such as: What play modalities is this child drawn to? Is this activity appropriate given the child's current development? Does the child have the ego strength to tolerate or stay with an open or direct exploration of feelings, thoughts, or experiences?

Consideration should also be given to the possible therapeutic powers of play activated by the activity. For example, does the activity draw upon direct or indirect teaching? Does it encourage self-expression or evoke cathartic release of feelings?

Oftentimes therapists are surprised by the power of a technique, which underscores the importance of understanding the strategy or technique through previous training or in vivo, role-play exposure to the strategy. It is also the therapist's responsibility to understand the change mechanisms underlying a technique and be able to link these mechanisms to their theoretical model and the therapy process. For example, some techniques are ill suited at the early stages of treatment, as there is limited trust or safety in the therapeutic relationship.

Finally, there is the consideration of how the therapist introduces an activity and the degree to which they immerse themselves in the activity. The video of Lynde, working with Ellis in Quadrant II, illustrates these critically important factors. In our experience, the technique itself does not foster movement or change, it is the practitioner's skillful use of self and the manner in which they apply or modify the technique in the moment, remaining responsive to the client, that lends therapeutic potency to the technique. Lynde's playful introduction, followed by her ability to immerse herself and join the play, is what made the activity a "hit" for Ellis.

ILLUSTRATIVE CASE STUDY:
VIDEO QUADRANT II SEGMENT—ELLIS

Download the case examples video and transcript from https://library.jkp.com/redeem using the code RTECPZF.

At the beginning of this play segment, Lynde says that she has an idea for a target-shooting game. To set the context for this activity she remarks, "Sometimes I get some angry feelings, and the angry feelings I call Mr. Mad." Next, Lynde draws a picture of Mr. Mad, stating that he often sneaks up and tricks her into getting angry with people. Her introductory comments set the stage for a structured game based on an externalization approach. Although Lynde's suggestion may at first appear intrusive, considering that in previous sessions she engaged in a co-facilitative role testing Ellis's readiness to explore certain feelings, Lynde's shift to a directive and structured activity is largely congruent with the way her role has gradually evolved in the therapy process.

In the next few turns, Lynde increases the emotional intensity by commenting that she is going to stop Mr. Mad from sneaking up and tricking her. When her dart strikes the target, she emphasizes this by stating, "Got his sneaky teeth!" Interestingly, Ellis's actions begin to parallel Lynde's progression of intensity. For example, after Ellis's first dart strikes Mr. Mad, Ellis appears to erase a larger part of Mr. Mad's face than he intended to, so he draws back certain parts on the face. Ellis comments, "Well now he's a little less mad." However, when his next shot misses the target, Ellis approaches Mr. Mad and remarks, "I'm gonna get him. I'm tired of him tricking me."

Noticing that Ellis appears to be tolerating the intensity surrounding this activity, Lynde suggests that for the next round they will have to tell about one time when Mr. Mad snuck up on them and made them "really mad." Ellis volunteers to draw a new picture of Mr. Mad, commenting, "This time he's not going to be as confident though." In fact, Ellis draws a larger face than the first Mr. Mad. Although Lynde notices this, rather than elaborating on the nature of the difference, which might pull Ellis out of the moment and risk losing momentum, she simply reflects, "Mr. Mad looks a little different this time."

As the session progresses, the level of intensity increases due to the emphasis Lynde places on self-disclosure. Ellis's disclosures quickly unfold to the point where he mentions a situation where three bullies trapped him in a washroom. The level of conscious processing also increases at this point as Ellis comments, "That really made me mad." Lynde's response contains the message that what happened didn't really seem "fair." Although this is an empathic comment, it also focuses Ellis on specific components of his experience, namely that what happened was hurtful and unfair. This appears to be a hit, as Ellis's voice tone increases, and he remarks, "I'm gonna get Mr. Mad now." Furthermore, Ellis remains with the construct of fairness, by discussing a time when he felt blamed for accidentally dropping one of his mother's glasses. Lynde mirrors this by stating that she also feels mad when she is blamed for things she didn't do.

Interestingly, in his next turn, Ellis erases Mr. Mad, even though there were many facial parts remaining. This likely signifies that the level of intensity increased to the point at which Ellis needed to pivot away from the play. Astutely, Lynde modulates the intensity by recalling that she still needs to put up the points for the game. Ellis is then declared the winner, which is consistent with the overall structure of the activity.

Some theoretical approaches would take issue with the fact that a winner was declared, as this could introduce an evaluative or possibly judgmental component to the relationship. However, we see that for the majority of this session the primary emphasis is the relationship, exemplified by Lynde's tracking of Ellis's feeling states and her use of reflective and supportive comments. As planned, the element of competition was introduced only after Lynde had first assessed Ellis's ability to tolerate the intensity of such an approach.

THE *WHEN*: CONSIDERATIONS FOR THE PLAY THERAPY PROCESS

Therapists often use structured activities as an adjunct to a Non-Directive Play Therapy approach (Jones *et al.*, 2003). A therapist using this combined approach often introduces structured activities that are less emotionally intense during the beginning stage of therapy, as the child has not developed a sense of safety and trust in the relationship. Once these elements are established, and the child has moved to the working stage of therapy, the intensity of activities may be increased to bring focus on and direct energy to the core goals of therapy. In discussing the function and characteristics of intensity of session activities, Jones *et al.* state:

> Intensity is defined as the extent to which the session topic, structured exercises and techniques do the following: (a) evoke anxiety in the client; (b) challenge the client to self-disclose; (c) increase awareness; (d) focus on feelings; (e) concentrate on the here and now; and (f) focus on threatening issues. (2003, p.35)

It is important that therapists consider these elements to ensure appropriate pacing of activities. For instance, a role-play activity may evoke too much anxiety for a child if it occurs early in the therapy process. Similarly, mutual storytelling activities designed to foster self-disclosure may be met with a defensive reaction if the story is too close to the child's situation and the child does not yet feel safe in the therapeutic relationship. In the case of the adaptive doll play described previously, play sessions were initially based in Quadrant III, *Non-Intrusive Responding*. This approach provided the child with an opportunity to first develop comfort in the relationship. It also informed the therapist about the child's ability to tolerate certain levels of intensity.

As discussed by Hambridge (1955), the media selected for structured play should relate to the child's issues and must be sequenced in a manner that moves from less to more intense material. Danger (2003) postulates that adaptive doll play offers a developmentally appropriate avenue for gradually strengthening the child's ability to share anxiety-provoking experiences and gain a sense of mastery.

Another important consideration is the child's need to "set the stage" in play by arranging materials or by contributing to the development of certain ideas for the play scenario. Chazan (2002) refers to these actions as pre-play activities, which are characterized by the child's exploration, manipulation, or creation of symbolic meaning to toys or objects, in preparation for more elaborate play. The importance of these activities should not be overlooked when working in Quadrant II as they provide essential information about what kinds of characters or activities the child is drawn toward, what adventures or storylines are of interest to them, and the forms of emotional representations that are most meaningful to them. Essentially, these activities provide children with opportunities to represent their experiences and offer an emotional bridge or pathway that supports problem-solving.

Although Quadrant II denotes a directive and structured approach, this does not mean that activities are devoid of a shared, collaborative process. Even the briefest of play insertions that a child makes, through character actions or narrations, informs the therapist about the child's emotional pathways and the logic used to test or evaluate outcomes or choices illustrated in the story scripted by the therapist.

THE *WHO:* CLINICAL APPLICATIONS

When working in Quadrant II, therapists must carefully examine the child's play skills as well as other moderating factors that support or negatively impact the child's participation in structured activities. Readers are advised to consult the Child Moderating Factors Scale (Appendix A) to become familiar with these factors, particularly those that relate to the child's ability to manage activities with heightened levels of emotional intensity.

This quadrant is well suited to working with children who encounter difficulties with self-regulation and have impoverished coping skills. Regarding the first area, there is now a large body of research that relates emotional self-regulation to social competence, linking reduced or diminished levels of control to behavioral difficulties (Bronson, 2000). Thus, children who struggle with self-regulated functioning need specific help to learn how to control arousal levels and to express emotions appropriately. They also require assistance in developing problem-solving skills.

The information-processing model of Garber, Braafladt, and Zeman (1991) asserts that self-regulation occurs in a rapid sequence, often at a level that is not entirely conscious. In the first step of this process, there is the perception of an emotion and the recognition of the need to regulate that affect. In the second step, the child interprets that emotion and comes to realize its cause and determine who or what is responsible for altering it. The third step involves goal setting, during which the child decides what needs to be done to manage or alter the affect. The fourth step is response generation, which involves thinking about choices or concrete actions that can be taken. In the final step, the child takes action.

The sequence of self-regulation parallels the processes involved in problem-solving. It also relates to the overall play therapy process, which is about helping children make meaning out of their experiences and emotions. In Quadrant II, self-regulation and problem-solving activities often occur through role-plays, games, or other structured techniques. In the fourth and final phase of Adlerian Play Therapy, the therapist is noted to shift roles, moving toward a direct, "teaching oriented" function. Kottman (2003b) indicates that this shift helps children consolidate new perspectives on their lifestyles. During this phase, the therapist might use role-playing, or other teaching tools, to help the child develop a specific set of skills, such as negotiation skills or strategies for sharing. For the emotionally dysregulated child, these skills are essential to their ability to cope in social situations and help ensure success in future relationships.

Quadrant II is also well suited to children who need to build a repertoire of adaptive coping skills. As noted by Schaefer (2003), techniques embedded in a Cognitive-Behavioral Play Therapy approach appear to be effective in addressing anger-control issues as well as problems related to anxiety. Structured Play Therapy, or those approaches using elements of release therapy, is also commonly used for adjustment reactions. For example, Jones *et al.* (2003) indicate that children struggling with divorce may benefit from structured drawing activities that provide opportunities for self-disclosure, as this sets the foundation for establishing greater self-awareness and supports the development of coping skills.

While younger children may not have the cognitive flexibility or sophistication to benefit from certain structured techniques, because they are operating within the preoperational stage, Knell (2003) asserts that children at this age are capable of making cognitive changes, as these normally occur within the context of everyday parent–child interactions. Thus, it is important that therapists consider how to make developmentally appropriate adaptations of structured play activities to optimize growth and change. It is difficult, sometimes impossible, to design the perfect activity. Fortunately, play offers the child experiential opportunities to make meaning; if the play activity is useful and developmentally appropriate to the child, then the processes of assimilation and accommodation will occur, supporting shifts in their cognitive schemas.

SHOULD I STAY OR SHOULD I GO? INDICATIONS FOR WORKING IN QUADRANT II

The following six indicators offer reference points for evaluating potential movement to or from this quadrant.

Indicator 1: Therapeutic Process

Like Quadrant IV, Quadrant II is typically accessed after the therapeutic relationship has been formed. Having said that, some children are ready to address problems, worries, and concerns in an open, exploratory fashion and may immediately discuss and process these matters at the outset of therapy. A therapist would likely stay in this quadrant as long as the child continues to remain engaged in the directed activity, or discussion. When the child appears immobilized or demonstrates a need to gain distance from the activity it is time to *go*. The child's age and stage of development must be considered in selecting activities and in the processing of those activities.

Indicator 2: Responses of the Child

A child will exhibit the following responses if they have the capacity to be working in Quadrant II: the child remains engaged in the structured activity or exercise and begins to insert their own elaborations; the child appears to make use of the activity outside of the therapy session and demonstrates increasing levels of adjustment; and the child exhibits greater levels of awareness of themselves, others, and/or their experiences. A therapist should leave if the child appears overwhelmed or is emotionally disengaged from the activity. Although some children are compliant to therapist-led activities, they may not gain any significant benefit from the activity.

Indicator 3: Child's Play Skills

Children with high and/or restricted play skills can benefit from therapeutic interventions in Quadrant II. Children who are concrete in their processing style may benefit from activities that provide a framework for making meaningful connections between thoughts, feelings, and experiences. Those children who demonstrate high levels of imaginative play may readily undergo internal differentiation of schemas. Therapists may also stay in this quadrant when the child has high verbal abilities and shows a need to talk about their experiences. Similarly, children with high levels of problem-solving ability may be driven toward Quadrant II. If children are non-responsive or robotic in their response to structured interventions...*go*.

Indicator 4: Child's Drive and Direction in Therapy

Movement to Quadrant II, *Open Discussion and Exploration*, is indicated when the child drives the therapeutic agenda to be more consciously addressed. When working in a less-directive manner, children sometimes provide an indication of their need for open discussion by becoming very literal in their play, stopping the play and talking, or providing a narration of the play. Other children are driven toward symbolic representations of their experiences and do not require conscious processing for resolution or reorganization.

Indicator 5: Context of the Presenting Issue

Children with significant processing difficulties, or who are very literal or concrete in their thinking style, may benefit from structured therapeutic activities, such as therapeutic board games, feeling card games, or sandplay re-enactments. Additionally, children who have been traumatized often benefit from structured play activities that relate to the troublesome event. When properly structured and paced, these activities bring focus to certain dissociated thoughts and feelings, as they facilitate the reorganization process. Traumatized children also need safe and contained means of verbalizing their experiences and require validation of their feelings. Quadrant II supports conscious levels of processing through various ways, including interpretive comments that link play themes to feelings and experiences. *Stay* in this quadrant when the child's responses indicate an ability to tolerate conscious levels of reprocessing; *leave* when the child's responses indicate a need for greater distance and/or the child experiences difficulties with processing troublesome experiences at a more conscious level.

Indicator 6: Timelines and System Parameters

Some children may benefit from time-limited, structured, experientially based activities. In fact, non-directive treatment approaches may be less efficacious for children who present with concrete processing styles, or high play skills with accompanying verbal skills, or specific adjustment issues. Parents and referring third parties, such as agencies, understand and support directive therapy approaches which provide another element of support and reinforcement for the child. If the appropriate emotional, developmental, and cognitive preconditions are present to work in this quadrant, the therapist should *stay*. If not, no time limits or systems parameters will be enough for effective therapy delivery through Quadrant II, *Open Discussion and Exploration*.

MOVEMENT WITHIN THIS QUADRANT: ILLUSTRATIVE CASE STUDY—HALEY

Download the case examples video and transcript from https://library.jkp.com/redeem using the code RTECPZF.

The final segment of this video case example occurs when Susan, Haley's therapist, indicates that she has an idea for addressing the problem of children behaving in a "mean" way toward Haley at school. Susan directs the play, moving from an initial, role-play re-enactment using figures in the sandtray to a problem-solving discussion, where modeling techniques are used to help Haley rehearse new strategies. Although Susan structures a large portion of this play segment, careful inspection of her wording reveals a collaborative approach. For example, Susan states, "I have an idea of how we can deal with that problem."

During the role-play re-enactment phase, Susan structures the activity by asking Haley to develop a playground scene in the sandtray. Susan prompts Haley to make it look like her setting at school to ensure that this activity is relevant and meaningful to her. Once the scene is set, Susan directs the activity further by asking Haley to demonstrate what happens at the school playground when she wants to play with her friends. When Haley verbally describes how her friends act, Susan asks Haley to "show" her what happens. As discussed previously, this is an important intervention because it establishes an emotional experience or pathway for problem-solving. With children, this is best accomplished by having them role-play an experience, as it helps them differentiate certain feelings and may eventually lead them to consider options that feel right. As illustrated by point A in Figure 9.1, this moment is structured and directed by the therapist, and the child is invited to remain at a moderate level of consciousness/self-awareness. However, as the therapist is not highly immersed in the play, point A is positioned near the middle area of this quadrant.

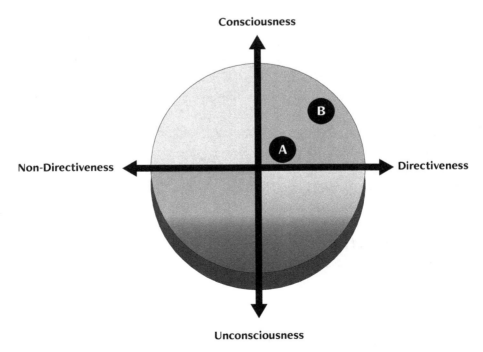

FIGURE 9.1: THERAPIST MOVEMENT IN QUADRANT II

As the scene evolves, Susan asks Haley to consider whether there are other students on the playground to play with, aside from the "mean" kids. Haley indicates that there is one student who used to be her friend until she wanted to play with the "cool kids." Susan persists by asking Haley what might happen if she asked this girl to play. Haley responds, "She'd probably say well...I wanna play with cool kids, because I don't wanna play with the nerdy kids." This scenario is then role-played, with Haley representing her character as moving off to a corner after Susan's character states that she just wants to play with the cool kids. Some therapists might have bypassed this step, as Haley had already identified that it was unlikely that this individual would join her in play. However, Susan's persistence models the importance of exploring possibilities; it represents that there are choices and emphasizes that it is okay to take a risk and to ask others if they want to play. This is further represented in Susan's question as to whether there might be someone "nicer" who would want to play. This appears to prompt Haley to consider another student on the playground. When asked what this person would say if approached, Haley tentatively responds, "I'm not sure." Susan then asks, "How do you want me to play it today?" This phrase communicates to Haley that she still retains the responsibility for making choices in their play. It also highlights that there are various possibilities that might occur, which is important to model when working with children who are feeling emotionally stuck and have low levels of risk-taking or persistence.

Despite these strategic comments, Haley returns the responsibility to Susan, stating, "You can decide." At this point, Susan has the boy character state that he is tired of playing on the swings and wants to join the other group of kids at the slide. This response likely reflects the reality of Haley's playground situation. However, Susan continues with a problem-solving approach by asking Haley to once more look at her options, such as whether there is someone else standing in the group who might change their mind and play with her. Haley identifies someone, but reveals that she normally wouldn't ask this individual.

Susan continues to facilitate Haley's exploration by suggesting that they try this in play to find out what might happen. This time, Susan's character indicates that they are busy but remarks, "I could probably play with you tomorrow at lunch if you wanna do that." This is a carefully crafted response, as it does not present a magical solution. Instead, it represents that a positive outcome is possible. Accordingly, Susan probes to find out whether the idea of asking an individual such as the one identified in the play would be something that Haley would be willing to practice and, most importantly, whether Haley believes it might work. This appears to be a hit, as Haley states that it could work! In this play segment, the therapist is verbally active, outside of the play, but also immerses herself in the play as she animates characters and makes use of her emotional self. The level of structuring and immersion places this further to the right in this quadrant, as represented by point B in Figure 9.1.

Throughout this segment, Susan refrained from offering an immediate solution or answer to Haley's playground dilemma. Instead, Susan's use of role-play re-enactments prompts the development of a collaborative problem-solving approach. This leaves Haley with several important messages. First, that she has options or choices at the playground. Second, that she is capable of thinking through which option is relevant and worth trying. Third, her feelings provide important signposts that help guide her in the problem-solving process.

KEY POINTS

- One factor that distinguishes Quadrant II from Quadrant IV, *Co-Facilitation*, is that the therapist brings structure and sequence to the play activities; they are a director *and* facilitator of the therapy process.
- Numerous play therapy models, such as Adlerian, Gestalt, Ecosystemic, and Cognitive-Behavioral, use prearranged or structured play activities to bring focus to or stimulate and deepen play activities.
- An open dialogue of thoughts and feelings often leads to the exploration of "choices" through active problem-solving or the rehearsal of new coping strategies.
- Decision-making concerning the *who*, *what*, *when*, *why*, and *how* for this quadrant is often rooted in an understanding of the ways in which affect organizes experience, thinking, and behavior.
- There is an underlying belief in Cognitive-Behavioral and Ecosystemic Play Therapy models that problem-solving processes provide a corrective experience in therapy, enabling the child to generalize what they have learned in therapy to other areas of their life.
- Children with high and/or restricted play skills can benefit from therapeutic interventions in Quadrant II.

⊚ **Chapter 10** ⊚

PREPARING PARENT FEEDBACK

Hand in hand we walk this path together.

The parent feedback and conceptualization forms video accompanies this chapter; along with the transcript, it can be downloaded from https://library.jkp.com/redeem using the code RTECPZF.

Parents are a critical part of the child and play therapy process; children are known to have better therapy outcomes when their parents are involved (Bratton *et al.*, 2005). For the purposes of this book, we use the term "parent" when describing a day-to-day caregiver for a child. It is recognized that a parenting role may be fulfilled by a legal guardian or a delegated person such as a stepparent, a grandparent, or multiple caregivers living together who each perform a parenting role as in the case of polyamorous family systems. Family is broadly defined as one or more adults who take on a purposeful role in caring for and helping to raise a child. Play therapists tend to be attracted to the field based on their interest, comfort, and often a preference for working with children. What makes children's therapy unique is that in addition to the child, the therapist must work with the parent(s) and the systems of which children are a part. It is not enough to schedule an hour for a child therapy session because there are many other responsibilities in addition to the face-to-face time with a child. The role expands to consultations with schools, childcare providers, and possibly child protection workers or lawyers and the court. Sometimes play therapists will interface with other therapists involved with the parents. If the parents don't live in the same home, parent updates and/or consultations may often occur twice. If there are multiple caregivers or practitioners involved, the play therapist may need to coordinate case review meetings. Planning and conceptualizing must consider the *who*, *what*, *when*, and *how* of parent feedback.

CONCEPTUALIZING PARENT FEEDBACK: THE FOUR STEPS OF PREPARATION

1) The Who

One of the first questions a play therapist should ask is, "Who is my client?" In child therapy the legal client is the guardian(s) of the child. The "client" is the party who has the authority to sign the consent-for-treatment form. This can get complicated because sometimes a legal authority such as Child Protective Services (CPS) can be the legal guardian and you are working with "delegates of authority" for a child such as foster parents. This means your client, in addition to the child, will be CPS. You may view the child as the secondary client or the primary recipient of services, but ultimately, play therapists have a primary obligation to the guardian(s) when delivering therapy services to children. When considering the question of "Who will be involved?", it becomes clear that the answer is "it depends." Who is identified as a significant party or a legal guardian involved in the case? Play therapists must consider guardianship from a legal involvement point of view. In Canada, for instance, a child can have more than two legal guardians. It is essential to know and understand the legal jurisdiction in which you as a play therapist work. Play therapists ask, "Will there be one or more parents involved in the process?" and then identify the parties at the beginning of the service. The only way to make the decision not to include a legal guardian is if one of the parties has sole decision-making authority provided by way of a court order. Once contacted, some legal guardians are not interested in being involved, but the decision not to be involved must be documented and the play therapist still needs consent for treatment from this parent. If another significant party who is not a legal guardian would like to be involved, this will require consent from the legal guardians.

It is important for play therapists to ask at the beginning of service if there is a current court order and, if there is one, request a copy for the file. Once the therapist decides who will be involved, it is documented. There can be no "Who?" without considering the child client. Play therapists provide services to children, and although children have no legal ability to make decisions about themselves, children are identified as a central client at the outset of any play therapy intake. The description of the child and the reasons for referral are provided by the parent at the beginning of treatment but children also contribute to self-descriptions and reasons for coming to play therapy. Play therapists tend to spend most of their clinical time with a child client. Typically, play therapy is considered child-centered and family focused. Even if a play therapist conceptualizes that it is best to do Family Play Therapy, the child remains centrally important, and a child client must agree to attend treatment.

What about other family members? Will you see siblings from the same family? Although there are some practitioners who would prefer not to see siblings for a variety of reasons, we support seeing more than one child in the family. Families are systems, and dividing treatment across multiple therapists may disrupt an integrated approach. Parents can also receive multiple suggestions that may be quite confusing to the parenting process. The family would also have to rely on more than one practitioner to conceptualize the family issues and dynamics. If you have a colleague in the same office, there may, at times, be good reason to divide the roles. Consent for consultation and coordination would be necessary so that the family does not experience confusion and you do not work at cross purposes with another practitioner. Seeing a parent for personal therapy at the same time as seeing their child for play therapy would be a dual role conflict. Play therapists do, however, see parents individually for parenting issues and parenting consultations. When a parent moves in the direction of wanting to process a current or past *personal* issue, play therapists make referrals to an individual therapist.

2) The What

Once you have established *who* the parent(s) are, an intake meeting is scheduled with the parties either individually or together. What will you talk about in the first meeting? There are several components to the initial parent meeting (Cates *et al.*, 2006). It is suggested that the therapist address the following areas:

- Establish rapport with each parent.
- Gather information about the child and family system.
- Gather information about the presenting problem.
- Explore culture and the unique makeup of the family.
- Explain confidentiality.
- Provide parents with a tour of the playroom.
- Explain that you will meet with parents to provide ongoing feedback and suggest feedback meeting frequency/timing.
- Explain the play therapy process (provide a handout explanation to take home).
- Help parents describe a way to introduce play therapy to their child (include this topic in your handout as well).

Establish an initial treatment agreement or contract, with an identified review or update process. What is your role? Will you be a consultant to parents? A facilitator of family play interventions? A model for parents on how to engage in child-led play? An individual play therapist for the child? A formal assessor? A preliminary play-based assessor and treatment provider? A parent coach? Play therapists may begin as individually child focused and, at some point, move toward including a parent(s). In any event, identify your role at the beginning of your time with the parents. Document in your notes that you clarified what role you will take with the family and that if your role changes you will make it explicit. This is considered clinical contracting. You will likely continue to contract with parents throughout the process. When you shift what you are doing and don't make it explicit, you put yourself at risk of being misunderstood and you will likely confuse the family members. If you move from an individual play therapist role with a child, the child needs to be included in this decision. Simply inviting a parent to the next child session without consulting with the child and gaining agreement would be unethical.

What can you share with a parent? What is meant by confidentiality, consent, and assent? Play therapists have legal obligations. Confidentiality in children's play therapy is identified as *private but not secret*. This means that children's time with you will generally be kept private except for the four hurts:

- They are getting hurt by someone.
- They know someone who is getting hurt.
- They are going to hurt someone.
- They are hurting or going to hurt themselves.

This explanation may need to be provided in pictorial form for younger children and should be provided in the presence of each parent with the child present. It is at this time that the therapist contracts with parent(s) *not to question* their child after sessions. You should tell the child that their parents may want to know how they are doing, that you will let the child know what you have learned about them before talking to their parent(s), and that they can help decide what you can and cannot share (with the exception of the four hurts). Typically, play therapists share general play themes and overall progress with parents, and they don't expose the specific details of the play sessions. Children have a right to be included in what will be said about them. Therapists will adjust how to consult with a very young child and may identify (with the child) positive things learned about them and ask the child if it would be alright with them if the therapist shares this with their parent(s).

Adults can legally consent for treatment for themselves and if they are legal guardians, they can also consent for treatment of legal minors (children under the age of 18 years). Consent is considered the act of giving informed legal permission for something to happen or an agreement to do something. Although children can't provide consent, they *can* provide assent which is an informed agreement or permission to participate in counseling. There are many creative ways that play therapists ensure a child has provided assent, including presenting prepared visuals that explain the therapy role, the play therapy process, and *private but not secret* and limits of confidentiality. Some children and youth don't want to participate, and although parents may still want their child to receive services, it would be important not to engage in a coercive assent process. Some children are uncertain or anxious and need additional assurance of the process and may need to try play therapy with the knowledge that they don't have to continue if they really don't want to. Providing children with a voice and ultimately a choice in agreeing to the process is essential.

What information can you provide to parents after meeting with a child? Once you have consulted with your child client about the basic things you would like to share with parents (generally this may be related to progress made or perhaps there is a special need or feeling a child would like you to share), you will then look to other pieces of data that help you to conceptualize the child using the Parent Feedback Conceptualization Form (Appendix D). Parents tend to appreciate the detailed attention and consideration brought forward about their child. The scale also helps to identify areas of strength, which is most important when working with children and their families. The next area of information to provide to parents is related to a child's overall presentation and communication. The Case Conceptualization Form (Appendix E) is a useful tool in this regard, as it helps identify specific elements of play themes and responses of the child. The following questions can be addressed:

- How did the child engage in the play therapy process?
- What play themes emerged? How did play themes shift over time?
- What needs, thoughts, or views did the child communicate?
- What are the markers of therapeutic growth?
- What elements of the child's temperament were present during play sessions?
- What is the personality of the child (leader, follower, cheerful, bright, etc.)?

Constructing answers to these questions in combination with the child moderating factors provides the practitioner with a way to create a feedback summary. By looking at the variables and questions, a road map for next steps will begin to form.

3) The When

Timing is always a consideration when providing parent feedback. Parents need to hear from you early in the therapy process, and therapists should aim to create a parent feedback meeting(s) plan at the outset of treatment. One suggestion is to see a child between two to four times and then set a parent meeting. Some children need more time to show or tell you about themselves through play so you may add one or more sessions to this plan—but if this is the case, initiate a touchpoint with the parents to let them know their child needs more time. The quick return to parents helps them to be partners in the process and alleviates uncertainty. It is also clinical judgment that sets the timing and type of parent involvement, however. Goodyear-Brown (2021) notes:

We want to include parents as partners in every instance in which it is clinically sound to do so. The science seems clear enough; inviting parents into the therapeutic process can maximize treatment gains, but how and when in the course of treatment? This is where the art of therapy is required...as they [clinicians] ask the question: "What can the system hold?" (p.xi)

Ponder the question, "What can the system hold?" Think about the family dynamics, family level of safety, openness of parent(s), parenting approaches, mental health issues, and individual member functioning. These factors all contribute to when and with what frequency you will see which family members. There are times when you can't leave contact with parents until you meet for a proper feedback session. If this is the case, you may choose to provide email updates or meet with parents on, say, Zoom for a purposeful face-to-face update. Sometimes it is clear that children are distressed and they need something immediate from a parent. Holding, encouragement, nurturing, and/or structuring of the child may all be possible imminent needs.

4) The How

How to provide parent feedback is where creativity, skill, and heart meet. Each parent will present in a unique way, and each will have a particular presentation or observable way of interacting with you. Parents are just people who come from a particular attachment organization and parenting experience themselves. Before delivering information to parents about their children, it will be important to identify a parent's style of interaction with you so that you can deliver information that meets where the parent is coming from.

PARENT PRESENTATION STYLES

Through our years of practice, we have identified 11 types of interactive presentation styles. When thinking about ways parents interact with you as a practitioner, you will also consider the likelihood that parents may present with a blend of a couple of different styles. Another consideration when giving feedback to more than one parent at a time is that you will likely be working with two primary styles versus one. This requires a creative feedback process. The following highlights possible parent styles and suggested ways to organize your feedback. The *Expert Parent* (EP) is a highly knowledgeable parent or one who believes themself to be knowledgeable. This parent usually comes in with identified knowledge or has researched you, play therapy, or various mental health topics. This parent may also be in the same field or a closely related field to you. Expert Parents bring a special focus on already knowing a lot. You will typically know that you are working with an Expert Parent because they will tell you what they know and possibly question what you know. This style of parent will likely test your knowledge and ask you to share examples of your work. These parents like to know about your background and sometimes ask you for your résumé. These parents want assurance that you know what you are talking about.

Providing feedback to the Expert Parent would include the use of clear linear points and academically focused information. It is useful to share research or reference materials that connect to things you have learned about the child. This could include references to child development or books of interest that connect to the presenting problem that the parent may be able to review. Being less process focused and more structured in your presentation with these parents is usually appreciated. These parents want to know that you have made significant connections between what they originally identified as the presenting problem and what you are observing in their child.

The *Deflector Parent* (DP) does not identify a particular problem at the outset of the process. These parents are often referred to as "rubber fence" style people, where there is no particular problem identified—even though they have come to see you. This style of parent may deflect blame onto others with little or no thought for their role in the dynamic. Goodyear-Brown (2021) views Deflector Parents as those who carry much "shame and negative self-talk," and therefore deflect responsibility onto others, including their children. Deflecting saves these parents from experiencing their own feelings of inadequacy.

Providing feedback to the Deflector Parent may include using visual aids to restate the intake issues and discussions that took place during the initial meeting. Provision of a pictorial pathway of treatment using various metaphors that may engage the parent would be helpful. Using a whiteboard or a flip chart offers a place to focus that is away from the vulnerability of a face-to-face discussion. You may also invite the parent to engage in elaborating on the visuals by inviting them to add to the picture, which increases their involvement and potentially their sense of self-efficacy.

The *Passive Parent* (PP) would like you to tell them what to do and yet they may have trouble following through with any suggestions you provide. Passive Parents would like you to take on the roles they should have. These parents don't like to be challenged and would prefer to step back and hope that you take over. They may need a lot of nurturing themselves and may draw you into their feelings of helplessness. These parents often present as uncertain about their own sense of self and can easily be stressed by being asked to provide more structure or guidance for their child.

Providing feedback to the Passive Parent would include connecting with the parent and parent issues, worries, and concerns. What would assist the parent to feel more of a sense of assurance and success? Passive Parents have been used to others taking over and are often attracted to those who are strong-willed and structured. Some Passive Parents have a more internalizing way of being and the idea of stating their needs or having expectations of their children feels too demanding. These parents need you to break down some small achievable actions to take. Modeling ways of limit-setting or role-playing with this style of parent, so that they may experience a felt sense of what it would be like to *do* something different, is very useful. For the Passive Parent, it is all in the practice of "doing".

The *Aggressive Parent* (AGP) tends to present with anger or blame focused on the therapist or "other(s)." This style of parent may have been through many other services and not felt heard, or the parent may be reactive or easily frustrated when not hearing what they would like to hear. These parents often use emotionality (particularly anger) to manage situations where they feel out of control. Frequently, Aggressive Parents negatively trigger therapists and call on a concentrated effort on the part of the therapist to remain neutral with humor and empathy. Aggression can come in the form of direct or indirect blame and projection. Indirect aggression can arise through describing your actions in an affidavit, reporting you to your professional organization after you have worked with the person, or behaving in obstructionistic or behavioral ways toward you or others directly. Aggressive Parents may write long critical emails to you pointing out all of the ways you are not helpful.

Providing feedback to the Aggressive Parent requires the therapist to feel firmly grounded and not intimidated. When working with Aggressive Parents, you must find points of intersection with a parent's issues and concerns. A point of intersection can occur when you listen carefully to the language used by the parent, and you find a point of agreement in the concerns presented. An example may be that the parent complains about the child's attitude and behavior and then contradicts this by saying, "And thankfully this doesn't seem to happen at school." The therapist then joins the parent by saying, "No, you're right it seems that Jennifer *can* manage her behavior at school!"

The *Process-Focused Parent* (PFP) goes around and around talking about what is happening but never seems to see an end (or be interested in one) or pick up on the therapist's goals or objectives. This parent can be frustrating for the therapist, as therapists are engaged to provide a road map and a way to address a presenting issue. The parent often repeats a concern without seeming to hear the actions the therapist is taking. These parents like to talk about what is happening rather than address what is happening. They may not be interested in a resolution; rather, they may be stuck in the problem.

Providing feedback to the Process-Focused Parent requires the therapist to use process diagrams and provide examples of other similar treatment situations for similar presenting issues. The therapist is looking for entry points to join with the parent as the parent describes how they see things working (or not working). These parents need to have an entry point identified in order to follow a new direction and possibly try new things with their child. Because process focused people are interested in why and how things are the way they are, it is also possible to join with them on "how" things change. It is not as direct an intervention as used with other styles of parents, but if these parents are engaged in a process toward change, they are usually quite motivated to try something different and to help you look for change. Norton and Norton's process-of-play-therapy diagram (2006) would be very useful to show these parents.

The *Solution-Focused Parent* (SFP) is prone to wanting you to tell them the answer with the expectation that you will "fix" the problem. These parents want a more-or-less expedient outcome. Their expectations need to be managed. You will want to emphasize how play therapy works and that success with a child happens at the pace of the child. Keep in mind these parents like outcome measures and outcomes in general. They are likely to be somewhat impatient with process-oriented discussions and prefer you to get to the outcome more quickly. They are likely to ask you to provide their child with "tools" to take away. They are not usually open to the idea that change is somewhat more complex due to the influence of multiple variables and that teaching their child a few simple strategies (tools) may not be enough for any enduring outcome.

Providing feedback to the Solution-Focused Parent may include an outline of the stages of play therapy using Norton and Norton's diagram (2006). This pictorial representation would be quite useful for this parent style. This appeals to the need to know what is happening and how the problem is addressed in play therapy. It combines the way a Process-Focused Parent approaches their child's presenting needs with the Solution-Focused Parent. If the Solution-Focused Parent knows there is a pathway, they will likely be quite supportive of the play therapist's efforts. The play therapist can use the diagram for multiple feedback sessions to anchor where the child is at in the process, which may be reassuring for the Solution-Focused Parent.

The *Collaborative Parent* (CP) is likely the easiest parent with whom to work. These parents are eager to work *with* you and are ready to be called on to be active participants or part of the therapy process. These parents are typically less defensive and more capable of being co-therapists and are eager to learn how they can assist. Collaborative Parents bring their own ideas to the process and are committed to their child's growth and development—even if it takes some time.

Providing feedback to the Collaborative Parent follows an egalitarian approach by using collaborative language such as, "together we can..." These parents are partners in the process. They are typically capable of follow-through and can tolerate progression and regression as part of what may happen for their child in therapy. These parents benefit from educational materials and can usually implement home-based activities with their children. Using step-by-step mapping and outlining the two roles (yours and theirs) helps to assure the Collaborative Parent. Collaborative Parents make your job easier, and the treatment provided ends up being more efficacious as it is known that parent involvement increases treatment success (Bratton *et al.*, 2005).

The *Conflicted Parent* (CONFP) either presents as "in conflict" with the other caregiver or exhibits an inner conflict perhaps as related to their own guilt about the way they have parented or some other related self-blame. Parents who are either in conflict or conflicted pose a challenge because their focus is typically not on their child, rather it is on self or other. Other is often the other parent, which increases the need for the therapist to become more of a manager of circumstances. The therapist has to be conscious of not becoming a target of blame or a personal therapist to the Conflicted Parent. Conflicted Parents complicate the process because they have their own needs that detract from the child therapy process. Play therapists have to work to not get drawn into a middle position by Conflicted Parents. This style of parent presentation often comes with agendas that are not always transparent or child focused.

Providing feedback to Conflicted Parents includes identifying and outlining multiple issues that contribute to making things confusing and complicated. Therapists will want to compartmentalize and organize competing issues of importance to these parents. Parent issues and child issues and needs can be presented visually so that the therapist can assist the parent to differentiate adult and child areas of concern and importance. Therapists will likely have to regularly restate their role as child therapist. Conflicted Parents often have difficulty hearing feedback from their children, and the play therapist may want to make use of the Parent Readiness Scale (Yasenik and Graham, 2016) to identify how ready the parent is to hear feedback about their child. This scale outlines nine variables related to parent readiness and includes: three *parent–child* items, three *parent–parent* items, and three *self* items. The lower the readiness score on this scale, the more the therapist will provide generalized feedback to the parent.

The *Control Parent* (CONP) attempts to control the therapy process, or you as the play therapist. This could include deciding when to come and who they will bring to a therapy session. A Control Parent may have been scheduled for a parent feedback session but without notice decide to bring their child for a child session instead. They may attempt to pressure a therapist to use a particular intervention or demand information from sessions. These parents can be quite certain they know what the process "should be" and sometimes end up intimidating a therapist into follow their agenda instead of the therapist remaining in charge. These parents need more structuring and contracting at the outset of therapy so that when they attempt to direct the process the play therapist can go back to the contracted agreement for review and re-contracting.

Providing feedback to the Control Parent (CONP) requires language that emphasizes the role of a play therapist as guide and manager of process. Establishing the process and parameters of the therapy is essential. Calling on some of the parent's ideas would be important because these parents need some form of purposeful involvement. You may also take what you have learned about a child and find areas that line up with the parent perspective. What can the control style parent take on as a task? You will want to consider making use of the control style to assist you rather than to directly bump up against the parent. Power struggles can easily erupt with these types of parents. Skill in providing feedback includes finding points of intersection and incorporating the parent need to feel included during the process. These parents are often harder to encourage to participate because they tend to be observers, organizers, and directors of processes rather than collaborators.

The *Insensitive Parent* (IP) presentation style means a parent does not easily read the cues of their child (or others) accurately or in a timely manner; this can include the therapist. Siegel and Hartzell (2003), in their seminal book *Parenting from the Inside Out*, refer to mindsight—"The ability to perceive our own minds and minds of others" (p.9)—which includes the ability to perceive non-verbal signals that help parents to accurately respond to their children. Signals include eye contact, facial expressions, tone of voice, gestures, and body postures. Parents with low sensitivity or ability to read cues may have a difficult time understanding the therapist's ways of conceptualizing their child or the child's needs. The child may be communicating needs that the parent misses. Parents may then have trouble being a part of the solution related to their child's therapy process.

Providing feedback to the Insensitive Parent requires the therapist to identify the parent's early parenting experiences and personal needs first, and, second, to link the child's cues with an interpretation of the need of the child. Feedback may include ways parents can look below the surface of their child's behaviors. What is the behavior telling us? Adlerian play therapists for instance help parents identify the goals of misbehavior, which is one approach that identifies what may lie below the behavior and looks at what the behavior is communicating (Kottman, 2011). Play therapists often ask about the fine line between addressing a parent's experiences of being parented and keeping the primary focus on the child with whom they are working. A systems theory approach is useful to avoid toppling over and solely working on the parents' family-of-origin issues in individual sessions. It is suggested to keep the focus on the parent–child system interactions. Some parents will require a deeper look at their own parenting experiences with another individual therapist, while others can remain in the systems approach to working on the interchange between them and their child. The symbolic use of miniatures in sand scenes is a very effective way to move the focus of feedback to a projective space (which provides a safe distance for parent involvement). The therapist can *show* the family system and symbolically identify child and parent needs. This is also a safe way to invite these parents in interactive reviews.

The *Abusive Parent* (ABP) presentation style poses a potential or actual risk to the child. These parents often come from harsh parenting experiences themselves, and when stressed, they react in ways they have experienced with their parents. It is not always clear what is happening in families where you suspect abuse. These parents are often wary and suspicious of your involvement or actions with their child. They combine with other styles listed above in that they also often present as controlling and insensitive. They sometimes seek therapy out of guilt, or they have been court ordered into a therapy process. They tend to control what the child shares in therapy, but as a play therapist, you may see metaphorical disclosures. When working with this presentation style, you will want to find a way to provide safety for the parent. These parents tend to be highly activated most of the time and their presentations demonstrate a sympathetic-autonomic nervous system state of either fight or flight. Therapists usually neurocept a feeling of dread or alarm themselves but there may not yet be a concrete reason for this experience.

Providing feedback to the Abusive Parent requires the play therapist to limit feedback to surface topics only and to keep all comments about the child and the child's process positive. Any early questioning of this presentation style will create high levels of alarm and trigger a potential retaliation or negative response. These parents need help, but until you know what is happening and have enough information from the child, it could be quite risky to bring any needs or issues the child presents to the surface. The feedback may be delivered to Child Protective Services before it is provided to a parent. Parents who have this presentation style will likely require some form of mandated services or a legal intervention at some point. Therapy for children of these parents may end up being a holding space until there is enough safety for the child to disclose enough for the therapist to seek further assistance. The main point here is you don't want to create more harm.

CONSIDER FUTURE NEEDS AND AN ONGOING TREATMENT PLAN

During parent feedback sessions, it is important to identify the next steps and define the following:

- How many more sessions do you recommend before getting back together again?
- *What* will you work on with the child and *what* approach will you take to work on the identified areas?
- Will you suggest some home-based interventions? What can you provide as guidance for parent interventions?
- Do you want to schedule one or more parent-only meetings as well as meet with the child?
- Do you want to prepare the parent(s) for parent–child sessions? How many

parent–child sessions might you recommend? How will you consult with the child about including their parent(s)?

- Will you check with the school or other important people involved in the child and family's life?
- If you are going to terminate services, will you gradually lessen the frequency of sessions or will you suggest developmentally sequenced therapy in the future? In some situations, you may return to the parents with a message of stopping therapy at that time.
- How will you terminate with the child? How will the child be involved in planful endings?

KEY POINTS

- This chapter has identified the *who*, *what*, *when*, and *how* of parent feedback. Additionally, parent presentation styles have been highlighted in combination with how a therapist might approach feedback with a particular parent presentation. Parts of this overview will be highlighted in the accompanying demonstration parent feedback and conceptualization forms video (and transcript) on the case of Ellis, which can be downloaded from https://library.jkp.com/redeem using the code RTECPZF.
- Part of the play therapist's role is to decide what can and will be shared with parents. Consider the role of consulting with children before delivering parent feedback. It is important to consult children throughout the span of the treatment process. When working with children and youth, understanding the terms confidentiality, privacy, consent, and assent are critical.
- The timing of parent feedback and parent involvement throughout the therapy process is another consideration for the play therapist. When providing feedback, review the 11 common parent presentation styles and consider providing feedback to more than one parent at a time. Each parent may have a different presentation or a combination of presentations.
- Play therapists must plan *how* to provide feedback. Each parent style requires a different engagement, entry point, and approach. As part of the feedback, future planning for additional therapy sessions and potential follow-up appointments are discussed.

◎ **Chapter 11** ◎

CASE CONCEPTUALIZATION: THE CASE OF ELLIS

The weave of the quilt reveals the hidden story.

PURPOSE AND USE OF THE CASE CONCEPTUALIZATION FORM

One of the supervisor's tasks is to understand the complex systems and processes embedded in the case and assist the supervisee to conceptualize these factors. The Case Conceptualization Form (Appendix E) is an integrative tool that can be quickly deployed to illuminate critical elements of the case, to provide the supervisee with a structure for organizing their thinking, and to foster a deeper understanding of goals and intervention strategies. This form integrates information and hypotheses the supervisee has been collecting through: Child Moderating Factors Scale (Appendix A); Degree of Immersion: Therapist Use of Self Scale (Appendix B); Tracking and Observation Form (Appendix C). Completing the form sets the framework for entering a collaborative learning space by supporting the supervisee in conceptualizing where they are at in the therapy process. Most importantly, it gives the supervisee ownership in the learning process.

It is helpful to ask supervisees to complete the form in advance of a scheduled supervision session. This prompts the supervisee to assume an active role in the process. In practice, the form can be discussed from the far-left box to the right, or in the opposite direction. At the outset, it is important to ask supervisees whether they are feeling confused or stressed by the case or if they are more concerned with specific questions, such as when or how to introduce a certain technique or strategy. The first concern suggests that it is likely more important to begin with the *Self* box so as not to get hung up on case details and background information. This orientation reflects an emphasis on helping the supervisee explore the relationship between the self and the client system, which often brings us closer to an understanding of underlying transference and countertransference issues.

◎ 164 ◎

Visually, the boxes in the second row have been purposefully placed under specific boxes in the top row as this helps the supervisee make conceptual links between the information in each box. For example, an understanding of the child's world view often comes through an exploration of thematic material. Similarly, an understanding of transference and countertransference surfaces through discussions of how a supervisee feels about working with the client/system. An understanding of resiliency and vulnerability factors comes from a review of background and contextual factors, under the *Content* subheading.

Both supervisees and supervisors have likely experienced case review sessions where much time is spent on background information, with little time remaining to formulate the issues and advance a new plan. From the perspective of Gestalt therapy, the Case Conceptualization Form helps explore the contact-boundary between the therapist and the client system. The concepts of *figure* and *ground* are also useful to consider. Figure refers to perceptions of experiences or reality that are currently in the foreground of attention. Ground refers to everything else around the figure. Ground is a more implicit part of the process and serves as a context for the figure; its relationship to the figure gives it meaning (Perls, Hefferline, and Goodman, 1951). Through the Case Conceptualization From, figure and ground are jointly explored with the supervisee, and from this process the "Gestalt", or what we perceive as real and meaningful, becomes illuminated.

PROCESS AND GUIDING QUESTIONS: ELEVEN AREAS FOR SUPERVISION

Each section of the form is described below. When possible, the form should be completed by the supervisee prior to supervision. Although supervisors may choose to sequence the discussion as they wish, the following sequences and guiding questions are commonly used at the Rocky Mountain Play Therapy Institute™.

To illustrate this process, each section includes questions or points that may have been raised by Lynde, the therapist working with Ellis.

1) Self Box

Therapist's degree of immersion is constantly considered throughout the play therapy process and is a central construct in this circumplex model. Underlying this construct is the belief that one of the fundamental change mechanisms is the therapeutic relationship. Accordingly, it is critically important that the supervisee be able to identify and articulate their use of self and, most importantly, how they experience their involvement with the case. This is often the most challenging and difficult part of completing the form. Supervisees are usually more comfortable talking about specific dynamics of the case than exploring how they *feel* about certain case dynamics.

Yet, without sufficient opportunities to reflect on their role and feelings, supervisees will forge ahead without the necessary level of self-awareness.

In working with this factor, supervisors must remain aware of the fact that they have entered a collaborative space. It is often more important that the supervisee *discover* how they are feeling rather than be *told* how they are presenting or managing with a client. The following questions can be used as a starting point for discussion.

GUIDING QUESTIONS FOR THE SELF BOX

- How do you feel about this client and others who are part of the client system?
- In what ways did your cultural self emerge in sessions with the child? What cultural opportunities did you take when working with this client?
- What do you like about this client? What is it about this client is challenging for you?
- How do you feel this case is progressing?
- When have you felt effective? When have you felt discouraged or challenged?
- How have you made sense of the challenges?
- What would you really like to say to certain individuals surrounding this case? What do you think they would do with that information?
- If you could change something about the client context, what would that be?
- When you think of your immersion in the play process, what areas of self have been easy to access? Which ones are difficult to access? What do you think might be either inhibiting or facilitating your immersion?

CASE OF ELLIS: REFLECTIONS BY LYNDE

- I enjoy working with this child and family. Parents are committed and eager to learn/help.
- I was aware that I bring an attitude of expecting respect from children and the belief that adults are to be treated in a certain way. I became aware of my experience of growing up with an authority hierarchy in my family of origin.
- Initially I felt challenged. Child presented as somewhat angry/irritable yet did not display aggressive outbursts.
- I was somewhat surprised by the initial question posed through puppet play: "Why are you here?" Once we moved to in-depth symbolic play it felt more comfortable and natural to become immersed in play. I felt my use of self expanded—physical self and emotional self.
- I am wondering if I should increase use of interpretations? I used linking interpretations and it seemed to be a hit.

For Appendix B, I rated my verbal use of self as low to moderate. As sessions progressed, the "here-and-now" discussion began to increase, as did my use of interpretations. My emotional use of self also increased—I became more immersed in the play, so I rated it moderate to high. I became more aware of feelings of sadness, for myself, as he began to disclose what happened at school. Overall, I felt my level of embodiment was moderate—I was aware of certain feelings during sessions. In terms of cultural use of self, I felt I was on the low end—I share a similar cultural background and there did not seem to be moments in play where there were opportunities or a need to introject. Overall, I feel I am mostly on track with my degree of immersion (total immersion score was 28).

2) Goals and Hypotheses Box

Goal setting is a fluid process, as goals often shift as the therapy process evolves. Accordingly, it is critical that the supervisee be able to articulate and refine treatment goals. Typically, goals encompass issues identified by the referral source. However, these goals are often broad-based, issue-focused statements that need to be refined and narrowed to carry meaning and provide direction in therapy.

The following points may help the supervisee focus on specific goals and the underlying therapeutic powers of play (TPoP). These points might be presented to the supervisee in advance of the supervision meeting for consideration and refinement.

GOAL AREAS FOR CONSIDERATION

- To increase the child's range of affect.
- To assist the child in verbally expressing feelings.
- To strengthen the child's ability to cope with specific feelings or situations.
- To help the child explore the nature and meaning of current relationships.
- To enhance the child's ability to relate to others (e.g., attachment organization).
- To expand the child's ability to get their needs met in adaptive, prosocial ways.
- To help the child explore and make meaning of troublesome experiences.
- To bolster the child's self-esteem and self-image.

THERAPEUTIC POWERS OF PLAY (TPoP)

For each goal area, ask the supervisee to identify which of the four primary areas of the TPoP the goal falls within: fosters emotional wellness; enhances social relationships; increases personal strengths; or facilitates communication. Next, ask the supervisee to identify which of the potential 20 TPoP might specifically be accessed, and through which play modality. As the TPoP are essentially trans-theoretical in nature and function as a *threshold concept* (Drewes and Schaefer 2015; Parson, 2021), discussion often deepens the supervisees' understanding of TPoP in general and how access to a specific TpoP enhances the therapeutic effect.

In supervision, time should also be allotted to helping the supervisee identify indicators of therapeutic growth. This often includes consideration of factors outside of the therapeutic context, such as school adjustment, friendship patterns, and family relationships.

CASE OF ELLIS: REFLECTIONS BY LYNDE

The following goals were identified by the parents:

- To help Ellis identify and cope with a range of feelings, including anger and frustration.
- I think the TPoP addressed by this goal fall in the domains of "increases personal strengths" (e.g., resiliency) and "facilitates communication" (e.g., self-expression).
- To examine the impact of incidents of teasing and bullying at school.
- I think the TPoP addressed by this goal fall in the domains of "fosters emotional wellness" (e.g., catharsis) and "facilitates communication" (e.g., self-expression).
- To assist Ellis in expressing his feelings.
- I think the TPoP addressed by this goal fall in the domains of "fosters emotional wellness" (e.g., catharsis) and "facilitates communication" (e.g., self-expression).

In completing Appendix A, I prioritized the following three child moderating factors: resilience, emotional expression, and world view. These factors seem to be consistent with the stated goals of the parents.

Parent consultation was requested to strengthen and support parenting strategies. My primary goals in parent work are as follows.

- To strengthen parents' capacity to engage in collaborative problem-solving when issues become "stuck" by building skills in reflecting feelings and responding to intense emotions.
- To increase positive levels of communication that recognize successes for Ellis.
- To recognize and facilitate opportunities to engage in family-based activities that strengthen relationships.

3) Supervision Questions Box

Ideally, the supervisee will complete Appendix A prior to attending supervision, as this form leads to the formulation of questions and goals by considering client moderating factors and how these interact with the dimensions of directiveness and consciousness.

The following questions exemplify some of the basic issues that come forward at this point. It is often helpful to share these questions in advance with the supervisee to help shape and refine questions specific to the case. Growth in case conceptualization skills is often represented by growth in the depth of questions, moving toward higher levels of self-reflection such as reflecting on use of self, along with a deeper understanding of movement within and between quadrants and use of TPoP.

GUIDING QUESTIONS FOR THE SUPERVISION QUESTIONS BOX

- Which quadrants have you been working in? Did you choose or facilitate movement between quadrants? If so, why?
- Should you become more or less directive? Why?
- Should you move toward higher levels of awareness/consciousness? Why?
- How would you know if it is time to move or shift between quadrants?
- Does it seem that there is no movement occurring? How might you be getting in the way?
- What have you noticed about your degree of immersion? Should you become more immersed in a certain area (e.g., emotionality)? How might you do this?
- What should you be tracking thematically?
- How might you tell whether an intervention is a hit or a miss with this child?
- How should you involve parents and other team members at this point in the process?
- Do you need to clarify your therapeutic role or stance? To whom?

The descriptive analysis section of the Tracking and Observation Form (Appendix C) can be used in parallel to examine the "road map" of movement across quadrants. As well, it can be used to examine the impact of therapist-led shifts and the nature of the child's response (e.g., protest, ignored, moderate-to-high responsiveness).

CASE OF ELLIS: REFLECTIONS AND QUESTIONS POSED BY LYNDE
Should I continue to work in Quadrant II or return to Quadrant III, giving him more distance?

I'm not sure whether the externalization of "Mr. Mad" was a hit. How can I tell?

I used two types of interpretations—reflective and linking. He seemed to respond. Should I move to bridging interpretations as I have noticed a rise of consciousness in play (and verbalizations about his bullying experiences)?

I need to book a consult with the parents. What should their role be at this point? What can I say about progress as we have only begun to talk openly about feelings and his bullying experiences?

4) Goals and Hypotheses Box

After considering the child's present pattern of functioning and development (e.g., social development, emotional development, cognitive development, behavioral functioning, and developmental stage of play), the supervisee should be asked to prioritize these issues and develop hypotheses about the sources or factors that impact the child's current functioning. In certain cases, these factors might become goals of therapy. In other cases, the impact or outcome of these factors is the focus of intervention. For example, constrictions in a child's emotional response style may become a focus of treatment. In this case, the goal is to assist the child in verbalizing and labeling their affect and to recognize variations in their affect. This work might extend to parents and teachers by discussing strategies that help generalize/encourage self-expression.

CASE OF ELLIS: REFLECTIONS BY LYNDE

- *Hypotheses*: Thematically, Ellis is demonstrating movement from feeling powerless and now seems to feel there is the possibility of help/support (external resources) and perhaps personal power (internal resources). Ellis likely has an underlying need to feel safe/secure in relationships and this has been shaken by his bullying experiences. I feel it has been difficult for Ellis to recognize and "own" the negative feelings that came from his bullying experiences, which is also partly related to longer-standing challenges with expressing feelings (i.e., he tends to internalize).

5) Process Box

Therapeutic processes can be examined from a broad stage/phase viewpoint or from the perspective of a single session. The Tracking and Observation Form (Appendix C) offers a detailed breakdown of the play process from a single-session perspective. For example, it addresses issues such as the child's capacity to direct and maintain play activities, the child's ability to complete play sequences, and the nature of play inhibitions, disruptions, and endings. The descriptive analysis (road map) section may be transposed onto the case consultation form to highlight specific examples of movement (or lack of) in the play therapy process. Questions are raised as to not only the amount of time spent in certain quadrants (and why) but also what factors triggered decisions to initiate therapist-led shifts between or within quadrants.

Understanding the play process from a stage perspective often informs us as to what is unfolding during the single session. Although there are model-specific conceptualizations of stages in the play therapy process, a somewhat universal framework emphasizes three basic stages: 1) engagement/beginning stage; 2) working stage; 3) termination stage.

As described by Moustakas (1982), troubled children often move from diffuse negative feelings to ambivalent feelings that retain elements of anger/hostility. Eventually they develop clear and distinct feelings along with realistic attitudes. While this perspective provides the supervisee with a compass to look for changes in direction, caution is required when applying stages to specific children, as there are limitless variations in presenting issues and client/contextual variables. Keeping this in mind, movement in the play therapy process is generally indicated when the child is able to express feelings (verbally or symbolically) with greater focus and intensity. In many cases, children move from exploratory safe play to symbolic play that is representative of their view of self, their families, or their experiences. During supervision, attention must be given to the supervisee's use of self and immersion in the play, as these factors either enhance or inhibit movement from one stage to the next.

As children often need to test for protection before they are willing to move to the working stage of therapy, the supervisor should help guide the supervisee to examine instances in which limit testing (or testing for safety) occurred. Supervisees may mistakenly believe that because the child tested limits with clean-up and no longer engages in limit testing at the end of sessions, they have moved from this stage. While this is possible, highly traumatized children frequently need to re-establish feelings of safety and acceptance; seldom is testing of this nature a one-off occurrence.

The following questions can be posed to the supervisee to support a conceptualization of where they are at in the therapy process.

GUIDING QUESTIONS FOR THE PROCESS BOX

- What types of limit testing have you observed? What is the nature of the child's response to your limits?
- What defense mechanisms are used by this child? Why are these important to the child?
- Have you observed any shifts in client moderating factors? If so, which ones?
- How would you describe the current therapeutic relationship? How would you rate it in terms of degree of connection (see Appendix A)? Which indicators did you consider in this rating?
- How much time is spent in "safe play" or set-up during the session? What is the significance of this?
- What, if any, shifts have occurred in the child's world view?

- What do shifts, inhibitions, or disruptions in play sequences tell you about the therapy process?

CASE OF ELLIS: REFLECTIONS BY LYNDE

- I feel we are in the working stage. Child has moved from expressing diffuse/negative feelings (as he did with puppets) and is now more specific in expressing feelings in relation to situations in his life (e.g., bullying at school).
- Initially, play scenarios were brief and short (not fully mediated/closed), particularly when the emotional content became more intense.
- Child responded well to Quadrant III—reasonable play skills and able to lead the play. Also responded well to therapist entering the play (Quadrant IV). We have accessed sandplay, puppets, and games.

6) Interventions Box

In the process section, the supervisee is asked to engage in a descriptive analysis regarding the sequence of movement between quadrants and estimate the amount of time spent in each quadrant. Mapped on to this should be the types of interventions used, including interpretations, as well as the play modalities accessed, such as therapeutic storytelling, games, etc. By asking the supervisee to identify the sequence of these interventions, it will become increasingly clear as to how they make sense of the range and timing of their interventions. The supervisee may also be asked to outline the relational and affective markers noted in each quadrant (see Appendix C).

Interventions are not limited to in-session activities. Questions should be posed concerning how others are included in the treatment plan and what their response has been. For example, the role of parents, teachers, and foster parents should be explored. The following questions help guide the discussion process.

GUIDING QUESTIONS FOR THE INTERVENTIONS BOX

- Why did you decide to begin your work in this quadrant?
- If you facilitated movement between quadrants, what did you notice about the child's response (e.g., protest, ignore, degree of flexibility)?
- Did this intervention deepen the play? What are the markers of this?
- What levels of interpretation have you used? What was the sequence of these? What was the child's response?
- How has your level of immersion shifted over time? Was this intentional?
- What made this intervention a hit? What are the indicators of this?
- What have you learned about the child's world view through the interventions?

- How does this intervention relate to the child moderating factors that you previously identified and/or prioritized?

CASE OF ELLIS: REFLECTIONS BY LYNDE

- Road map (from Appendix C)—The process began in Quadrant III and then moved to Quadrant IV. Next, Quadrant I was entered from Quadrant III. The last session was in Quadrant II, using an externalization strategy.
- The shift from Quadrant III to Quadrant IV was partially initiated by child (during sandplay). Child seemed to accept therapist's use of characters and efforts to increase emotionality (a "hit" I think?).
- I think Ellis's world view is shifting through child-led play scenarios.

7) Themes Box

The Tracking and Observation Form (Appendix C) is designed to assist supervisees in tracking relational and affective markers as well as thematic representations in play. Themes are seldom one-off occurrences. Rather, they are represented throughout play segments and reflect the child's underlying thoughts and emotional experiences. It is important to track the recurrence of themes as well as how they evolve over time.

GUIDING QUESTIONS FOR THE THEMES BOX

- What general repetitive themes have you tracked in the play?
- What primary emotions are attached to the themes?
- Are play segments involving a theme resolved or are there abrupt endings and disconnections? If so, what significance or interpretive meaning can you identify?
- What characters/roles are embedded in the themes (e.g., maternal or paternal figures, friends, mysterious characters)? What significance do these roles hold?
- What is the intensity of affect attached to the themes? Has this shifted over time? If so, how has it shifted?
- Is the theme grounded in some form of literalness/reality/experience for this client?

CASE OF ELLIS: REFLECTIONS BY LYNDE

- Themes include loyalty/betrayal, power/control (imbalance), rejection/insecurity, and victimization.

As noted on Appendix C, there were initially more play disruptions. During the last session, using an externalization game, there was another somewhat abrupt ending—he wiped off "Mr. Mad" as if to say he was "done" and didn't want to discuss it further.

8) Child's World View Box

This construct comes from a phenomenological perspective or approach, which emphasizes how individuals perceive their environment and how they operate within it. By taking a step back from assuming there is a right or wrong way to view an experience, a phenomenological stance encourages the supervisee to understand the idiosyncratic world view of the child and its impact on the therapy process. A world view can be broad and encompassing or narrow and constricted. It can also be positive or relatively pessimistic and dark. The following guiding questions may assist the supervisee to more deeply consider a phenomenological perspective.

GUIDING QUESTIONS FOR THE CHILD'S WORLD VIEW BOX

- How safe does this child feel?
- Who or what functions as a safe haven for them?
- Does this child think that supports are available or accessible to them?
- What are the primary needs of this child? How have these needs been met?
- What tensions or worries might they hold?
- How does the child see themselves as functioning in the world? What parts of self are valued? What parts are devalued? Is there an authentic self represented?
- Do they believe they have internal resources to cope?
- Does the child hold a future orientation? What do they see or hope for?

CASE OF ELLIS: REFLECTIONS BY LYNDE

- Child's world view: "I am small and not very powerful. Others can hurt or boss me around and I am powerless to stop them."

I think that Ellis is beginning to shift from powerlessness to incremental experiences of empowerment in the play scenarios.

9) Content Box

While it might seem that the sky is the limit here, it is important to capture the critical pieces of background information, otherwise the supervision process becomes bogged down in meaningless case details. Keep in mind that as supervisor you can streamline the process through the range of questions you ask. In turn, this supports learning and reflection, as supervisees begin to realize what pieces of information are necessary and what elements are extraneous. Although it is helpful to begin by asking about the presenting problem and the history surrounding it, care must be taken to direct the discussion toward those factors that are most relevant.

GUIDING QUESTIONS FOR THE CONTENT BOX

- What is the identified primary referral issue?
- When did this issue first surface? Did it lead to developmental interruptions? Consider onset, intensity, frequency, and duration of the identified issues.
- What are the secondary issues?
- Under what conditions does the issue(s) improve or worsen?
- What is the impact of this issue on the child? What is the impact on family and other relationships?
- What is the counseling/intervention history? What were the outcomes?

A brief exploration of family history is necessary and tools such as a family genogram can quickly capture this information.

GUIDING QUESTIONS

- What is the familial ethnocultural identification? What factors will you consider regarding the culture of the family system?
- What issues have been reported in the spousal and sibling subsystems?
- How is this family coping with their current stage of family development?
- What is the parenting style and history surrounding this style(s)?
- What is the scope and nature of their support network?

Next, ask about important facets of the child's developmental history. Embedded in this are questions about *major disruptions* in development or caregiving (e.g., divorce, out-of-home placements, age of onset of trauma/family violence). These are important to record as they often signal that the child's emotional and relational development has been truncated or impacted at a certain age/stage.

GUIDING QUESTIONS

- How did this child manage with the core developmental and emotional milestones?
- What do you know about the child's temperament? What role has this factor played in the referral issue?
- At what age did major changes or stressors occur?

- What impact did these factors have on the child's adjustment and attachment organization?
- Is there an abuse/trauma history? What are the known indicators?
- What is this child's sexual/role identity?

It is critical that an awareness and sensitivity to culture are maintained throughout the therapy process. While not all elements may be readily understood at the outset, continual reflections about our cultural self and the client's help ensure that cultural sensitivity remains at the forefront of our work.

GUIDING QUESTIONS

- What cultural understanding do you have of the child and the child's family?
- In what ways does the child identify the "self"?
- What beliefs and values are demonstrated through the play?
- How does the child and/or child's family view your cultural presentation?
- What cultural similarities and differences are there between the child and their family; child and you; and/or child and child's family system and you?
- How does the culture of the child impact the therapy process?

CASE OF ELLIS: REFLECTIONS BY LYNDE

- Nine years-old, Grade 4.
- Intact family: Ellis is the middle child. Older sister 12 years; younger brother 4 years. Not much time spent playing together.
- Developmentally "on track." Plays some sports.
- Two school friends moved in the past year. No consistent friendship group at school but has positive relationships with neighbor friends.
- Three known incidents of bullying at school: two on playground, one in a school bathroom.
- Some reluctance to attend school. Mother currently describes him as angry, somewhat aggressive, and perfectionistic.
- Described as small for his age and sensitive about this.
- Parents note that he has an "independent style." He likes to play on his own terms.
- Child emanates the hard-working, independent belief system of the parents.

10) Resiliencies and Vulnerabilities Box

Resiliency is commonly taken to mean an individual's ability to see problems as obstacles versus barriers. Those with a resilient mindset often attempt to learn from mistakes and face issues in a problem-solving manner. Resiliency derives from certain innate factors such as temperament characteristics, attachment organization (affective and relational capacity), and problem-solving capacity. Resiliencies can be reflected in the ability to be socially connected with friends and/or family members.

The following list, although not exhaustive, may prompt an examination of the child's resiliencies and vulnerabilities. These same factors may also be explored for caregivers.

RESILIENCY AND VULNERABILITY FACTORS

- Physical health and wellness.
- Temperament.
- Locus of control/sense of control over life.
- Active versus passive response style.
- Hope and dreams versus despair.
- Self-image and self-esteem.
- Cognitive abilities.
- Cognitive appraisal of self (evaluation/perception of stress level; evaluation of one's resources to cope; coping strategies).
- Ability to have fun/sense of humor.
- Availability of a confidant or support to whom child ascribes positive motives.
- Openness versus secrecy.
- Problem-solving capacity.

CASE OF ELLIS: REFLECTIONS BY LYNDE
Resiliency factors:

- Bright and creative.
- Supportive family.
- Doing well, academically.

Vulnerability factors:

- Emotionally reactive behaviors—pushes others away.
- Bullying experiences—eroded self-confidence/self-esteem.
- Not strong at expressing feelings in a prosocial/adaptive manner.
- Tends to be more "alone" in his play activities (perhaps tied to temperament).

11) Transference and Countertransference Box

Even when a supervisee believes they have been working in a non-intrusive manner by using facilitative/reflective responses, they are still making use of the "self." Accordingly, it is critical that the supervisee remain aware of possible transference-countertransference issues. Sometimes awareness surfaces when a supervisee discusses hits and misses. For example, they might either personalize a child's non-responsiveness (e.g., seeing it as a total miss) or misattribute the child's positive response to something the therapist did (e.g., seeing it as a therapist-generated hit).

Depending on the theoretical orientation of the supervisee and supervisor, issues of transference and countertransference may be differentially emphasized. For example, a phenomenological approach to play therapy emphasizes that the play therapist is mainly responsible for understanding and interpreting the child's play (Mook, 2003). Within this approach the therapist plays an active, encouraging role to facilitate the child's play-based expressions, verbally or symbolically. At the same time, the therapist operates from the viewpoint that the child is deeply involved in trying to understand their play scenarios and may require distance from this process. When a therapist moves to Quadrant IV, *Co-Facilitation*, they are often utilizing soft hypothesis testing and interpretations, which have the potential for elaborating the play. Therapeutic processes such as transference and countertransference are often activated in Quadrant IV, as therapist use of self is also heightened.

Supervisees must be prepared to differentiate emotions that are projected from the core of the child's needs/issues (transference) from those related to core (and potentially unresolved) issues in themselves (countertransference). Ideally, supervisees need to assess internal feeling states, to analyze the play, and to use these insights to understand the less conscious process of the child. This is where the supervisor has a role in supporting supervisee self-awareness and exploration. Transference and countertransference processes should be explored and embraced versus shut down or seen as a therapeutic shortcoming. Allan (1997) suggests that awareness of these issues may point to various directions of exploration.

Interestingly, Moore and Chow (2022) place countertransference into the framework of polyvagal theory, emphasizing that it may show up through words used by the therapist as well as through feelings and our nervous systems. When feelings involving countertransference are directed back toward the client through facial expressions, tone of voice, etc., the therapist's response may evoke feelings of shame or guilt rather than a shared sense of co-regulation (Moore and Chow, 2022).

GUIDING QUESTIONS

- What meaning did this symbol, theme, or play sequence hold for you? How has it resonated for you?

CASE CONCEPTUALIZATION: THE CASE OF ELLIS

- What was your immediate interpretation of this segment/play activity? Has this shifted? Why or why not?
- What else did you observe in the child in terms of emotionality?
- What aspects of self have or have not been accessed for immersion? Why?
- What personal links or associations have you made to the thematic material?

CASE OF ELLIS: REFLECTIONS BY LYNDE

Possible transference:

- Child may see me as a teacher or an adult who wants to change/correct his behavior.
- They may also see me as another adult who failed to support him—anger is being transferred.

Possible countertransference:

- At times I want to pull back, maybe more than I should, so he doesn't think I am trying to teach him something or change/correct his feelings.
- In response to his anger, and I think some of the hurt he is beginning to express, I feel like I need to avoid, sidestep, or maybe even tippy-toe around more intense feelings. It makes me feel a bit uncomfortable not knowing how intense his underlying feelings really are.

SUMMARY

In discussing the case of Ellis, Lynde has brought forward clear hypotheses as well as observations and reflections based on the tracking and reflection tools that are part of the Play Therapy Dimensions Model. Importantly, Lynde's discussion indicates an awareness of her use of self, an understanding of Ellis's immediate responses, and the degree to which her use of self, over time, has facilitated and perhaps deepened the therapy process. This level of understanding only comes after a therapist takes time to reflect on several elements, including use of self and child moderating factors.

Lynde must now consider how to provide an overview of the therapy process to Ellis's parents while inviting their participation during the next phase of therapy. Lynde must simultaneously consider what the next steps will look like in the therapy process. For example, should she remain working in Quadrant II? If we examine the "Should I stay or should I go?" indicators for this quadrant, as discussed in Chapter 9, we find that there are several positive indicators for remaining in this quadrant. For example, Ellis appears to have reached a point where he is better able to directly communicate about his hurts and, in fact, initiated brief statements about these experiences. While Ellis, and all children, have a speed limit regarding how fast they can go in consciously processing their experiences, this is not to say they wouldn't benefit from structured play activities that bring focus to disowned or dissociated thoughts and feelings, as this helps facilitate the reorganization process. The key factor here is providing acknowledgment and validation of expressed feelings. As illustrated in the video, Lynde provided brief statements that seemed to be accepted and tolerated by Ellis, and he also appeared to tolerate interpretive comments that linked play themes to his known experiences. Additionally, Ellis has an involved, supportive family who are available to comfort and support him as he begins to express more underlying thoughts and feelings. Certainly, Ellis is at a stage of development where he has the cognitive skills necessary to identify and express feelings directly.

In Chapter 10, we discussed how parent feedback is formulated. The parent feedback and conceptualization forms video also provides an example of how the parent feedback and consultation process might unfold with a case such as Ellis's.

KEY POINTS

- The Case Conceptualization Form (Appendix E) is an integrative tool that supports self-reflective practice. The form should be completed prior to supervision meetings and can be reviewed in a sequence that best fits the priorities for supervision.
- The guiding questions illustrate key points for consideration. The theoretical orientation of the practitioner, and phase of development of the supervisee, should drive this reflective process.
- The case of Ellis illustrates how specific sections of the form might be completed. However, the clinician's theoretical orientation will ultimately drive the weighting of factors that contribute to case conceptualization.

◉ **Chapter 12** ◉

UTILIZING THE PLAY THERAPY DIMENSIONS MODEL
In Supervision

*The Ferris wheel moves us round and round until
we see the world from many places.*

WHY USE THE PLAY THERAPY DIMENSIONS MODEL FOR SUPERVISION?

The Play Therapy Dimensions Model offers an organizing structure to assist all play therapy supervisees to conceptualize, plan, and intervene with clients. Although play therapy supervisors have access to numerous models of supervision, there are few, if any, that apply to play therapists specifically. As emphasized by Tholstrup (2001), supervision models generally provide a process to deliver theoretical knowledge, reliable frameworks, doubt and insecurity management, and techniques and intervention strategies. All of these elements help avoid the danger of random eclecticism. Supervisors can simply add the Play Therapy Dimensions Model to their preferred general supervision framework.

The model does not require the play therapist to use a specific therapeutic approach, therefore supervisors can use the Play Therapy Dimensions Model to supervise those trained in one or more approaches to play therapy. Play therapists are encouraged to view their interventions on a continuum of directiveness and consciousness, no matter what their original training. Many play therapists may not be aware of the subtle ways in which they intervene with clients *within* their identified approach. The Play Therapy Dimensions Model therefore helps the play therapist identify specific movements within, for instance, a Non-Directive Play Therapy session. Even within a particular approach, the Play Therapy Dimensions Model assumes that a continuum of directiveness and consciousness exists.

The Play Therapy Dimensions Model helps play therapists to expand their thinking regarding ways of intervening with clients. It supports learning about the array of approaches available to play therapists. The four quadrants allow for a varied use of self as a play therapist which helps practitioners identify areas in which they may choose to work—perhaps for the first time. A number of play therapy approaches/models fit in each of the four quadrants. In the play therapy literature, most overviews describing play therapy approaches include the following: Child-Centered Play Therapy, Filial Play Therapy, Psychoanalytic Play Therapy, Gestalt Play Therapy, Adlerian Play Therapy, Cognitive-Behavioral Play Therapy, Jungian Analytical Play Therapy, Prescriptive Play Therapy, Family Play Therapy, group play therapy, Ecosystemic Play Therapy, Phenomenological Play Therapy, Object Relations/Thematic Play Therapy, Ericksonian Play Therapy, and Theraplay (attachment-enhancing play therapy). Although play therapists are not necessarily highly trained (or supervised) in all of these approaches, it is recommended that they acquire a basic understanding of each approach so that they know what they *are* and *are not* doing during a play therapy session and why. The Play Therapy Dimensions Model is useful in encouraging both new and seasoned play therapists to identify their approach to play therapy. If another approach is more fitting to a particular child, the practitioner may be encouraged to elaborate her training. The Play Therapy Dimensions Model reminds the therapist that the best approach taken with a client should be driven by client need and a well-thought-out philosophy of treatment.

The Play Therapy Dimensions Model encourages the therapist to look at both the client and therapist moderating factors. All children are not the same, although it is understood each needs to be viewed from a developmental framework. Beyond development, the unique qualities of both the client and therapist drive therapeutic planning and process. What do practitioners need to understand about the self and the client before and during therapy? If we do not understand the play skills of the child, or miss identifying the child's level of resilience or ability to communicate, or fail to identify the child's attachment organization or current support network, will we offer the child the best therapeutic experience? What about the therapists? What is their experience level? How aware are they of how they use themselves in therapy? What is their connection to the client? How confident are they when working with particular presenting problems? Do they identify therapeutic issues at the outset or not? These questions and others guide play therapists' practice and their therapeutic activities.

The supervisor can quickly identify the supervisee's process in the understanding of and planning for client sessions when using the Play Therapy Dimensions Model. The three supervision tools, the Child Moderating Factors Scale (Appendix A), Degree of Immersion: Therapist Use of Self Scale (Appendix B), and Tracking and Observation Form (Appendix C), all assist supervisees to organize their thinking about a client in order that they may thoughtfully engage in the therapeutic process. The supervisor may use each form to assist a supervisee to identify therapeutic goals or to identify areas where more supervisory assistance may be required. The forms are helpful to the supervision process as the supervisee can complete them in preparation for supervision sessions. The supervisor can then conceptualize the case quickly and avoid the supervision trap of, "too much time spent sharing too much content." The supervisee is expected to participate in the evaluative process. The forms will also help the supervisee to make therapeutic decisions prior to the supervision meeting, which helps to increase independent practice and decrease a heavy reliance on the supervisor to *answer* all of the questions. Without an adequate framework, this development cannot happen. The Play Therapy Dimensions Model can assist each therapist to move to an enhanced level of practice—no matter what the level of experience of the practitioner.

HOW TO USE THE VIDEOS

Download the videos and transcripts from https://library.jkp.com/redeem using the code RTECPZF.

Video 1 Overview: Cases of Ellis and Haley

The first video is divided into two distinct parts. The first part, demonstrated through the case of Ellis, introduces the four quadrants: Quadrant I, *Active Utilization*, Quadrant II, *Open Discussion and Exploration*, Quadrant III, *Non-Intrusive Responding*, and Quadrant IV, *Co-Facilitation*. Each of the quadrants is arranged in relation to dimensions of consciousness and directiveness, in that the therapist will be either more or less directive and/or will bring therapeutic matters more or less to the conscious awareness of the client. The video exemplifies each quadrant by showing session clips of a child and therapist. During the case study of Ellis, it may appear that the therapist should choose a single quadrant in which to work. This is, however, not the purpose of the demonstration. The purpose is to slow the process down so that the supervisee may study segments of interaction and make specific observations of the potential use of self and the corresponding response of the client in *each* quadrant. Even within each quadrant, a therapist may be working on a continuum of directiveness and consciousness. The first half of the video helps the supervisor to clearly point out the different ways of approaching a client. The supervisee can study each quadrant in a more concentrated way.

Through the case of Haley, the second part of the video demonstrates the potential movement between all quadrants during a single session. This part of the video does not suggest that this is the way all sessions should be conducted; rather, it exemplifies that therapeutic activity in one or more quadrants during a single session may be possible and, for some clients, may be clinically most appropriate. Supervisors may use this video segment to help supervisees identify what they are doing during their own sessions and, more importantly, why. Most supervisees (regardless of their original training) tend to make use of their intuition, which is what allows them to enter the therapeutic dance with a client. In order to supervise effectively, however, it must be acknowledged that intuition is only the initial drive that helps the supervisee make decisions. After various therapeutic decisions have been made, it is in supervision that the supervisee and supervisor discuss the direction and appropriateness of those decisions and consider other contributing factors for future sessions.

Both parts of the video can be used in a stop-and-start manner to observe critical therapeutic points. In the first part of the video, Ellis and his therapist demonstrate a number of examples of therapeutic decision-making. How and when the therapist uses her voice and emotionality, physical self, verbalizations, and interpretations can be examined and discussed. After looking at each play segment, supervisors could ask the supervisees to provide their observations of the various responses of the child to the therapist. This examination can help supervisees become more attuned to the therapeutic process when *they* are in a session.

The second part of the video also provides an opportunity to briefly study pivotal points in a session as related to therapeutic timing. The supervisee, once the factors that differentiate the four quadrants have been identified, will then be ready to examine the quadrants in relation to an entire session. Each point of movement between quadrants can be "frozen" on the video for the purpose of discussion. There are other choices the therapist could have made. Why did the therapist choose to move from Quadrant III, *Non-Intrusive Responding*, to Quadrant IV, *Co-Facilitation*, at that particular moment? If the therapist had stayed in Quadrant III, what hypotheses could be generated as to how the child would have responded? Again, it is the thoughtful analysis that increases the supervisee's ability to case "conceptualize." Due to high client caseloads, therapists often find themselves "flying by the seat of their pants" when delivering treatment. Good supervision and supervision tools can help to minimize this problem. Even when a supervisee cannot get approval to video, or for other reasons cannot video, a clinical training video can be very useful in supervision.

Video 2 Overview: Case Conceptualization and Preparing for Parent Feedback

The second video is a supervision session using two new forms: Case Conceptualization Form and Parent Feedback Conceptualization Form. In this video, the supervisor walks through the various areas of consideration to help the supervisee articulate what she has learned about Ellis and then how to take what she has learned into a parent feedback session. The usefulness of the forms is demonstrated as the supervisee organizes her thinking and prepares "how" to share useful information about Ellis's progress to his parents. The following skills are demonstrated:

- Use of the Case Conceptualization Form and exploration of each of the domains on the two forms.
- Identifying salient issues in play therapy sessions.
- Articulation of process issues using the Play Therapy Dimensions Diagram.
- Use of the Child Moderating Factors Scale items for discussion.
- Identification of what Ellis is communicating during play sessions.
- Creative thinking about how to give feedback.

Video 3 Overview: Case of Ellis—Parent Feedback

The third video is a midpoint parent feedback session related to the case of Ellis. In this session, the therapist provides a verbal and visual feedback process to Ellis's parents Don and Donna. The following skills are demonstrated:

- Utilizing and organizing information gained through the Child Moderating Factors Scale.
- Formulating the child's presentation and communication style during therapy.
- Review of the original presenting concerns.
- Organizing key points to share with parents.
- Modifying feedback to match parent styles (Collaborative Parent and Solution-Focused Parent).
- Creating and presenting the follow-up plan.

AIDING SUPERVISEES TO USE VIDEOS/VIDEO REVIEW

The value of video recording cannot be underestimated. Many therapists are reluctant to video. The personal learning is incredible, however, due to the fact that we cannot take in all aspects of ourselves while we are with another person. The frequency with which therapists "get in the way" of their clients is high—or at least higher than initially suspected. It is difficult truly to know about how a supervisee makes use of themselves without the ability to watch that person in a live session.

There are specific ways to encourage supervisees to use video. The following suggestions increase comfort in doing this.

- *Role-play with your supervisee*: The supervisor plays the child and the supervisee plays the therapist, and then they reverse the roles. Be sure to video all mock therapy segments. The more the supervisee is before the camera, the more at ease they will be.
- *Video yourself*: As a supervisor, be sure that you have videoed a number of sessions that you can show to your supervisee. Never ask your supervisee to do something that you yourself are not comfortable doing.

- *Show your own "blooper" videos*: These are parts of clinical sessions that you have had where you think the direction or timing went wrong. Humor helps supervisees to feel more comfortable, and it lets them know that you are human.
- *Ask supervisees to choose a video they* don't *like*: Ask supervisees to record a number of sessions and choose a video they really don't like. Ask supervisees to identify a few different moments in the video that they would like to have done differently and provide a couple of alternative interventions.
- *Ask supervisees to choose a video segment they* do *like*: Ask supervisees to bring a segment of a therapy session that they do like to supervision. Celebrate moments that went well.
- *Make video accessible*: Set up a video system in your office that is not complex or cumbersome. Therapists will use videos when they don't have to jump through hoops to gain administrative approval or follow complicated set-up procedures.
- *Assist supervisees in getting approval to video*: Assist supervisees to rehearse talking to parents and children about being videoed. If supervisees are nervous about videoing, they are not likely to get approval.
- *Have fun and provide a format to review*: Have fun watching the videos and provide the supervisee with a format to evaluate or discuss the video segment.
- *Train supervisees to find significant video segments for discussion*: Watching an entire video together can be a waste of supervision time. Sit down on one or two occasions to go through a video and assist the supervisee to find significant therapy segments to present for discussion.
- *Ensure supervisees formulate questions prior to supervision*: Ask supervisees to come up with a couple of questions for use in supervision related to their videos. This will help guide the discussion and enhance the supervisee's conceptualization skills.

USING THE PLAY THERAPY DIMENSIONS MODEL TO REVIEW VIDEOS

When assisting the supervisee to review the videos, it is effective to have the four quadrant diagram (Figure 3.1) available to look at. The following questions will help guide the video review:

- What quadrant are you working in? Using the four quadrant diagram, indicate what part of the quadrant you were working in.
- What play therapy approach are you using? What factors contributed to your choice in therapy approach?

- What quadrant did you begin to work in? Did you consciously remain working in this quadrant or move to a different quadrant? What factors influenced your decision to shift?
- What do you notice about your use of self in this video segment? Refer to the Degree of Immersion: Therapist Use of Self Scale (Appendix B).
- What do you notice about the client?
- Considering the context of the client story, what do you think is happening in this video segment? What themes are being represented?
- If you had been more/less directive in this session, how do you think the client would have responded?
- Can the client tolerate more direct discussion about the presenting issue? If so, what are the indicators? If not, what are the indicators?
- Will you stay working in this quadrant? If so, why? If not, why not?

A DEVELOPMENTAL MODEL OF SUPERVISION

Skilled supervisors typically utilize a general model of supervision, but it is rare to find a model that relates specifically to play therapists. The Play Therapy Dimensions Model can easily be added to any global supervision model.

The Rocky Mountain Play Therapy Institute™ identifies a developmental approach to supervision as a preferred approach when reviewing a supervisee's clinical work. Viewing the supervisee from a developmental framework is consistent with viewing children and families from a developmental approach. Everyone appears to be on a growth continuum, with no stage being better or worse than another; rather, it is "just where one is." Many developmental models (in addition to facilitative, behavioral, skills training, and reflective approaches) of supervision are cited in the literature and have generated a considerable amount of research interest (Milton, 2001). For example, in reference to developmental approaches, specific levels of development have been identified, ranging from novice (Level 1) to expert (Level 3 and above). This view may be seen as too simplistic by some, based on professional practice consisting of a wide array of skills, knowledge, and expertise. Having been influenced by the work of Stoltenberg, McNeill, and Delworth (1998) and other developmentally focused supervisors, we have found it useful to conceptualize therapist development as occurring in three phases, with corresponding degrees of expertise and capacities for assuming clinical responsibility.

Phase I: Beginning Play Therapy Training

It is during this phase that supervisors will notice the therapist demonstrating high motivation to move quickly from novice to expert. There is a great desire to learn the *best* or *correct* approach to dealing with clinical problems. Due to the fact that play therapy is a specialized form of therapeutic intervention with children, supervisees quickly realize that adult therapy training is not easily generalized to this population. Most institutions do not provide full programs in child and play therapy; rather, both students and seasoned therapists interested in working with children have typically been exposed to a single, non-practice-based play therapy course. Learning about the power of play and the symbolic nature of the *child's* way of communicating cannot be rushed. The unique skill set and personal awareness necessary to work with children is not something one can achieve by fast-tracking the learning process. Students of various backgrounds studying at the Rocky Mountain Play Therapy Institute frequently present their wish to finish the program more quickly. This request is discouraged, although students may at times be disappointed. This is just an example of motivation in Phase I to move from the novice developmental stage. The high anxiety and, at times, uncertainty about the process drive the desire to quickly develop a skill set during this phase.

During Phase I there is a high level of dependency on the supervisor for consultation and direction. The supervisee is often looking to the supervisor to "just tell me what to do," and therefore is less process oriented and more task and technique oriented. Self-awareness is typically limited while self-focus is high. This is not to say that the Phase I supervisees do not have self-awareness; rather, they are typically preoccupied with how they are doing as a play therapist. When learning a new skill set, it is difficult to simultaneously hold all parts of the greater whole in mind. Consequently, it is easy to "get in the way" of the client during Phase I development.

Phase I supervisees are therefore also quite apprehensive about being evaluated. Because of an inevitable preoccupation with how they are doing personally, supervisees are often relatively unaware of their strengths and weaknesses. Sometimes supervisees' confidence levels exceed their skills, while others demonstrate an emerging skill with little confidence. Either way, the emerging confidence theme is critical, and as supervisors, we need to identify activities to assist in all areas of therapeutic functioning. Stoltenberg *et al.* (1998) describe numerous domains of functioning including: intervention skills competencies, assessment techniques, interpersonal assessment, client conceptualization, individual differences, theoretical orientation, treatment goals and plans, and professional ethics. We would add that inherent in each of these domains of functioning are special considerations and issues related to working with children in the context of their families. Examining professional ethics in relation to treating children, for instance, is more complicated than ethics related to treating adults. There is little formal training in identifying special issues related to minor-aged primary clients who do not choose or pay for their own therapy.

During each therapeutic phase of development, the supervisor must be able to provide evaluative feedback to the supervisee regarding special issues in all domains of functioning.

BRIDGING ACTIVITIES

Bridging activities are purposeful supervision activities designed to increase the skills, knowledge, and experience of the supervisees and, in our developmental model, are critical to assist in the growth of the play therapist. The play therapy supervisor may choose a number of play-based activities to facilitate supervision during each phase.

During Phase I, critical objectives of the supervisor include the following.

- *Spending extra time with supervisees in general*: Be available informally as well as formally in scheduled supervision sessions. You are a play therapy supervisor—have fun! General sharing of new games or activities you have tried in therapy, discussions of fun you have outside the play therapy environment, and creating an open, playful environment over lunch or breaks can all be ways to spend extra time with Phase I supervisees.
- *Increasing the intensity and frequency of theoretical discussions*: Use video examples of play therapists in the field demonstrating various theoretical approaches of play therapy. The Play Therapy Dimensions Model case examples video is useful when discussing theories and where on the continuum of directiveness and consciousness those theorists find themselves primarily working. Discussions that take place during group supervision can be particularly helpful for Phase I play therapists. Sharing different approaches and ways of addressing different-aged children with varying developmental needs can be very useful.
- *Encouraging exploration of personal practice models*: Personal practice models are typically richly informed by an accumulation of clinical training and of personal and professional experiences. It is during Phase I that supervisors should encourage supervisees to begin to consider what they bring to the play process and what approaches are immediately "fitting" for them. Playful, creative activities can be developed to assist supervisees to begin to explore their personal practice models such as creating a personal mandala using art supplies or utilizing clay to design a shape that represents their own practice model. Written practice model exercises can be developed to help with this exploration as well.
- *Encouraging exploration of cultural use of self*: Assist the supervisee to develop a personal cultural mosaic. Right from the beginning, we bring ourselves into the therapy process. Individual differences and important values, beliefs, and orientations carried by the play therapist impact a client's cultural understanding of self. Consider intersectionality (interconnected and overlapping social categorizations) in treatment along with cultural opportunities that may arise during a given session to address important cultural issues.
- *Providing a format for reviewing videos*: Videoing can be very intimidating; therefore, we developed a guideline for using videos. This is an important

experience for the therapist. Until therapists see themselves, it is difficult to be objective or to truly know how they use themselves in a session.

- *Introducing play therapy techniques*: There are many resources that list hundreds of play therapy techniques. Why then do people repetitively attend conferences in the hope of "gaining a new technique"? Simply stated, new techniques help people to feel more confident (and sometimes renewed). During supervision, techniques can be introduced within the *context* of a child client. The important awareness about techniques is that not all techniques work with all children, and the greatest learning comes from knowing more about what to do when. Meaningful use of play techniques will increase the supervisee's overall clinical development.

- *Demonstrating practical skills*: Supervisors must get involved by making use of case questions in a practical way. Role-playing by getting the supervisee to play the client and the supervisor to play the therapist can be very effective. If you have a video camera handy, video the role-play as well. Reviewing this together can be fun and a great learning opportunity. You may also get permission for the supervisee to observe your session with a client, or you could video the session and have the supervisee watch it afterward. At the Rocky Mountain Play Therapy Institute, we have a rotating team where each therapist individually has a chance to go in and out of a role-play session. Supervisees get to "try on" new techniques and approaches without the concern of harming child clients. The therapist or supervisor playing the child provides feedback to the play therapists.

- *Providing self-development exercises*: We have created a number of self-development exercises over the years with the aim of increasing the awareness of supervisees in relation to their comfort when working with different children, parents, systems, and supervisors. Additionally, written and experiential exercises regarding personal practice issues and past issues related to personal play experiences are helpful.

- *Giving positive, supportive feedback*: Supervisees are on a learning curve during Phase I, so let them know what is going well. This is the time when mistakes are inevitable, and supervisees need to find ways to manage their anxieties. Supervisors must find ways to consistently provide structured, constructive feedback.

INDICATORS OF MOVEMENT FROM PHASE I TO PHASE II

Growth indicators for the developmental stage of Phase I include: a slight decrease in the supervisee's need for play therapy techniques; a shift in focus from being self-focused to being client focused; a slight increase in autonomy and greater levels of confidence (especially in relation to taking on more complex cases); increased comfort in utilizing tools and techniques; and greater independence in problem-solving.

As noted by Stoltenberg et al. (1998), it is at the end of the first phase or level of development that a supervisee may present as wanting to advance directly to the third phase or level. This is viewed as impossible and is compared to deciding to skip adolescence and move directly into adulthood. Although conflicted in nature, Phase II is a necessary step for the consolidation and organization of layers of learning. Movement from Phase I to Phase II is similar to the disengagement of the adolescent with their parents. An emerging independence is observed, combined with the intermittent need for dependency, structure, and guidance.

Phase II: Imitation of Experts

It is during Phase II that the play therapist enters with a whole kit of shiny play therapy tools and begins to use them with more variation and elaboration. In Phase II, play therapists demonstrate a separation/autonomy conflict. At times, the conflict can lead to a false sense of autonomy and confidence. When things go well, they go very well, and when they do not, the Phase II therapist's confidence is shaken. The ambivalence is further emphasized by the play therapist's fluctuation between thoughts of extreme incompetence and thoughts of not needing any help at all. During this phase, therapists typically ask for help with difficult clients. It may be that they have asked for more challenging clients, or as a supervisor, you have assigned more difficult clients. Regardless, their abilities are being challenged within one of the domains of functioning. As a supervisor, you can identify Phase II supervisees by their propensity to be evasive and non-accepting of your suggestions for some of their clients and their contradictory need to rely on you fully for others. This phase is highlighted by the desire to grow and take risks while at the same time preferring the safety of what is already known. The Phase II supervisee is still highly motivated, only now in a selective way.

The supervisee's awareness of the client and the client's needs have increased, making it possible for the supervisee to understand the client's world view. This can be both therapeutically valuable and personally devastating. The inherent vulnerability of children evokes a sense of fragility or vulnerability in us and, at times, makes us question the meaning of life. It is during Phase II that play therapists are challenged to be in touch with their own childhoods. The child client's reality tends to collide with the therapist's reality, which creates numerous internal conflicts that must be reconciled. This heightened awareness of the client and how the client presents trauma in play therapy adds to the complexity of the supervisee's development. It is in this stage that the supervisor learns about the supervisee's tolerance, patience, and capacity for empathy. One of the confusing aspects of Phase II is that the expectation for integration of broad-based knowledge is much higher, and the relief of feeling competent is churned up with additional pressure to keep adding to the learning experience. The ambivalent nature of this phase of therapeutic development leads to intermittent uncertainty and, at times, intermittent feelings of frustration that get projected onto the supervisor.

BRIDGING ACTIVITIES

During Phase II, critical objectives of the supervisor include the following.

- *Encouraging risk-taking and creativity*: Supervisees are encouraged to try new interventions and to adapt textbook techniques to better meet client need. Provide the supervisee with some examples of times you have changed or elaborated a technique or intervention to maximize its usefulness. Supervisors can provide supervisees with material that may enhance a play therapy session. For instance, if there are new Theraplay activities the supervisee has developed that require art supplies, or if a particular character is missing from the sandtray shelves, encourage the supervisee to make it out of clay so that it is immediately available. There are many ways to encourage the play therapy supervisee to stretch skill levels with parents, for instance. Support the Phase II supervisee to grow beyond their comfort zones.
- *Shifting supervision from "tell me" to "show me"*: During Phase II, it is time to stop providing all the suggestions. Supervisees are encouraged to demonstrate their dilemma, need, or question, and this takes role-playing, video review, and case discussions to a new level. Phase II supervisees are, when challenged, able to answer most of their own questions. Having a format for case discussion is very helpful for both the supervisor and the supervisee. Play therapists can gain from experiential supervision, which means that the supervisor may provide materials (clay or art) or opportunities to go directly into the playroom for the supervision session.
- *Decreasing the level of the supervision structure*: During Phase I, supervision structure needs to be high, but as supervisors enter into Phase II, more independence is encouraged. Part of the message is that you have a belief that the supervisee can operate independently but with support. Without letting go to some degree, the supervisee cannot grow or develop. This is similar to the type of letting go experienced during the adolescent stage of development. Each supervisee will present with individual differences that will inform you of how much support is necessary.
- *Expecting mixed success*: It is important for you as a supervisor to understand that although in one case the supervisee has gained in experience and confidence, it will not necessarily generalize to all other cases. As a supervisor, you must manage your own feelings of frustration and help the supervisee strike a balance between growth and risk-taking. Errors in clinical practice can be reframed as positive. As a supervisor, your role is to help to manage all

ethical and legal matters in order to allow the supervisee to experience clinical errors and successes with greater ease and acceptance. As a supervisor, you will often find supervisees putting in extra time and energy into cases that they have conceptualized well. The cases they do not understand well are the ones on which you need to spend time to assist them to develop a framework for intervention.

- *Emphasizing the therapy process versus techniques*: During Phase II, the process of therapy is a key focus. Helping supervisees answer the questions, "In what stage of therapy am I?" or, "In what quadrant am I working and why?" is important to this stage of development. The play therapist begins to evaluate the *who*, *what*, *when*, *why*, and *how* of play therapy. Techniques are already available to the supervisees; now they need to be more evaluative as to why they may choose one technique over another and explain where this choice *fits* in this stage of therapy. Getting the supervisee to map the therapy activity can be a useful intervention when emphasizing the process of play therapy in particular. The Child Moderating Factors Scale (Appendix A) is another useful tool for helping the supervisee focus on the process.

- *Doing more co-consultation*: Phase II supervisees can deepen their learning by directly consulting with their supervisor and offering their own insights and suggestions to the supervisor's cases or cases of other team members. Sharing thoughts and approaches to various cases can increase the supervisee's ability to take risks. The Rocky Mountain Play Therapy Institute provides a formal opportunity for group consultation for play therapists. A framework is provided to conceptualize cases in addition to video reviews and playroom demonstrations. Learning from the experience of others enhances development.

- *Assigning more complex cases*: Phase II supervisees need to be challenged, and the only way for them to gain experience is to learn by doing. In most practice settings, a range of client issues and problems are presented, from adjustment difficulties to more pervasive, long-term entrenched difficulties. In child therapy, the same continuum exists. Children's difficulties are, however, made more complex by their rapidly changing development. Play therapists need to have the opportunity to work with many children from a broad spectrum of presenting issues to help them to move from Phase II to Phase III. Experience cannot be rushed, only accumulated. It is during this time that supervisees are highly ambivalent and, at times, unsure if they have chosen the right career. It is important, when assigning cases, that the supervisor expect a level of fragility regarding the Phase II supervisee's confidence and sense of competence. Feedback during this time must be skillfully delivered to ensure that supervisees can retain a sense of success but still learn from their experiences.

- *Providing more supportive confrontation*: Having already pointed out the inherent internal conflict for Phase II supervisees, it is critical that the supervisor does not avoid challenging the supervisee. This is the opportunity for growth, and it is during this phase that the supervisee is responsible for sorting out the case, deciding what will be done, and implementing a case plan. Ethical practice demands that we are all able to defend our work or decisions. Supportive challenging is essential to help supervisees reflect on their practice and use of self so that they can integrate this learning back into their practice model.

INDICATORS OF MOVEMENT FROM PHASE II TO PHASE III

The Phase II play therapists are ready to move to Phase III when they are observed as having integrated the learning objectives of both Phases I and II and can now fully evaluate the self and the client. Treatment clearly flows from assessment on a consistent basis. There is evidence of a developed conceptual framework for looking at child clients. The ambivalence has diminished, and the supervisees offer more in the way of collegial interaction. There is more of a primary interest in how they fit into the conceptual framework, and they are more interested in self-evaluation and self-exploration. There is an emerging openness to different conceptual frameworks, and supervisees begin to own their decision-making around clients. It is possible for the supervisee to work more independently and access supervision when necessary. It is not as likely that the supervisee who is moving to Phase III will take things personally when a difficult situation with a client does not work out.

Phase III: Advanced Play Therapist

The Phase III therapist presents consistently as clinically stable with a high degree of autonomy. It is during this phase that the therapist may identify an area of specialization. The Phase III therapist has accumulated a broad knowledge base and is focused on continued development of a conceptual framework. Also, the Phase III therapist is open to diverse ways of conceptualizing cases.

It is your job as a supervisor to begin to shift your thinking and behavior yet again to prepare to supervise the Phase III therapist. This is not the end of Phase III; it is the beginning. Therefore, it is important not to simply remove yourself and view the supervisee as an independent practitioner. Continuing to provide all of the support offered to the Phase II therapist in addition to setting the stage to provide additional growth opportunities is essential.

BRIDGING ACTIVITIES

During Phase III, critical objectives of the supervisor include the following.

- *Giving the supervisee more independence*: Don't go away; just allow for more independent decision-making in every way that you can without ignoring your job as overseer. As a supervisor, you have the ultimate responsibility for the clients. Build in ways for supervisees to access supervision without feeling as if they are "regressing" to seek you out. It takes a highly skilled supervisor to supervise Phase III therapists. Your job is to continue to find ways to "get out of the way" while being there for the critical moments.

- *Focusing on global client and supervisee issues*: As a supervisor of a Phase III therapist, you will be able to engage in more systemic, political, legal, cultural, and social discussions in addition to continuing to provide more individual case-specific consultations. This focus adds to the depth of discovery and the continuation of self and other awareness. Play therapists are typically faced with limitations that are often related to one of the above issues. Children have little power when it comes to their own treatment. We are often witnesses to matters that appear to be out of our control, but Phase III therapists have now acquired more skills and resources to find ways to use their professional influence to initiate change. Global discussions are necessary for therapists to debrief and create meaning so that they can remain mobilized and empowered to stay in the counseling field.

- *Spending more time referring to spirituality*: In a world that is full of complexities, child and play therapists are one of the helping professions that are exposed to the minute details of both internal and external pain, suffering, and confusion. As mentioned earlier, as supervisees develop, they become increasingly aware of themselves and their clients. As a supervisor, you can develop tools to help lead discussions in relation to personal well-being and the "magic" of play therapy. Supervisors need to assist therapists to create spiritual meaning as well. How we use ourselves extends beyond the Play Therapy Dimensions Model. How do we speak about the unspeakable? Some of the unspeakable issues are profoundly positive, while others are profoundly negative. Helping therapists talk about their experiences of children's spirituality is of particular relevance to play therapists, as they often witness many complex symbolic representations. Giving permission for this level of discussion is important to the development of the expert therapist.

- *Continuing to build co-collaborative relationships*: Evaluation is more often shared at this point. The Phase III supervisee can now clearly identify the goals for supervision. It is your job to identify all of the domains of functioning and, with the therapist, identify areas of focus. Supervisees in this stage of development will not be functioning at a Phase III level in all areas. There are times when the relationship will appear more consultative, while at other times it will be more supervisory. Your role is to encourage independent thought and processing, without losing track of the fact that supervisees are continuing to attempt to integrate new ways of looking at themselves as well as taking on greater levels of responsibility.

- *Continuing to make use of experiential activities*: The Phase III play therapist has typically gathered some experience using a number of play therapy interventions and techniques. It is at this point that play therapists may be able to design their own techniques and tailor them to the client. The supervisee is never too experienced to learn experientially. The continued use of art, play, and sand as a part of the supervision process is highly recommended. This ensures that therapists will not become stagnated in their work with children. Working with children uses a different level of energy than working with adults. Play therapists continue to need appropriate expressive outlets through supervision.
- *Challenging and providing supportive confrontation*: You cannot grow without being challenged. This is particularly true for Phase III therapists. They are more capable than Phase I and II therapists of withstanding the questions and pressures of defending their work because their personal doubts are no longer disabling. This is essential preparation for any potential court work. The court does not care about your "phase of development," they just want to know why you did what you did. Furthermore, they want to know that you chose the best intervention or approach and that it was in the client's best interests. The next level of case discussion can occur here as you begin to help the supervisee address these issues.
- *Continuing to address all previous clinical objectives*: Choose to engage with the supervisee where necessary based on goals related to one or more fundamental domains of functioning which include: intervention skills, assessment techniques, interpersonal assessment, client conceptualization, individual differences, theoretical orientation, treatment goals, and/or professional ethics.

INDICATORS OF MOVEMENT FROM PHASE III TO EXPERIENCED THERAPIST

The Phase III therapist strives for stable, consistent functioning across all therapeutic domains. During the movement toward experienced therapist, the supervisor observes supervisees solidifying their professional identities. They have a heightened personal understanding, and they are more capable of monitoring the impact and interaction of their professional lives on their personal lives. You will often observe supervisees having developed an interest in a specialized area of treatment, research, or learning. They are more prepared to meet others as colleagues and can assert themselves regarding clinical decisions or case conceptualization. There is an emerging curiosity and a realization that the more they learn, the more they don't know. The movement from Phase III to experienced therapist does not mark a point of *arrival*; rather, it is a movement toward having a greater level of flexibility and openness to an endless sea of possibilities.

UTILIZING THE TRACKING AND OBSERVATION FORM

To provide a structured, more standardized way of monitoring and recording the multiple variables that occur in the play therapy relationship, the Tracking and Observation Form (Appendix C) was developed. The form helps the play therapist to review sessions by providing anchoring constructs for therapeutic activity. The form is divided into four main sections: 1) descriptive analysis, including the developmental stage of play and play processes; 2) relational and affective markers, including emotional range, self-regulation, and engagement; 3) thematic representations, including a menu of possible play themes; 4) summary, including the child's view of the world, emerging hypotheses, and a planning section.

There are many uses for the Tracking and Observation Form. We recommend that all beginning play therapists use it for every session. The value is that it provides an organizing structure which ensures ongoing development in the multiple ways of viewing a play therapy session. Phase I play therapists are typically learning what they should be recording as important or relevant. It is difficult for supervisors to teach this skill by dyadic instruction alone, because it becomes impossible for supervisees to memorize the layers of details of which to remain aware during a given session. The form then becomes a training tool that can lead supervisors and supervisees in case-related discussions. A deeper conceptualization of the client is derived after completing the form, and it gives supervisees language to use in defining what they see and experience. We have found that using this form with Phase I supervisees enhances their development and prepares them for Phase II.

Supervisees are more likely to deepen their understanding of the Play Therapy Dimensions Model by using the Tracking and Observation Form. It begins with a quick reference to the four quadrants. Play therapists are asked to draw the sequence of their movements between quadrants, and if they were directing the movement, they are asked to consider the child's response to their decision. The form concentrates on the child, and the child's experiences and responses. Keeping the child in mind is harder than it may seem. Both Phase I and Phase II play therapists struggle intermittently to remain focused on the client while remaining aware of the self.

When studying the vast body of knowledge related to children, it became apparent that finding a way to be inclusive and integrative when working with children would mean that therapists needed to have a global perspective with accompanying indicators of child presentation that ranged from "normal" to "severely maladjusted." Although students of play therapy were interested in the work, it was difficult for them to manage their broad-based knowledge in a meaningful way, without completely overlooking major factors. In addition to being expected to make use of their knowledge base, students were required to keep track of specific play processes. The Tracking and Observation Form helps the play therapist to organize this expectation.

Writing comprehensive summaries or reports for third parties is made easier by using the Tracking and Observation Form after each session. The only way to really track subtle change is to review a series of sessions in a standardized manner. Therapists ask the same questions each time, which helps to identify changes, play sequences, themes, resolutions (and lack of resolutions), problems, concerns, needs, and future direction. Play therapists can use the form subtitles to write summaries. Many third parties are suspicious of play therapy, and it may be that play therapists have not been as good as they would have liked in writing about the therapeutic power of play. The legal system demands that play therapists defend their approaches and work with children. It is important to understand that to those non-play therapists, the simplistic version of play therapy is that "a bunch of toys are used to get kids to talk and disclose things in an adult way."

The Tracking and Observation Form is also good for those therapists doing work for insurance companies or employment assistance programs. Notes taken after each session can often be demanded for review. A standardized case note is clear, is consistent, and removes the potential assumption of subjectivity. It is easier to write short summaries for companies when in the habit of recording in a standard manner.

Supervisors can gain a very quick view of a child's presentation by reading the form in advance of a supervision session. It allows the supervisee and supervisor to make the best use of the supervision time. Questions can be formed to help guide the supervisee to integrate the areas of focus in order to further conceptualize the supervisee's role in aiding the child. If there are conflicting pieces of information recorded by the therapist, the supervisor can formulate questions to further the therapist's thinking and conceptualization. Goal planning is considered at the beginning of the form as well as at the end, which immediately helps the play therapist to think about the context of the child's story and leads to holding that story in mind as therapy unfolds. Supervisors will be able to use the tool to evaluate the supervisee's insight and capacity to observe the details in play therapy sessions. If the supervisee has difficulty understanding the child's emotional range or self-regulation, for instance, supervisors will target that area as one to explore further.

UTILIZING THE CHILD MODERATING FACTORS SCALE

The Child Moderating Factors Scale (Appendix A) is a decision-making guide that comprises scaling and evaluative questions to aid the play therapist in making clinical decisions. It helps to answer the *who, what, when, why,* and *how* when using the Play Therapy Dimensions Model. The guide is divided into two main domains: 1) child moderating factors, and 2) the top-three factors to focus on during treatment. The goal of the guide is to increase the therapist's assessment and conceptualization skills.

Beginning with child factors, we know that each child is unique, and therefore we need to view all children in a consistent manner across multiple variables. The guide outlines 11 factors including: 1) play skills, 2) communication skills, 3) development, 4) emotional expression, 5) self-regulation ability, 6) attachment organization, 7) relational skills , 8) world view, 9) defense mechanisms, 10) resilience, and 11) support network. Play therapists are asked to provide a score on a scale of 1 to 5 for each of these factors. The therapist then looks for strengths and potential weaknesses in order to conceptualize the child. If therapists meet with caregivers prior to seeing the child, the therapist may be able to provide a preliminary score for most or all of the moderating factors *prior* to seeing the child. Once the child is seen, the therapist can revisit the scores and decide if they should remain the same. This can be done on the same sheet for comparison. Discrepancies between how the therapist and the caregivers view the child do occur, so it is important to flag these areas for future consideration and consultation. The Child Moderating Factors Scale decision-making guide is *not* meant for parents, teachers, or other professionals' use. It is a tool solely intended for the play therapist.

Knowing about child moderating factors is essential to case planning, pacing, and decision-making, and subsequently leads therapists to choose an appropriate quadrant in which to begin therapy. On an ongoing basis, the client informs the therapist about the need for movement; therefore, using the child moderating scales over time helps the therapist to decide when the client needs to move to a different quadrant. Just because a therapist starts, for instance, in Quadrant III, *Non-Intrusive Responding*, does not mean that the therapist must stay there. Some clients clearly present their need to discuss a concern directly and therefore need the therapist to move to Quadrant II, *Open Discussion and Exploration*. For example, if you notice that the child's play skills, communication skills, emotional expression, self-regulation, resilience, and relational ability are all very high, you may decide to work more directively with that child. When viewed together, the client moderating factors provide a comprehensive view of the child.

Where to Begin

The decision-making guide asks the play therapist to prioritize the top-three child moderating factors. This section asks the therapist to rate the degree of directiveness as well as the client's degree of consciousness (from the therapist's point of view). These scores help the therapist to make decisions about use of self in relation to client presentation. Through supervision, the play therapist can answer critical questions such as: Does the child have the skills to engage in a highly directive and/or conscious manner? Do I really know what the child's concerns are? Would it be best to work non-directively? Am I choosing to work in this manner because it falls within *my* comfort zone? Am I missing cues from the child? Are the child moderating factor scores changing? If so, what does this mean? Is my confidence increasing or decreasing? Do I need more skills or knowledge regarding this presenting issue? If so, how do I receive this support? Am I getting in the way of the child's progress? If so, how? If not, how am I enabling the child's progress?

The Four Quadrants

This section of the Child Moderating Factors Scale includes a brief menu of variables that help guide the therapist to choose the quadrant in which to begin and continue working. This short checklist can be used prior to each session because the child moderating factors are constantly in flux.

Phase I play therapists can begin to identify therapeutic entry points and build on their understanding as to how they affect the client. Phase II play therapists can immerse themselves in the study of the play therapy process. Phase III play therapists can use the tool to truly integrate use of self, techniques, theory, and process. Play therapists in each phase of development will use the decision-making guide at a different level. It is useful to refer to Figure 3.1 when utilizing the decision-making guide; it is good to have a visual reference when assisting supervisees to map the treatment process.

UTILIZING THE DEGREE OF IMMERSION: THERAPIST USE OF SELF SCALE

The Degree of Immersion: Therapist Use of Self Scale (Appendix B) is a self-evaluation scale that relates to therapist use of self across five categories. It was developed to assist play therapists to increase their awareness of the powerful impact they have on child clients. Because this is a difficult topic to address in a general way, specific therapist behavior and interaction are described as immersion. To what degree do you immerse yourself in the play? In order to answer this question, we divided how one *could* become immersed in a play therapy session into the categories: verbal use of self, emotional use of self, physical use of self, self-system, and cultural use of self. The more or less a therapist engages in these activities indicates the degree of immersion. We could not ask play therapists to score themselves without providing a rating of the child's response to their action or non-action. Therefore, as a part of each category rating, therapists must also rate the child's response to their level of immersion. Additionally, after each child rating, therapists must also provide three clinical indications as to the effectiveness of their use of self in that category.

Once play therapists have scored themselves on all five categories, they earn a composite score that indicates a total immersion score. This information can be enlightening to play therapists, even without the use of a video review. Some therapists are surprised by this score because they had not viewed themselves as "immersed" at all. After reflecting on each category (including the child's corresponding response), therapists can make some decisions about how to vary their behavior to better meet the child's needs and enhance the therapeutic experience. Through our supervisory experience, we began to realize it was difficult to help supervisees self-assess without providing them with a way to evaluate themselves on several levels. Use of the immersion scale in supervision has helped supervisees increase their awareness of the dynamic interrelatedness of the child–therapist interchange. Process of therapy is then driven by this important relationship. A close evaluation of what happens in the space between people in the play therapy room has helped supervisees identify why the process is either moving forward or stuck in neutral, or even regressing. The outcome for use of the immersion scale is not only an increase in awareness of the many levels of communication, but also an enhanced attunement to the client–therapist relationship. Degree of immersion is a concept considered throughout the Play Therapy Dimensions Model. The immersion scale asks therapists to identify the quadrant in which they were working during the session, and whether they moved from one quadrant to another. The critical question after identifying work in a given quadrant is, what therapist or child factors contributed to the decision-making? The immersion scale keeps therapists on track, asking them to continually reflect on the interaction between themselves and the client. This is what informs the highly attuned play therapist.

KEY POINTS

- Using the Play Therapy Dimensions Model Diagram during supervision offers an organizing structure for conceptualization and planning.
- Two video case examples of Ellis and Haley can be used to stop/start during supervision to identify activities in each quadrant as well as movement between quadrants.
- Case conceptualization is deepened through the use of two tools: Case Conceptualization Form and Parent Feedback Conceptualization Form. The video examples of the use of these tools are used to help supervisees deepen their understanding of their child client as well as how they might articulate feedback to parents.
- A model of "how" to use videos with supervisees is presented.
- Three phases of supervisee development are presented: Phase I: Beginning Play Therapy Training, Phase II: Imitation of Experts, and Phase III: Advanced Play Therapists.
- Bridging activities for supervisors to consider in order to support supervisee growth from one phase to the next are emphasized.
- The utilization of three scales during supervision sessions are reviewed.

◎ **Chapter 13** ◎

THERAPIST USE OF SELF

By the turn of the kaleidoscope a thousand ways of being are revealed.

What does therapist use of "self" mean? First, we shall visit the idea of self. The term "self" has been referred to for many years by many writers. Erwin (1997) notes that many authors of psychotherapy have referenced the self as a person, the ego, a set of self-representations, an inner agent, etc. Alternatively, constructionists view the self as constructed through interaction with others (Andrews, 1991; Cashdan, 1988; Mann, 1994). Cashdan (1988) states that the child's self is incrementally evolving through interacting and engaging with others. Interaction with others begins the formulation of how we begin to develop a self-concept. Things are communicated to us and about us through early relational experiences and initially we are told who we are. This sense of self is, however, viewed as fluid and shifting, and many writers believe that the self-concept adapts and changes in response to the environment (Andrews, 1991; Cashdan, 1988; Gergen, 2009; Mann, 1994; Peavy, 1996). The idea of self for the purpose of exploration here is reflected by Wosket (1999), who has distinguished between the person of the therapist and the therapist use of self:

> Because the person of the therapist pervades the therapeutic relationship, some aspects of who the therapist is unavoidably become accessible to the client to a greater or lesser degree. Therapists inadvertently reveal themselves through such aspects as dress, accent, age, voice intonation, skin color, involuntary changes in movement or facial expression, mannerisms, the furnishings and state of orderliness of the counseling room and so on. Yet inadvertent self-disclosure is not the same thing as intentional use of the self. (p.11)

It is the intentional use of self that is of interest here. Play therapists who will no doubt, as Wosket (1999) notes, "reveal" themselves to their child clients, must also make conscious use of themselves during play sessions. If it is to be followed that there is a fluid, in-motion quality to the development of self, then it is possible for play therapists to be purposefully useful, and in therapy imitate some of the natural parent–child processes that may be needed to assist in differentiation and rediscovery of a sense of personal empowerment, among other things (Winnicott, 1965). Use of self is therefore intended to have an impact on the child client as part of the essential overall process.

The focus on therapist use of self became vitally important to us after reviewing many hours of videoed sessions. What made play therapy "work" and look like "magic"? Certainly not the prescribed activity, the words used in the therapeutic reflections, whether the therapist worked in one dimension or another, or the quality of the playroom. It was the purposeful use of the qualities of the play therapist. It was timing and understanding. It was being present in a variety of ways that were mostly purposefully woven throughout the session with the child. It was clear when a therapist made a "hit" or a "miss" during the session. It was a dance on video that we could look at together and explore what had happened to either keep with the rhythm or take the dance out of step.

There are few places to receive training in the area of therapist use of self, and there are even fewer systematic guides to use of self (Wosket, 1999). This chapter attempts to raise the play therapist's awareness to the various ways one makes use of the self in a play therapy session. The play therapist uses their whole body when engaging in play. This adds to dimensions of adult-based work and offers more complexity to the therapeutic process. Evaluating the various ways play therapists use themselves in a given session is important due to not only the broad and multiple uses of self but also the need to relate on two planes at all times—with the child, matching where they are developmentally, and maintaining the adult "third eye" to track the process and content of the play session.

After examining a variety of play therapy theories in practice, it would appear that as important as it is to have a theory to work from, there is at least one cautionary note: if a therapist over-relies on the theory, the creative and spontaneous responses or ways of being with a child client will be lost. Writers referring to adult forms of therapy also note that as much as it is wise to have a theoretical framework, it is also important to be prepared to abandon the restraints of the approach to embrace the uniqueness of the person who is before you (Karasu, 1996; Maslow, 1982; Mann, 1994; Wosket, 1999; Crouch, 1997). Although great effort has been made to find the most effective approaches to play therapy and a variety of adult therapies, differential effectiveness appears to emerge as an outcome because a myth exists related to therapist uniformity (Kiesler, 1966). This being said, it leads us to look more closely and specifically at the use of self, from session to session. Each young client's unique presentation and way of interacting with the therapist will be a factor in the therapeutic dance. The therapist's way of interacting and being with the child and the child's responses to therapist-led actions will tell a story of the therapy process. Of course, it is expected that no two therapists are alike and no theory will always direct the process, therefore it will be important to track the therapist use of self for therapeutic direction.

WHAT ARE WE LOOKING FOR?

As a first step, we look at some of the obvious and not so obvious ways therapists immerse themselves in their ways of being with their child clients. The term "immersion" is meant to describe the various ways and degrees to which the therapist engages in specific behaviors, language (verbal and non-verbal), and emotions during the play therapy session. To immerse is to plunge or dip into—to move into something. Immersion can be experienced as deeply (perhaps intensely) immersed into the process, moderately immersed, or just dipped into the surface of the process. All forms of immersion can be exactly right depending on the child and the therapist and the dance that is occurring between them. The child will tell the therapist verbally and non-verbally if the immersion is in keeping with the dance or not. "Immersion" as a term for the description of use of self in play therapy is useful to help therapists identify when and if they should continue their way of responding in a given session.

Perhaps the literature on personal qualities of a play therapist points to some preconditions to potential use of self. Nalavany *et al.* (2004) added to what others have found to be important factors in their study of therapist qualities, competencies, and skills for play therapists. The research identified seven clusters of qualities: being attuned to and reflecting the child's verbal and non-verbal behavior and feelings; being sensitive to the child; being warm, empathic, genuine, and accepting of the child; being open to personal awareness and growth; having the skills for working with parents and families; having a theoretical understanding of the process of child therapy; and having a structured, intentional approach to the therapeutic process. Certainly, all of these factors will be helpful when evaluating the use of self, but again, these qualities alone do not reflect how the play therapist will actually *be* in relation to their client in the therapy setting.

Ray (2004) in her article on supervision of play therapists discussed basic and advanced skills of the play therapist and generally concurred with some of the findings of other authors (Axline, 1947; Guerney, 1983; Kottman, 2003b; Landreth, 2002; Moustakas, 1997; O'Connor, 2000). She noted:

> Basic skills include non-verbal skills of leaning forward, appearing interested, seeming comfortable, applying a tone congruent with the child's affect, and applying a tone congruent with the therapist's response. Basic verbal skills include delivering quality of verbal responses, tracking behavior, reflecting content, reflecting feeling, facilitating decision-making, facilitating creativity, esteem-building, and facilitating relationship. (Ray, 2004, p.30)

Ray (2004, 2011) goes on to say that advanced skills include enlarging meaning (facilitating understanding), identifying play themes, connecting with children, and limit-setting. Some of the core skills identified by Ray are highly model specific and are utilized by Child-Centered play therapists (Landreth model). The tracking and reflecting activities and ways of responding to children regarding esteem-building, for instance, may or may not be primary ways all play therapists work and therefore will not be targeted skills to develop for all play therapists. Even if play therapists from different models cross over in their skill sets, they may each evaluate how they approach the skills in different ways. Ray (2004) offers a tool for Child-Centered play therapists called the "Play Therapy Skills Checklist" which is helpful for those primarily trained as a Child-Centered play therapist. A more directively trained play therapist may need to evaluate their use of self differently. The question does not appear to be *what* skills will be more primarily used, but rather *how* will the therapist use their skills and how does the child respond?

As a way to assist all play therapists in tracking and evaluating therapeutic use of self, the Degree of Immersion: Therapist Use of Self Scale (Appendix B) was developed. The scale is useful for purposeful reflection after play therapy sessions, as practitioners can decide if the ways in which they made use of themselves was facilitative or interruptive to the process. By taking a closer look at the potential domains of therapist use of self, the play therapist can raise their awareness of what to pay attention to. The literature has reference to play therapy skills (Kottman, 2011; Ray, 2004; O'Connor, 2000) and techniques (Goodyear-Brown, 2010; Kaduson and Schaefer, 2003; Malchiodi, 2008; Rubin, 2008; Schaefer and Cangelosi, 2002; Lowenstein, 1999), but with the exception of Ray's (2004) contribution for Child-Centered play therapists, there is little reference to *how* play therapists reflect on the various ways they could engage in these activities.

To further explore how the play therapist makes use of the self in sessions, the following five main areas outline what the therapist could begin to identify and evaluate in a given session and in sessions over time.

1) VERBAL USE OF SELF
1.1) Here-and-Now Discussion (Open Discussion and Exploration QII)
Verbal discussion is related to the degree the play therapist was involved in talking directly to the child about their daily life or about a specific issue they came to counseling to address. There are a couple of ways verbal discussion may emerge in a play therapy session: 1) the child raises an issue, shares something about their life, and wants to talk directly and openly about something that is current in their life or something that is bothering them; 2) the therapist questions the child about their day or life

circumstances, or talks openly to the child about an issue of concern. The therapist may also talk to the child while the child plays. In both examples, the play therapist is working outside of the play therapy metaphor. Play therapists may find themselves in high levels of immersion in this domain when much of the session is dedicated to *Open Discussion and Exploration*. This may be exactly what the child needs to do, or they may tell you by changing the subject, ignoring you, withdrawing, or asking to leave the session, such that you change the degree of immersion related to verbal discussion.

Verbal discussion can be one way to immerse yourself that is familiar to you, as it is similar to that of adult counseling, which may in turn make you feel more competent. If the verbal discussion is led by the therapist, it is important to know why you are choosing a verbal approach and to read your child client's cues regarding their comfort and developmental ability to enter into a discussion. It may also be a way for you to gain some specific input from the child that you could not get any other way. In this case, it is also important to read the cues of your client and sensitively adjust the course of discussion or potentially return to the play and remain tracking the play themes and metaphors.

The pressure to "talk" to children is sometimes very high, based on parent or third-party requests. It is also important to realize most therapists who were first trained in adult forms of psychotherapy have learned that a core process of change emerges from what Beitman and Soth (2006) describe as "activation of self-observation." This means that therapists (no matter what specific type of psychotherapeutic approach they use) will assist clients to increase their self-awareness, which relies on consciousness. Consciousness requires utilization of particular brain structures in order to provide a framework to hold the emerging awareness. The difficulty is that therapists often forget about the developmental differences between children and adults, and the therapists' agendas to find verbal ways to increase awareness and to change maladaptive responses become paramount. Fonagy and Target (1997) state that self-observation is when a person actively scans their inner landscape (intentions, expectations, feelings, cognitions, and behaviors) and the ideas in other people's minds and what other people think of them. Prochaska and Norcross (2003) note, "all so-called verbal psychotherapies begin by working to raise the individual's level of observation [and] increasing consciousness...increas[ing] the information available to individuals so that they can make the most effective responses to the stimuli impinging on them" (pp.12–13).

When thinking about these statements about adult forms of therapy, it is important to consider the various ways of working with children and to at least evaluate the ways in which each individual child is approached regarding diminishing symptomology and increasing overall functioning. Knowing the child and the developmental abilities of the child will be a first step. Also, the play therapist has more options available to them to reach the same end as verbal therapies do with adult clients. This being said, it is re-emphasized that there is no single rule regarding verbal interaction in play therapy; rather, it is the child who will let you know if you are on track or not. Again, the therapist's model of training may dictate verbal use of self. The Child-Centered (Landreth model) will likely rarely make use of self in this way, while a Non-Directive play therapist (UK model) may. The Landreth model does not support asking questions of the child, and Landreth practitioners would not decide to enter the play, while the UK model would support working in the metaphor and inserting comments and at times entering the play with the child. Other models of play therapy make wider use of the continuum of consciousness and directiveness, and practitioners practicing in these models will make verbal use of self in sessions.

When examining this area of use of self, useful questions for consideration are as follows:

- Do I feel more effective when I hear specific feedback from the child?
- Can I gain their voice/input in another way?
- Do they demonstrate the ego strength and cognitive ability to engage in answering my questions?
- Does open discussion assist the child and in what way?
- Am I more comfortable with talk therapy generally?
- Am I following an adult model of talk therapy?
- Am I apt to move to open discussion when there is silence?
- Am I a highly verbal person and am I more comfortable with verbalizations?
- Do I believe that it is not until the child verbalizes their understanding or awareness that I have done my job?
- Do I completely avoid open discussion with the child because I have been trained to work in the metaphor or to only provide reflections?
- Am I pressured by outside agendas?

The integrative play therapist may draw on both directive, conscious ways and non-directive, less conscious ways of interacting with the child client. The most important consideration is to reflect on whether the choice you make as a therapist is useful to the child.

1.2) Reflecting and Tracking Statements (Non-Intrusive Responding QIII, Co-Facilitation QIV)

The use of reflective statements in play therapy is typically toted as one of the basic play therapy skills. Often referred to as tracking or reflecting, this skill is used in many approaches to play therapy, although the Child-Centered play therapists (Landreth (2002) approach) are often thought of first when referring to this skill. Adlerian, Jungian, Narrative, Prescriptive, Non-Directive (UK model), and Integrative therapists are among a few other play therapist practitioners that would also use reflective statements in play as a way to communicate that they are "with" the child. Landreth (2002, 2012) would say, "I see you, I hear you, I understand." Kottman (2011) listed a number of play therapists that she surveyed who noted that they do not use tracking in their work with children including Cognitive-Behavioral, Ecosystemic, Gestalt, and Theraplay play therapists. For those practicing in these ways, the use of self in relation to making reflective statements would be skipped and the practitioner would move to the next item on the scale. These therapists may find themselves using reflective comments, however, just not for the main purpose of demonstrating being *with* the child as described in Child-Centered Play Therapy (Landreth model).

Reflections in play therapy relate to non-interpretive statements made during the course of play that reflect a child's behavior, play content, and feeling states. There are no rules to tracking play activity; rather, the therapist must make decisions about the frequency and timing of tracking and reflecting. Reflecting is exemplified by the avoidance of asking questions of the child or naming items before the child has identified or named an item.

Ray (2004) states that the word "tracking" is used when demonstrating that the therapist is following the behavior of the child in the session. She notes it is a way for the therapist to, "immerse him or herself into the child's world" (p.32). The therapist will make verbal statements such as, "You are pouring that in there," or, "You are looking for something to use," etc. These statements are used in a timely way to demonstrate that you *see* the child and that you are *with* them.

Reflecting content is when the therapist paraphrases verbal statements and comments made by the child such as, "You have one of those things at home too," after the child says, "This is the same as the one I have." Reflecting content demonstrates too that you are with the child. Reflecting feelings is also a verbal response given to the child by the therapist after the child demonstrates an action or behavior that is clearly laden with feelings. The therapist may say, "That makes you sad," after the child makes a statement in a sad voice through a puppet. This can be interpretive in that the therapist will be using the non-verbal information from the child to make these comments. The child is then thought to become more aware of the emotions which they are presenting, and this gives them a way to express their emotions more fully.

Facilitating decision-making is another reflective process that has been discussed primarily by Child-Centered play therapists but is also honored by other play therapy approaches. In the child-centered manner of facilitating decisions, the therapist will return the responsibility to the child so that the child may succeed at an action, such as, "You can use the blocks in most of the ways you would like," or, "You can decide what that will be," or, "Show me how you would like that to go." Other play therapists may assist children to meet the same types of decision-making actions but through more directive or structured activities. Either way, there will be a point of offering the child the opportunity to make decisions to help them meet their own objectives.

THERAPIST USE OF SELF

Esteem-building and encouraging reflections may also be an observed therapist action. The play therapist in the child-centered way of working would not provide praise; rather, they would reflect on the child's behavior and provide encouraging statements such as, "There, you did that all on your own," or, "You knew exactly how to do that!" The child may struggle with something, but the therapist will refrain from stepping in and assisting the child and will instead make encouraging statements such as, "You keep trying that and you're not giving up." Other play therapy approaches may use these statements as well as praise-oriented statements. Either way, it will be important to know your child client and to know why you are doing what you are doing. Ultimately, is what you are doing useful to the child? Relationship-building reflections may include statements made about the child's response in relationship to the therapist. The child may be angry with the therapist, and the therapist will need to decide how to respond in a relational way. The Child-Centered therapist may choose to say, "You are really angry at me right now." Other practitioners may make reflective statements that have both a component of a statement and a component of a wondering question. Reflections could include positive comments about the relationship, "You are having a lot of fun with me right now," or, if you are not child-centered trained, you may use language that includes you by using the words "we" or "I."

Facilitative reflections may be made to deepen or, as Ray (2004) notes, enlarge the meanings of play interactions. Ray gives an example of, "You always make sure to play with the mommy doll" (p.34). Typically, Child-Centered play therapists are more cautious about providing interpretations in play, but other approaches such as Adlerian, Gestalt, and Ecosystemic Play Therapy do use more interpretive statements to enlarge the meaning of the play scenario. Play therapists may stay in the metaphor and provide a reflection about a character as well, such as, "Wow, that guy sure is mean." These reflections are not directed by the child, so the timing and decision-making around what you say and why you say it are important.

The child's response tells us many things about the ways in which we use ourselves. Consider the following questions before rating yourself:

- Did you vary your tone and expression when making reflective comments?
- Did you track too closely with too many comments?
- Did the child correct you or ask you why you were making comments?
- Did your comments appear to enhance the play process or did they get in the way?
- Did the child begin to repeat what you were saying about the play?
- Did the child pivot from the play, turn their back on you, or otherwise try to shut you out as a result of your reflections?
- Did you vary what you were tracking and reflecting?
- Were you purposeful in what you were tracking and why?

- Did you reflect feelings through the characters in the play?

The scale asks you to identify the effectiveness of the different ways you may use yourself in the session. You will have to be aware of what the child is doing in response to you by later rating the child's response and providing three examples to support your rating. High responses mean your use of self was a hit and helped to facilitate the play and the relationship. Low responses observed from the child are considered a miss, and you can make adjustments to your use of self in this area in the next session.

1.3) Restating Content (Non-Intrusive Responding QIII, Co-Facilitation QIV)

Restating content is another core skill used by most play therapists regardless of their theoretical orientation. It is considered a form of paraphrasing or verbally reflecting back to a child client something they said as part of the play activity or something they shared with you. Restating content can assist a child to clarify an understanding of the self (Landreth, 2002). A child may be playing with some family doll figures and say, "These ones are really bad!" and the therapist would restate, "You think those ones are bad!" Reflecting is not simply repeating *exactly* what the child just said; rather, it is about adding a feeling or shortening the comment made by the child to reflect the important part of what was said. Reflecting, tracking, and restating content are basic core skills to the play therapy process. The relationship between the child and play therapist is built on these therapeutic interventions, as the child is aware that you are there and involved in following their play. The play can be sequenced and organized when a play therapist can find a way to balance these skills in a given session. How did the child respond to you restating content? Consider the following questions before rating yourself on the scale:

- Did the child ask you why you kept repeating them?
- Did you find ways to paraphrase salient parts of what they said?
- Did you notice the child elaborate the play or become directly oppositional and/or agitated with you?
- Did you notice yourself using tracking too frequently?
- What was your tone like when restating content? Animated? Flat? Monotone?
- Did reflecting content distract you from following what the child was showing you in the play?

1.4) Interpretations (Active Utilization QI)

The use of interpretations in play therapy varies depending on the play therapy model from which you practice. Many play therapists use interpretations in their work with children but are unaware they are doing so because interpretations are often made by making comments through the play metaphor. For instance, "That princess is angry," is an interpretation of a child who has not said the princess is indeed angry. In this instance, an interpretation of the princess's feeling state is noted out loud by the therapist even if the child has not themselves verbally identified the princess as feeling anger. This is an interpretation that stays in the play and does not directly link the princess as potentially being a part of the child but allows the child to contemplate the princess's anger.

Providing interpretations is one of the verbal uses of self. When using interpretations, play therapists find themselves working in Quadrant I, *Active Utilization*. Interpretations are verbal comments made by the therapist after observing repetitive play themes and play scenarios. These verbal comments are meant to utilize the play material to assist a child to develop a new understanding or meaning by bringing a link between play and the child's lived life to conscious awareness. O'Connor (2002) notes that there is a strong correlation between children's mental health and their use of language, and in part, a child's language acts as a bridge from action to symbol to thought. O'Connor emphasizes that language plays a central role in the therapy process.

Psychodynamic, Ecosystemic, Jungian, Gestalt, Prescriptive, and Adlerian play therapists are a few of those who will at various times provide interpretive comments with the intent to raise the awareness of the child client. O'Connor (2000), in his model of Ecosystemic Play Therapy, focuses on providing a child with an alternative cognitive understanding of their issues or problems. His five-stage model of interpretations includes: 1) reflection of thought, feeling, or motive; (b) pattern: point out a pattern of behavior over time; (c) simple dynamic: point out a child's unexpressed thoughts, feelings, and motives in their behavior; (d) generalized dynamic: point out how a pattern is transferred across settings and interactions; and (e) genetic (historical source connections). This interpretation model exemplifies the purposeful use of raising content or feelings to assist the child to make a conscious connection. O'Connor believes that it is reasonable to make use of the evolving cognitive development of the child as part of the therapy intervention. Because we are conscious beings and use consciousness to interrupt maladaptive patterns of behavior and feeling states, assistance in bringing forward the material that is at the edge of being available to the child is supported by many play therapy models. Types of interpretations in the Play Therapy Dimensions Model include: reflective interpretations, linking interpretations, and/or bridging interpretations. Chapter 8, which describes *Active Utilization*, identifies the three increasing levels of interpretations used by some practitioners in therapy. When using interpretations in play therapy, the therapist looks for appropriate therapeutic moments, is aware of the child's development and ability to hold an interpretive comment, and understands a child's support system. Raising consciousness in children's therapy requires the fundamental development of play skills for it to be useful and not shut the child down. How did the child respond to your interpretations during the play? Consider the following questions before rating yourself on the scale:

- Do you believe that interpretations are valuable to the play therapy process? Or has your training led you to believe that interpretations may get in the way of the process and may even be damaging?
- Do the tone of your interpretation and timing seem appropriate?
- Did the child pivot from (abruptly stop) the play?
- Did they outwardly reject or correct your comment, e.g., "No, the princess isn't angry"?
- Did the child seem to incorporate your interpretation and did the play elaborate because of it?
- Did the interpretation offer them an opportunity to disclose something to you that they had not previously disclosed?
- Do you tend to overinterpret what is happening in the play and then make interpretive statements to gain validation of what you think you are seeing?
- Did the interpretation lead to open discussion and exploration?
- Do the tone of your interpretation and timing seem appropriate?

2) EMOTIONAL USE OF SELF
2.1) Emotionality (Non-Intrusive Responding QIII, Co-Facilitation QIV)

Emotional use of self is considered in two ways: the emotions that are inserted into the play by the play therapist (emotionality) and the play therapist's personal emotional experience (emotional self). We will reflect on *emotionality* first. This scale asks the therapist to rate the degree to which they provided emotionally based responses, either using high levels of consciousness (direct statements made) or low levels of consciousness (staying in the metaphor of the play). Emotionality is identified as when and how the therapist inserted emotions in the context of the play. Adding emotional intensity to the play session may be observed in the form of increasing the emotional emphasis assigned to a character, "There he is, he's coming faster and faster," or by providing a voice to an action or character—either assigned to you by the child or you may be adding to the play through co-facilitation of the play. The therapist has to decide how intense to be, what they may add (either with words or with actions), and what the duration of the emotional insertion will be. You may only do this through using reflective statements or you could be purposely elaborating the play by remaining in the therapy metaphor. Regardless, you will be thoughtfully adding a part of the emotional "you" to assist the child

212

to explore deeper or varied emotions of characters used in play. Additionally, you communicate to the child that you are aware of feelings which *they* may have had. This provides the emotional distance for the child to be able to integrate uncomfortable or dissociated feelings that they potentially need to reorganize and own. Therapists find themselves using their emotional selves throughout play sessions partly because of the therapeutic need to be attuned and empathically connected to their child clients.

Ryan and Courtney (2009) are recognized for bringing the term "congruence" to the play therapy literature. Ginsberg (2011), in his response to Ryan and Courtney, notes, "Congruence, defined as an inner state on the part of therapists in which outward expressions of feelings consistently match therapists' inner feelings, is seen by Rogers as an essential component of accurate empathy with clients" (p.110).

Ryan and Courtney (2009) differentiate between child and adult models of therapy, however. They emphasize that children present in therapy at various levels of development and play therapists tend to work non-directively, thus allowing children to lead the play and fully work in the play metaphor. Children do not self-refer to counseling and are therefore not typically conscious of their difficulties nor are they coming to therapy to purposefully self-actualize. Ginsberg (2011) comments on the fact that the play therapist must become, "skillful in being genuine" (p.110). We would concur with this comment because the ways in which the therapist weaves an accurate reflection of empathy and unconditional positive regard will often occur within the play therapy metaphor. Ryan and Wilson (2000) in their earlier work provide examples that illustrate this process in role-plays (or dramatic play). The child may, for instance, direct the therapist to "be the mother figure," and the child plays the child of the mother and during the exchange explores their relationship with their abusive mother. The therapist may not bring the issues to consciousness by making direct statements about the link between the child's play scenario and their real experiences with their mother; rather, the therapist will *be* the mother and reflect in character the shame of the mother while in role, all the while remaining in connection with themselves outside the role. Through these congruent emotional exchanges, the child is able to integrate ways of viewing the "real" mother and is empowered by having a skilled play therapist congruently reflect the potential realities and feeling states that may have been pushed away or dissociated from the child's view of their mother. Play therapists know that it is difficult for children to hold contradictory and conflicting feelings about caregivers, particularly when the caregiver behavior has been abusive. Unique to the play therapy is that recovery and the integration of reality occur *through* the play.

We view congruence as an important part of the emotional use of self. Those working from different approaches to play therapy may in fact express congruence in varied ways. Ginsberg (2011) notes the differences, for instance, between other

Non-Directive play therapists through references to the, "Guerney and Landreth models" (p.110). Although all the non-directive models of play therapy generally follow Rogers' (1957) focus on congruence and accurate empathic responding, different practitioners place a different emphasis on their use of self with child clients. As previously noted, there is no one way to be congruent or to use emotionality in play therapy, but it is important to understand what you are doing and why. When rating the emotionality scale, questions to consider include the following.

- Did your emotionality match that of the child's?
- Did you emphasize or intensify an emotional response (directed or not directed by the child) and what was the response?
- Did you have a strong feeling and not express it (in or out of the play)?
- Did you over- or under-respond emotionally given the play scenario?
- Did you notice the child pivot away after your emotional response?
- Did you remain in the play and demonstrate congruence concerning your response?
- Did you exit the play and become too directive by raising consciousness to the situation because of your needs?
- Did you follow the child's instructions for insertion of emotionality into the play situation?
- Did you use emotionality embedded in reflective statements?

This area of use of self is critical to the play therapy process. It is one of the primary ways play therapists intervene in the play. It is a core skill that lies close to the therapist and is highly related to the child–therapist relationship. Play therapy techniques, or the play therapy approach alone, will not elicit growth and change in a child; rather, it is the varied ways the therapist moves with and through the techniques and/or approach as they connect with the person of the child that provide the restorative experience. Both directive and Non-Directive play therapists must be highly attuned to their own responses and respond in facilitative ways. It is our belief that being aware of what you are doing during a given session will assist you to modify your responses in ways that enhance therapeutic growth and recovery.

2.2) Emotional Self (All Quadrants)

We all bring our own emotions into sessions with clients, and therapy with children is no exception. In fact, many therapists report higher levels of sensitivity toward their young clients partly because children are inherently a vulnerable population. The use of self emotionally is demonstrated in play therapy sessions through the therapist's voice tone, cadence, intensity, volume, and rhythm, in addition to facial expressions and gestures. What was the degree to which you were personally emotionally involved during the session? This may include your awareness of feeling a particular intense emotion or noticing yourself shutting down, becoming numb, or temporarily losing track of following the client. You may become aware of a personal experience, or a personal memory may be triggered. Tracking your internal emotional experience is an important part of understanding what is happening in a session. Your emotions may create an over- or under-responding during your involvement with the child. You may want to find a way to address various feeling states that emerged during the session either in ongoing supervision or in personal therapy.

When rating emotional self on the scale, consider the following questions:

- Did you notice your feeling states during the session, and if so, what did you notice?
- Did any memories of your own experiences emerge during the session?
- Did you notice where in your body you felt an emotion?
- Were you generally unaware of any personal feelings during the session?
- Did you notice yourself withdraw and shut down at any point during the session? If so, did you become numb?
- Did you over-express an emotion that did not fit with the emotion of the child?

3) PHYSICAL USE OF SELF
3.1) Physical Self (All Quadrants)

The play therapy literature does not specifically address the use of physical self and its influence in a session. Ironically, much attention is placed on the physical space in which play therapists work, and tools of the trade such as play therapy toys and different play mediums, but not on how you make use of these items and spaces with your physical self in mind. Turn off the sound on your video camera and watch your session. You will see that you are making moment-to-moment choices of how you manage proximity, movement, touch, and physical energy in the therapy room. You may see yourself moving away from the child when it is apparent you need to move toward the child. You may find yourself drifting and becoming disengaged. You may find the way you use your physical self makes it difficult for a child to make contact with you. Alternatively, you may be very involved and perhaps at times too involved. You may see yourself getting in the way of the play rather than being part of the play process. You might block activity by becoming too active and dominant. You could become obstructive by lying on the floor beside the child, meaning your body positioning stops the child from moving around the room. Play therapists' styles of being in play are as varied as the child client's styles of being in play. Style variations are not the issue, but how you as the therapist may need to vary your style to better serve your client *is* the issue.

Part of the restorative experience for children in therapy includes physical movement and touch. Some play therapists avoid direct contact with their child clients due to fear of the child misunderstanding their intent and subsequently disclosing abuse by the therapist. Others work purposefully with physical proximity and touch such as Theraplay therapists (Munns, 2000) and non-Theraplay therapists working with attachment-related concerns with children and families. Whether you work purposefully with touch or not, it is important to become aware of the ways you respond to touch and movement instigated by the child. Is what you are doing facilitative or rejecting? Are you finding ways for children to have a new physical experience that is restorative or that reorganizes previously abusive physical experiences?

Play therapy is one of the most physical therapies. It requires many decisions to be made by the therapist, including how physically assertively you play and move around the room. Decisions are often quite purposeful especially when working with a child's regulatory system. The child's physicality and use of their body to assist in providing them with a new felt experience (for instance, of a calm body feeling) may be facilitated as a result of different degrees and levels of movement in play. The therapist then needs to decide what they will do alongside the child or how they will demonstrate or role-play action with a child. These decisions need to be quite consciously made, and the therapist must know themselves and their own regulatory system. It is, for instance, possible for the therapist to become overly stimulated and dysregulated themselves during the play session. It is also possible for the therapist to under-respond and become somewhat immobilized by the action of the child. As a function of trying to set limits indirectly, some therapists have been observed to withdraw and use their bodies (turning away or dropping the play sword) to set a boundary rather than to be congruent in setting limits.

Because we are physical beings, it is common to observe a child's play action or the therapist response as "embodied" or physically represented in the play. This would be of interest to keep in mind and record later. You may experience during a session, or later observe in a videoed session, a pervasive sad feeling state that emerges and is then spontaneously embodied or represented by you and the child becoming less animated, with a drooped posture and downcast facial expressions. Jennings (1995) notes this as a purposeful part of her work as a play therapist who uses embodiment, projection, and role. Therapist use of physical self during role-play may look different to that of the therapist out of role. There may be reasons to increase intensity and intentionality physically while in role.

In evaluating the physical use of self, it may be useful to explore the following questions:

- Were you fully present physically?
- Did your physical movements match the child's? If not, was that purposeful?

- Did you obstruct the play through the use of your physical self?
- Did you move around enough or were you constricted in your use of physical self?
- Did the child need more or less physical action in the play?
- Did you touch the child? If so, how and why?
- Did you set limits through the use of your physical self or are you using a more direct limit-setting process?
- Did you use touch to set limits? If so, how and why?
- Did you notice your body actions and facial expressions as facilitating the play?
- Were you aware of your own emotion regulation and did you manage this through congruent use of your body in space?
- Were there examples in the session where emotions or issues were embodied? If so when and why?

4) SELF-SYSTEM
4.1) Embodiment (All Quadrants)

Embodiment is a representation or expression of something in a tangible or visible form. To embody something that may be happening between you and a child client or to embody something you think is happening within a child, or yourself, you must have an awareness of your self-system. Exteroception (the awareness of our external world such as sound, sight, smell, taste, and tactile features of objects) is one area of awareness. Interoception (awareness of what is going on in our bodies), neuroception (autonomic response by the nervous system registering danger or safety), and proprioception (awareness of where our bodies are in space) are a few considerations when assessing the self-system. To what degree were you aware of your self-system in the presence of the child? In some circumstances during play therapy, you will find yourself feeling a sense of what is happening and feel the energy and power of the connection or bodily awareness of yourself and the child. Other times, you may be unaware of what is happening and in fact feel quite removed and possibly numb and disembodied (separated from or existing without a feeling of bodily connection). Embodiment in play therapy is one of the important ways that therapists bring their energy into the space. It is difficult to describe and powerful when felt.

Consider the following questions when rating your self-system:

- What did you notice in the external environment during the play session?
- What sensations, feelings in your body, and level of your internal energy did you notice?
- Did you externalize a feeling or energy state during the play through, for instance, a gesture or reflective statement?

- Did you notice how your body was moving and taking up space in the playroom?
- How did your awareness and presence in the space impact the child client's awareness or connection with you?
- Did you feel relatively shut down? Numb? More in your head than in your body?

5) CULTURAL USE OF SELF
5.1) Cultural Self (All Quadrants)

Consider your multicultural orientation (Davis *et al.*, 2018). How do you honor the multiplicity of truths and experiences of others? Your identity includes your views, meanings, participation, or membership in a group (race, ethnicity, socioeconomic status, age, gender, sexuality, religion, education, language, education, occupation, and political ideology), which collectively arrive in the play therapy setting (Gil and Drewes, 2021). Cultural awareness requires self-awareness and self-exploration as well as the awareness of other. Bringing your cultural self forward requires a purposeful use of self in play sessions as well as in your work with parents. It requires you to be curious about the cultural identity of your client(s).

How do you collect information from parents at the beginning of the process? It is important to include cultural identity questions during intake so that you can learn about salient identities and related meanings held by family members. What do you notice about the child's cultural identity? There are typically opportunities to engage in cultural comments or ways to enter a child's cultural expressions in the play process itself. Sometimes you may be reflecting racist comments made by a child versus letting the comment slide by, for instance. Finding entry points to engage in emerging cultural representations in play is an important skill.

Cultural use of self is more than simply knowing yourself and being curious about other; it is also about human rights and social justice advocacy (Ceballos, Post, and Rodriguez, 2021). A multicultural orientation takes into account systemic oppression and inherent power differentials that exist in society. Some children you see will be living in marginalized situations where their voices are limited and self-concepts are negatively impacted. Play therapists provide environments where children are able to gain a sense of personal empowerment and voice. Consider the following questions when rating yourself on the scale:

- To what degree were you aware of your cultural self in the play therapy session?
- What cultural representations did you observe in the play metaphor?
- Did you raise any cultural references made by the child to consciousness during the play session?
- Do you understand the child's family culture?

THERAPIST USE OF SELF

- What beliefs were you aware of surfacing during a play therapy session or a parent session?
- What did you notice about the child's self-concept and how is this tied to the cultural identify of the child?

KEY POINTS

- The Degree of Immersion: Therapist Use of Self Scale covers five key areas: 1) verbal use of self, 2) emotional use of self, 3) physical use of self, 4) self-system, and 5) cultural use of self.
- After rating the self on the five areas, the therapist evaluates the child's responses and provides three examples to defend the rating. The child's responses help the therapist to modify their use of self. The scale focuses on increasing the play therapists' reflective capacity and sense of intero- ception, exteroception, proprioception, and neuroception in play therapy sessions.
- A child's response may be *low*, related to the therapist actions (indicating a relative "miss" in the therapeutic use of self), *medium* (moderate response to the therapist use of self), or *high* (a "hit"—a significant response to the therapist use of self, and the child's play elaborates and deepens). Total immersion scores can be identified, but the score itself does not indicate that the therapist should change what they are doing.
- The scale assists therapists to modify their use of self item by item. For some items, the therapist will remain immersed in the same way for the next session; for other items, the therapist will alter their use of self.

Chapter 14

SETTING THE COMPASS: THE JOURNEY TO SELF-AWARENESS

The world of land and sea—how far is it back to me?

Beyond the theories, models, techniques, and approaches is—you. It has been said, "The longest journey is the journey inwards" (Hammarskjold, 1964, p.65). Play therapists are swept back into the world of children, and the play therapy experience has been repetitively referred to as "magical," "spiritual," and "healing." There is something that happens in play therapy that can never be written about or explained in words; yet we are all witness to it.

As therapists, we hold a belief and faith that change is possible, even when the odds seem insurmountable. Continuing to hold on to this philosophical belief is difficult at times. Skilled storytellers such as Joyce Mills (1999) provide us with the inspirational metaphor of the transformation from caterpillar to butterfly. In her eloquent way, Mills tells the story of imaginal discs, "These imaginal discs are our inner resources, interests, skills, and past learning—just lying dormant and, in a sense, just waiting to be awakened...to be released" (p.73). The caterpillar does not overtly present evidence of imaginal discs, but, "cells of change contain and protect all of the mystery that transforms the caterpillar into the butterfly" (p.73). This metaphor is meant for us just as much as for our clients.

PLAY TIME: KNOW YOURSELF AS A PLAYER

There is no way to enter into the playful world of the child without revisiting your own childhood. *You* in your adult state and *you* in your child state enter the playroom together, whether you are consciously aware of this or not. Mills and Crowley (1986) note that making contact with your childhood and your child within is essential in order to greet the child client with compassion and understanding in therapy.

We would add that compassion for your child within is critical. As your child state meets child clients, there will be an unspoken impact. How can you access *your* child part of self while remaining clear and thoughtful in your adult state? This is the challenge of the play therapist.

The Playtime Exercise (Appendix F) was developed to specifically address the therapist's past experiences of play. Having observed many students being intermittently drawn to, or repelled by, particular play objects, it became clear to us this behavior was part of a childhood response set. We began to ask ourselves: what toys did students play with as children? We purposefully asked the question, "Did you have toys as a child?" Knowing supervisees come from diverse backgrounds, it may be possible that toys were not a part of their experience as children. If toys were not a part of childhood, how will the therapist relate to the playroom? At the Rocky Mountain Play Therapy Institute™, a main focus of beginning play therapy training is to form a relationship with the *playroom*. Getting familiar with where the toys and objects are and what is attractive to the therapist is an important activity. Play therapists are encouraged to provide adjectives to describe items with which they are comfortable and uncomfortable so that they may begin to link any past experiences with the present.

During a play therapy training, a cohort was asked to go into the playroom, explore the toys in any way they would like, and just notice what they were drawn to and repelled by. Sally, a play therapy student, walked into the playroom and looked around but did not touch any of the toys. She then sat in the middle of the room and looked at objects from a distance. When everyone was finished and had joined her on the floor, Sally began to cry. She wanted to touch the toys, but she realized that in her family, toys were precious and breakable, therefore she was not allowed to play with them; rather, she had been permitted to look at them. Sally was startled that she had an overwhelmingly negative reaction to the cave that was part of the playroom, and she noted that she thought it was "scary." She wondered why any child would want to play in it. Additionally, she felt she would never play with the swords or Nerf guns, because the children in her family were never allowed to have play weapons growing up, and she feared she would not have a clue how to play with them in therapy.

In contrast to Sally, Joanne completely explored every inch of the playroom. She looked closely at things and dumped out baskets containing many of the small items. She touched most things and commented on her tactile experience throughout. Joanne noted that she loved the cave and thought it would be a great place for children to hide; for her, it engendered feelings of safety and protection. Joanne grew up with brothers and noted that she thought playing with swords, puppets, and building materials would be most comfortable for her. She claimed that she did not like dolls, dress up, or "girl stuff" such as Barbie dolls. Joanne went on to say that she did not believe Barbie dolls presented good role models for girls.

Both therapists experienced the same playroom environment completely differently. We want to know about the play experience of the therapist because of the intermittent, overwhelming nature of the stimulus pull toys and play objects elicit. This response is defined as a strong, sometimes unconscious association with past play or real-life experiences with all the accompanying feelings and physical sensations. A stimulus-pull response will also occur for child clients. Therapists must be aware of how various toys affect them and how they will manage past childhood experiences in order to avoid imposing their experiences on the child client. Play therapists can interrupt the therapy process by injecting their own likes and dislikes (verbally and non-verbally) for certain play objects or play activities.

Years ago, I did co-play therapy with a colleague. We realized soon during our work together that we approached play in extremely different ways. She was spontaneous, impulsive, excitable, liked to catch people off guard, and used every space in the room. I was quiet and more reserved, and we realized later that I overcompensated for her style by creating order and taking up less space. This led us to ask about the degree of control our caregivers exercised over our play as children and whether caregivers' degree of control affected how we approached play therapy. This turned out to be a very important question that later led me more closely to observe a supervisee's energy level, boundaries, and limit-setting ability during training. The Playtime Exercise (Appendix F) asks play therapists to rate themselves regarding the degree of control imposed on their play by caregivers. Exploring this answer helps build personal awareness and answers the question of why a supervisee may fall on a continuum of expressiveness ranging from unrestricted limits and boundaries to highly restrictive limits and boundaries. This awareness helps play therapists adjust their behavior to better accommodate the style and approach of the child client. Additionally, play therapists must often help set limits for some children, while others require permission to explore and express themselves.

Reflecting on if and how your family took time to play together is also important. If play as a family group occurred, then what kind of play was it? Some families were focused on physical activities like swimming, skating, or other outdoor sports, while others recall indoor activities such as board game nights or no family play at all. You must remember what the socioeconomic and sociocultural environment was during your childhood years because many factors contributed to the way in which your parents were *supported* in parenting you and, in fact, playing with you. How play was understood in your family has helped to formulate what you believe about play today. Every possible belief about play has been described, from play is fine when the work's all done, to play is important and essential, and play promotes mental health and personal growth. Consequently, some therapists highly value family playtime, and some do not. Every play therapist has a belief about play (outside of the play therapy room) that must be understood before entering the practice of child and Family Play Therapy.

Lenore Terr (1999) wrote about why adults need to play. About defining play, she said, "For an activity to be play, it must be lighthearted. When people are playing, there is a sense of good-humored, spirited, even sparkling pleasure. There is an infectiousness to play. It beckons us to join in" (pp.29–30). Although people refer to some activities as play, Terr would say the description cannot be considered as such if there are frightening, extremely competitive, and/or harmful outcomes to another person attributed to the activity. This is an important consideration for play therapists. Many people drawn into the field of therapy have had difficult childhoods, and therefore, as an old client once said to me in a poem, "Don't expect tales of balloons and teddy bear picnics." Sometimes, descriptions of play made by therapists do not actually meet the definition outlined above. We must be willing to fully explore our play experiences if we are to provide safe, play-based experiences for our clients.

The Playtime Exercise (Appendix F) asks several questions that lead to the interactive and relational nature of play therapists' personal experiences. It is critical to know how rigid or flexible your thoughts are on, "What does it mean to be a member of a family?", "What do you now value or devalue about certain family activities or functioning?" and, "What are your expectations of the families with whom you work?" There is a story told of Mohandas Gandhi who had dedicated his time to working in a village, serving the poor. A friend asked Gandhi about his humanitarian intentions, and Gandhi said that he was not at all intending to be purely humanitarian, and in fact, he was in the village to serve no one but himself. He said he would find his own self-realization through his aid to the village people. Gandhi's response is related to the fact that as we serve others, we are working with ourselves. This wisdom, at least partly known to us as therapists, emphasizes the need to know ourselves so that we can truly *serve* others. Otherwise, we risk imposing our values, thoughts, and need for resolution for our own childhood pain on clients.

Play therapists who are themselves parents can be particularly vulnerable when working with children, particularly abused children. We have found that therapists' vulnerability can increase if their own children are close in age to their child clients. This can be due to over-identification based on the direct pathway to empathic feeling states. The closer you are to your client circumstances, the greater the risk of countertransference. This is defined as consciously or unconsciously seeing oneself in the client, over-identifying with the client, and/or meeting one's needs through the client.

"Vicarious trauma" is a term describing the cumulative transformative effects of working with traumatized individuals (McCann and Pearlman, 1990). McCann and Pearlman studied the impact on therapists who treat adults who have survived trauma, torture, and abuse. They found that the inner experience of the helper is altered due to constant empathic engagement. Empathy requires us to engage and connect to another's pain by drawing on our own experience. Phase I play therapists are typically vulnerable to feeling overwhelmed and affected by their clients' stories because they are just beginning to understand themselves in relation to the client, and they may have fewer internalized structures to help them process what they are observing and experiencing. We want play therapists to immediately be aware of the risk they face when working with children, and we also want them to identify the dynamics related to doing this work and having their own children. For those who do not have children, we encourage them to reflect on the experience *they* had with caregivers and how they would do things differently or how they would do things similarly. The impact of play therapy work is such that it triggers responses related to the ways you have thought about yourself as a child, caregiver, and family member.

KNOW YOURSELF AND YOUR TEMPERAMENT

Know that your choices in play have also been influenced biologically. Terr (1999) has reviewed the work of several researchers who indicate that although you may have been influenced by your parents, there is genetic evidence that suggests that you also have a unique drive in the way you play and behave. Cloninger (1998) theorized that (in addition to previously identified chemicals) there are four behavioral building blocks and four interior brain chemicals that influence the inborn qualities of temperament, which in turn influence play behavior and ways of being. He identified the chemical dopamine as related to novelty-seeking traits, norepinephrine (noradrenaline) as related to harm avoidance, acetylcholine as related to reward dependence, and serotonin as related to persistence. Each child has a different level and combination of these chemicals which appears to be related (at least in part) to what the child is drawn to select for play activities.

Your identified activity level, physiological rhythm, adaptability, approach to/ avoidance of new or novel activities, emotional intensity, general mood, persistence, distractibility, and sensory threshold make up the most well-known characteristics comprising temperament (Thomas and Chess, 1977). Combined, these characteristics help to define your behavioral style or the way you *prefer* to interact with the world. Typically, a temperament scale is used at some point during therapy with children, but have you rated yourself on the nine characteristics defining temperament? Your temperament is, at least in part, genetically encoded, and therefore you must work with your style when understanding yourself as a play therapist. Phase I therapists, for instance, are particularly vulnerable to over-identifying with the style of their supervisors. It is essential for each play therapist to know themselves in terms of levels of extraversion and introversion, emotional style, and overall temperament in order to truly develop a therapy style that is unique and authentic. Graduate students are often observed trying to replicate the style of a well-known therapist by watching videos and providing demonstrations of their own rendition of "Dr. Jones's" interventions and techniques. The replication may or may not be possible based on the therapist's unique makeup. Knowing yourself relative to your temperament can lead you to greater self-awareness as a play therapist. It is then that you understand why some colleagues and clients are more difficult to relate to than others. You can be less judgmental with yourself and others and find ways to manage differences. Everyone has special talents and interests, so it is important to identify what these are for you.

Karen, a soft-spoken, cautious, internalizing play therapy trainee, was working in a dyad with her colleague Mandy, an outspoken, gregarious, self-proclaimed risk-taker. There could not have been a better combination for learning about individual differences. Karen was never going to replicate the innate style of Mandy and vice versa. Both affected the other in dramatic ways, however, and they needed to become attuned to the way each of them related to their world and the world of the other. They also needed to ask themselves how they would enter the world of play with a child who would present in these unique ways. Karen came to understand that her quiet nature triggered anxiety in Mandy in that Mandy did not get enough feedback from Karen to know if she *liked* her or wanted to be with her. Mandy learned that her outgoing way of relating took up a lot of emotional space, and Karen had trouble finding a way to enter into relationship with her. Mandy thought that Karen didn't really want to *play*, while Karen was intimidated by Mandy's desire to move from one play activity to another in a more aggressive manner. In general, Karen needed more time to "warm up" to the play environment, while Mandy "jumped right in." The therapists preferred playing with different types of toys, and when they did engage in a joint activity, they realized they liked to use the play objects differently. Each person found themselves, at various points, pivoting (or exiting) from the play. They came to realize that these responses likely took place during sessions with child clients, and they had previously attributed changes in play sequencing and process to the child only. Together, they identified what would happen in therapy if they were not acutely aware of the internal responses they each had to the other's behavioral style.

"Pacing," "timing," "mirroring," "engaging," and "reflecting" are all terms used in play therapy. Difficulty achieving these therapeutic activities increases when you are relatively unaware of how you use yourself in therapy and fail to identify the degree to which this is hardwired. It is hard work to maintain an awareness of your style in addition to all the other factors discussed in relation to knowing yourself. You will, at times, go against your natural instincts to provide a comfortable therapeutic environment for your child client. At least you can be kind to yourself when you realize adapting your style does not mean that you are losing touch with your authenticity.

KNOW YOURSELF CULTURALLY AND ETHNICALLY

Before you walk into the world of another, know the fabric of your world. It is frightening to find therapists using their own values, practices, and traditions to make recommendations for others. Do you primarily identify with your parents' heritage and cultural origin? Or do you identify with the country of your birth? O'Connor (2000) notes, "While it is important to understand the nature of a culture as a whole, the importance of assessing the degree of meaning cultural membership has for a specific client cannot be overemphasized" (p.73).

Culture includes any identifiable group that shares and passes on from one generation to another customs, beliefs, values, and language. Religion, social class, gender, sexual orientation, physical disability or ability, and age are also often specifically referred to in cultural definitions. As a competent play therapist, it is important to understand individuals and families from *their* identified ethnic and cultural reference point and to utilize the client's defining language or terminology. This aspect of information gathering is often overlooked or added as an afterthought at the end of a parent interview. There are times when working with a child's and family's cultural and ethnic identity is central to therapy. Knowing the degree to which culture is a key factor to consider is essential. Ray *et al.* (2022) link three important concepts to play therapists and the play therapy process: cultural humility, cultural comfort, and cultural opportunity. Cultural humility is an attitude of openness to "other" in relation to cultural identity, and an honoring of multiple " truths". Cultural comfort refers to a play therapist "leaning in" to conversations about a child's and family's cultural identity and the ongoing reflection on the therapist's thoughts and feelings about the conversations. Cultural opportunities are likely the least addressed in play therapy as this refers to play therapists consistently engaging in opportunities to explore a child's or their parent's cultural identities. This could occur both in and out of the metaphor of play. There is much to know about diversity and a practitioner's multicultural orientation, which is a "way of being." It is the ability to identify and respond to cultural markers, understand the self in the moment, and respond in a culturally sensitive manner to a client (Davis *et al.*, 2018). Beginning with an analysis of yourself will help you to identify individual and family practices that you have accepted as the norm. You may not have thought of this norm as specifically belonging to you and your cultural group. How does your group membership affect how accepted you feel in the larger or dominant culture? Effective therapy intervention includes an awareness of the specific characteristics that define you and your cultural group membership. Variables such as the family hierarchy, role assignment, degree of group enforcement of formal and informal rules, extended family versus nuclear family functioning, and individualism versus collectivism require consideration.

During an advanced clinical training on culture and therapy, I experienced a dominant culture bias. Most of the class identified with belonging to a nuclear family system. I was asked to role-play a traditional Jewish mother married to a white Protestant male who had suddenly lost a child. I presented my extended family story, indicating that my mother and grandmother had arrived and were now living at the house. Relatives were visiting daily, and the group was grieving together. My grandmother, the matriarch, oversaw the household. I presented as stressed and overwhelmed. My husband also presented as stressed, and he wondered if there could be a break from the relatives. Although there were rotating therapists and many "time outs" called to debrief with the therapists, each therapist directed me (as the grieving Jewish mother) to set clear boundaries and, "ask the relatives to leave in order to give me and my husband some space." Their directives around creating boundaries were well intended, but no one asked about the Jewish traditions related to grieving in general, nor did they ask about my family's practice specifically. This was an important lesson for me. Even in role, I was offended and felt misunderstood. It felt as though there was no way to inform the "helpers" that in fact they were making me feel worse and increasing the tension I felt with my husband. The couple's ethnic practices were never fully explored. Intercultural marriage, Jewish and Protestant traditions, extended versus nuclear family functioning, family hierarchy, family roles, and general practice regarding death of a family member were never explored.

To increase your cultural sensitivity, answering the following questions is recommended:

- What aspects of my personality, values, and beliefs result from my cultural group membership?
- How does my cultural group membership influence my relationships?
- How does mainstream thinking have an impact on my personal and professional development?
- How might my cultural group membership have an impact on my clients' perceptions of me?
- How might my cultural group membership have an impact on my perceptions about my clients?
- Do my clients need to maintain a level of silence in order to protect them from mainstream bias, prejudice, or persecution? Can I relate to this need?
- Do I understand cultural differences related to play?
- Do I understand cultural differences related to parenting?

O'Connor (2000) states:

Two types of knowledge make it more likely the therapist will be successful with clients from diverse backgrounds. One is knowledge about how to modify the therapeutic process to suit a given cultural group. The other is knowledge of the culture itself and the way it is manifested in the system(s) in which the client is embedded. (p.81)

Without modifications to therapy, play therapists risk imposing values and standards on children that are not consistent with those of their parents. This can place children "at risk" with their families. Since the COVID-19 pandemic, Gil and Drewes (2021) pointed out there is "a renewed focus on systemic racism, societal injustice, and the inequality" (p.2). The complexities of the internet and internet abuse worldwide are also a critical consideration when working in a multicultural orientation.

Ritter and Chang (2002), in their study, "Play Therapists' Self-perceived Multicultural Competence and Adequacy of Training," found that play therapists perceived themselves as, "somewhat competent to competent" regarding multicultural competence. Interestingly, the same therapists rated their training as below adequate. Although there was no significance between the number of years of practice and a therapist's perceived multicultural competence, there was a significant relationship between the number of multicultural courses taken and the therapist's perceived multicultural competence. Generally, play therapists rated themselves as having the highest competency in multicultural awareness and terminology, and least competency in racial identity development and multicultural knowledge. The study emphasized the need for ongoing multicultural training and questioned the discrepancy between the therapist's perception of their competency and their reports of inadequate training. Ritter and Chang (2002) indicate three dimensions of multicultural competence: knowledge, awareness, and skills. Additionally, therapists need training in racial identity development and multicultural terminology (Holcomb-McCoy and Myers, 1999).

Play therapy training in multiculturalism should also include a study of types of play including child-rearing games, songs, practices, and family roles in play activities. Play therapists are expected to provide culturally diverse interventions to clients, as is reflected in the Association for Play Therapy's *Play Therapy Best Practices: Clinical, Professional and Ethical Issues* (2022).

KNOW YOURSELF WHEN WORKING WITH PARENTS

Play therapists cannot work with children without working with parents or caregivers. The complexities of relating to parents are many and require therapists to know themselves and their own values about what it means to be parents. Depending on the work setting, you will likely be exposed to grandparents (or other family members), caregivers, career parents, foster parents, single parents, divorced parents, parents where one stays at home, adoptive parents, and stepparents. This is a diverse caregiver group, and each requires a slightly different skill set. Child and play therapists face a particularly challenging job, especially with the identifying label of "play therapist," which lends itself to defining the focus of treatment as *child* focused.

Who is your client? This must be clearly defined for the therapist and the parents. Following your professional association's ethical guidelines is only part of the process when working with parents and children. Children cannot live alone; therefore, how to view them in relation to their families, communities, and cultures is very important. The other critical elements have to do with your *interpretation* of the roles you believe parents and caregivers should have. Many adults make such statements as, "I'll never do to my children what my parents did to me." Play therapists are highly susceptible to vigilantism. Even the most well-meaning therapist is capable of trying to "save" children from their experiences or blame and discount parents. This is not to say that children do not need protection from ongoing abuse; rather, it is important to know how to engage and work with all parts of the child's system.

In our supervision experiences, we have witnessed supervisees become angered and disgusted with a variety of caregivers because of some of the following presentations:

- Caregiver lack of understanding and ability to change the view of the child.
- Foster parents who appear to be motivated by money with little regard to the child and their emotional needs.
- Adoptive parents who *return* children back to the foster care system.
- Caregivers who are more concerned with themselves than with their children.
- Dismissive or neglectful parents.
- Parents who present as punitive and/or emotionally, sexually, or physically abusive.
- Stepparents who cannot accept the dynamics of inheriting non-biological children and subsequently reject them.
- Parents who blame their children for their own conflict and chaos.
- Divorced parents who place their children in the middle of their conflict because they cannot manage their own disengagement process.
- Caregivers who place their children in adult roles and demand they care for them.
- Parents who support the other offending parent and emotionally abandon their child—as happens in some cases of intrafamilial child sexual abuse.
- Caregivers who treat one child preferentially over another.
- Non-protective parents who do not provide safe environments for their children.
- Parents who try to align you against the other parent in the hope that you will support their opinion in court.

- Generally manipulative parents who require your services to ensure they are protected and supported—at the cost of their own children's needs and concerns.
- Absent/abandoning primary caregivers (mothers or fathers).

These examples represent a snapshot of the parents you will meet when delivering play therapy services to children. What feelings are elicited in you by reading the above list?

All of us would have some reaction to each of the statements, but as a person working with children, we encourage you to know your *salient* issues. Salient issues are those experiences you have had in your life that may be closely related to one or more of the above parent descriptions. We are all generally motivated to help others and to recover what has been lost to *us* as children. In some way, we feel making things "right" for another child may interrupt a cycle within ourselves. In his wisdom, Muller (1992) writes about grandiosity and humility and says:

> We make the mistake of thinking that the problems of the entire world are on our shoulders, and it's up to us alone to solve them. Well, we don't. I must remind myself that I am part of the struggle and that is all that is really expected of me...to celebrate small victories. (p.82)

Having a supervisor who can enter into discussions about personal, salient issues in relation to working with caregivers is essential. We are not suggesting that the supervisor enter into therapy with the therapist; rather, that they acknowledge the therapist holistically in relation to therapeutic work. We cannot leave ourselves at the door when we enter the therapy environment, therefore there is no way to become aware without identifying the emotional layers that lie dormant. We do not want these emotional landmines set off by surprise, otherwise there is no way to manage the explosion.

We have learned the most about how deeply embedded the emotional layers related to caregivers are when delivering play therapy training or conducting parenting assessments and parent–child observations. It is during this training that therapists have not been able to screen their punitive, negative feelings toward the parent examples. It initially caught us off guard. Later, we realized that our own experiences of being parented affect deeply the way in which we approach our clients. Without direct discussion of these varied experiences, there is no way to help therapists put their experiences into perspective and look beside and beyond the needs of the child within.

This therapist reaction can be described as a countertransference response. The play therapist is at as high a risk of a countertransference response to the parent as the therapist would be to the child. A study by Hayes *et al.* (1991) found five qualities that help therapists manage countertransference effectively: anxiety management, conceptualizing skills, empathic ability, self-insight, and self-integration. Not surprisingly, the qualities of self-integration and self-insight were the most important factors in managing countertransference. In their comprehensive work related to linking parents to play therapy, McGuire and McGuire (2001) remind us that in therapy it is the trusting and accepting relationship with parents and caregivers that is most important. Otherwise, as we have also experienced in our practice, parents will leave therapy and take their children with them. We need to build a therapeutic relationship with parents, while at the same time keeping them involved in the play therapy process. To achieve this balance, we need to find ways to work around strong emotional reactions that lead to alienation.

MAKING MEANING

Years ago, two wise First Nations Elders visited my supervision group. They had a peaceful, kind presence, and their words never left me. They said that they could not answer why a particular child or family faced the pain, sorrow, or loss they did, but that it was our job not to protect them from their experiences but to walk right through the middle of their realities with them to the other side. I am sure these spiritual leaders would have agreed with Muller (1992) when he said:

> Thus family pain broke us open and set our hearts on a pilgrimage in search of the love and belonging, safety and abundance, joy and peace that we were missing from our childhood story. Seen through this lens, family sorrow is not only a painful wound to be endured, analyzed and treated. It may in fact become a seed that gives birth to our spiritual healing and awakening. (p.xiv)

It takes a great leap of faith for us to view pain as a gift. But to stay in this field of practice for the life of your career, making meaning of what you do and maintaining a spiritual sense of that which is unspeakable, is critical.

As a therapist, making meaning goes beyond all of what you thought you could answer biologically, psychologically, emotionally, socially, and clinically. What about the child who against all odds becomes an adjusted, loving parent or a successful, contributing member of the community? What about the child who, it was said, "could never attach to another person," but later met the right person with whom to defy this assumption? What about the things we cannot talk about such as heart, spirit, or soul? As therapists, we have an inkling of this and call it "magic" because we can provide no explanation that would satisfy the scientific world.

All therapists have at times in their practices deeply understood the power of the relationship between themselves and their clients. They have, in fact, attributed the growth and development of the client to this alone. No technique or intervention could have brought about the dramatic change. I often think about the many cups of tea I have shared with adult clients over the years, and I have attributed healing to the sanctity of this ritual. I remember each person's tea preferences. Extremely hot weather in the middle of summer never interrupted this important sharing. That is when I discovered it was more than drinking the tea that was important. I can only hypothesize about the other contributing factors, but that would likely take away from truly being present and accepting the power of the exchange and the unfolding of a unique relationship.

We are often seduced by what Muller (1992) describes as grandiosity. Grandiosity encompasses the measure of your own importance. When you begin to view your work as indispensable to the continuation of the species, you begin to hold on to what Muller describes as a deep fatigue and a private suffering that no one can touch: "Only by letting go of our inflated sense of importance may we begin to find the companionship and healing that comes with being simply human" (p.77). We have all fallen into the trap of the illusion of our own importance. Those who practice humility teach us that working hard and doing good things for others are just an ordinary practice of being human. During our work at the training institute, we have met many play therapists who have begun to view themselves as the most important person in the child's life and the only one who can truly change the child's life circumstances. The trouble with this view is that it puts an unreasonable burden on the therapist with accompanying, inevitably negative consequences. Clients are influenced by many people during the time you are working with them. Who is to say that your job wasn't simply to make it possible for them to get what they needed from someone else?

Accepting that pain, suffering, and loss are a universal experience is part of making meaning in therapy. If you reinforce the view that a client is unique because of their life experiences, you may inadvertently reinforce the belief that it is their wounds that define them and, in fact, set them apart from others. There is no service in creating a chasm so vast that there can be no way to use our special combination of wounds, gifts, and talents as a bridge to unite us with others. There is a Buddhist story of a woman who was deeply grieving over the death of her child. She refused to accept his death and took him to many helpers to get some medicine to "make him better." Finally, she visited the Buddha and asked him if he could cure her son. The Buddha responded that yes, he would help her, but first he needed her to bring him a handful of mustard seeds from a house where no one had lost a family member or friend. The woman was thankful and set out immediately. She went from house to house, only to find that each household had lost a friend, mother, father, sibling, or child. It was only after this experience of sharing in the sorrow of others that

SETTING THE COMPASS: THE JOURNEY TO SELF-AWARENESS

the woman could allow herself to grieve. She was not alone, and the universality of her loss became apparent.

Why are you a therapist? Why do you want to work with children? These are difficult questions to answer simply. After considerable reflection, some therapists decide that they do not wish to continue working in this field of practice, but they can usually say why they initially felt drawn to the work. All work that you invest time in is typically meaningful in some way. You can spot those who have lost their direction and meaning. They are typically isolated from their peers, do not seek support, present with strong negative emotions regarding their clients, and/or project their unhappiness onto systems or supervisors. Finding meaning is one thing; keeping meaning is another. It requires having a trusting relationship with your supervisor and team members. If this is not available to you, then finding a mentor is essential. How, otherwise, do you make sense out of the life circumstances of the children you counsel? You cannot do this job alone and remain grounded. We cannot be in therapeutic practice without having discussions related to faith. We need one another to cultivate our resilience as therapists.

> If we seek our safety within ourselves and not in the manipulation of environment and circumstance, then our practice becomes a pilgrimage to uncover a deep and abiding faith in our own gifts, our own strengths and our own spirit. (Muller, 1992, p.28)

So we end where we began. The magic of play therapy is found in the dance between human spirits. No one can define it; everyone can feel it. Unencumbered by the intellectualized adult world, the child takes us back to the time when we could speak using no words at all and say more than we could imagine. We are awed again through the eyes of the child. Our own child within is awakened and we remember that the inner strength, wisdom, heart, resilience, and intuition that make us human is now, and always has been, available.

KEY POINTS

- It is important to know yourself as a "player." How do you access your inner child state? It is important to stay in the play with a child client while remaining in contact with your child self.
- The Playtime Exercise (Appendix F) is a way to explore your play history. As part of this exercise the practitioner is asked to identify their play approach with their own children or a child they know well.
- Knowing your temperament style is an important consideration for all play

therapists. Identify your activity level, physiological rhythm, adaptability, approach/avoidance of new or novel activities, emotional intensity, mood, distractibility, and sensory threshold; this all helps to define the ways you prefer to interact with the world.

- Spend time identifying your cultural "fabric." Consider cultural humility, cultural comfort, and cultural opportunities in play therapy.
- Working with parents and caregivers requires special knowledge and consideration. Provide a supportive versus vigilante approach when working with parents.

All Appendices can be downloaded from https://library.jkp.com/redeem using the code RTECPZF.

Appendix A

Child Moderating Factors Scale

The Child Moderating Factors Scale is composed of scaling and evaluative questions to aid you in making clinical decisions and help you to identify the *who, what, when, why*, and *how* when using the Play Therapy Dimensions Model. Please review your child client profile and score each of the following factors on a scale of 1 to 5. Ratings should be developmentally informed, taking into consideration the child's current age. Ratings should also be based on observations and/or information obtained through consultation, not based on what you might expect to see. The scale may be filled out after the first session and/or session to session. The scale will provide the therapist with an overview of a child's presentation and identify areas of potential need or focus for therapy.

PLAY SKILLS

Complexity of play refers to flexibility and originality within various types of play, including dramatic/symbolic play, exploratory/sensorimotor play, functional/relational play, constructive play, dramatic play, and games-with-rules play.

1	2	3	4	5
Low-level play skills noted for age of child. Pre-imaginative play skills are fragmented or inconsistent. Child's play is significantly delayed or demonstrates severe trauma response such as immobilization or constriction.		Moderate play skills—some flexibility and imagination in play ability observed. Pre-imaginative play skills are present.		High play skills—creative, imaginative, complex play themes observed. Child is spontaneous and can direct the play.

236

COMMUNICATION SKILLS

Child's total communication system, including verbal content, gestures, body posture, movement, and physical proximity, as well as quality, quantity, and effectiveness of communication. Includes language comprehension, language production, and pragmatics (social use of language—e.g., turn taking).

1	2	3	4	5
Limited communication skills—verbal and/or non-verbal difficulties noted. Limited demonstration of communication and self-expression.		Moderate communication ability—age-appropriate verbal and/or non-verbal skills that support reciprocal communication and self-expression.		High ability to communicate. Demonstrates well-developed verbal, non-verbal, and social communication skills that enhance conversations and self-expression.

DEVELOPMENT

Domains to consider:

- **Cognitive**: Problem-solving ability (i.e., ability to understand causal relationships, organize and sequence thoughts and actions toward a goal, and monitor or modify strategies as needed); conceptual and procedural knowledge; attention and memory (i.e., ability to sustain concentration and/or shift focus, and ability to imitate or recall concepts or procedures associated with routines).
- **Social/emotional**: Social cognition—ability to infer social causes and understand thinking of others. Essential for development of pretend play and higher-order thinking.
- **Sensorimotor**: Child's motor skills and underlying functions that support movement, motor planning, and modulation of sensation (which impact attention, activity levels, and emotions).

1	2	3	4	5
Significant delays/weaknesses in cognitive, social/emotional, or sensorimotor development.		Moderate delays, weaknesses, or instabilities in cognitive, social/emotional, and/or sensorimotor development.		Developmentally on track or advanced in one or more areas.

EMOTIONAL EXPRESSION (RATE VERBAL/NON-VERBAL)

Verbal or non-verbal communication of feelings, reactions, needs, or intentions.

1	2	3	4	5
Limited emotional expression verbally and/or non-verbally. Flat, non-responsive presentation.		Moderate emotional expression noted verbally/non-verbally.		High ability to express emotionally. Knows feeling language and is both verbally/non-verbally expressive

SELF-REGULATION ABILITY

Emotional regulation: Ability to regulate emotional reactions to both internal and external stimuli; includes ability to self-calm or self-soothe.

Behavioral regulation: Ability to control impulses, monitor own actions/reactions, and successfully exert control in accordance with social conventions.

1	2	3	4	5
Low ability to self-regulate—emotional lability, impulsivity, emotionally reactive, or abreactive, etc. Moves quickly along stress continuum with slow recovery rate.		Moderate ability, can manage to self-regulate most of the time. Dysregulation is mostly situational. Moderate recovery rate noted.		High ability to self-regulate—even under stressful circumstances. Rapid recovery rate noted.

ATTACHMENT ORGANIZATION (EXTERNAL REPORTS)

Attachment styles are organized by primary and secondary caregivers. A secure base is provided through a relationship with one or more sensitive and responsive individuals who act as an attachment figure meeting the child's needs and to whom the child can turn to as a safe haven when distressed.

1	2	3	4	5
Significant attachment difficulties noted—may be diagnosed as disordered. Caregivers may be unavailable/unresponsive or report significant relationship difficulties related to attachment.		Some attachment difficulties reported/observed. Has at least one primary or secondary attachment figure. Some level of security with that person observed or reported.		Secure attachment relationships reported/observed. No attachment difficulties observed or reported.

RELATIONAL SKILLS

Ability to read/respond to social cues, to interpret and adaptively communicate social information, and to maintain reciprocity in a relationship to establish a cooperative and/or complementary role.

1	2	3	4	5
Reported difficulties in numerous relationships—peers, family members. Significant struggles/deficits in relational and positive engagement skills.		Generally able to establish cooperative relationships. Minor difficulties may be reported with at least one significant relationship or relationship group.		High skill level for positive engagement with others. Good relationship skills reported overall.

WORLD VIEW: COGNITIVE SCHEMA

Personal/idiosyncratic world view: a set of beliefs, values, assumptions, and expectations about the world, communicated through direct verbalizations or symbolic expressions in play. Leads to specific/unique personal narratives or actions.

1	2	3	4	5
Child has negative world view, negative sense of self and others. Does not view world as a safe or supportive place.		May not trust others, views self as having little control or as needing to take control. Ambivalent world view—may be context-specific or person-specific.		Positive world view even in the face of adversity. Reframes experiences into the positive.

DEFENSE MECHANISMS

Unconscious ego defenses that protect the self. Ranging from primitive to more developed or complex psychological strategies that can relieve distress or become constricting if overused.

1	2	3	4	5
Significant defense mechanisms observed or reported. May be signs of reactive defenses such as denial, sublimation, dissociation, aggression.		Some evidence of defense mechanisms in place—may be context-specific or person-specific. The defenses are moderately adaptive or flexible and can be eased when stress lowers.		Adaptive use of defense mechanisms. Not interfering with daily functioning.

RESILIENCE
A resilient mindset relates to the capacity to withstand or recover quickly from difficulties. Includes both process (e.g., mental, emotional, and behavioral flexibility) and outcome of successfully adapting to challenging life experiences.

1	2	3	4	5
Low resilience—fragile overall self-definition and response pattern to adversity. Slow to recover from difficult experiences and defines self negatively in the face of these experiences.		Some evidence of moderate recovery from adverse circumstances. Selective ability to regroup.		High resilience—quick recovery with positive, non-debilitating outcome.

SUPPORT NETWORK
A network or individuals, groups, or institutions (e.g., schools) that are committed to supporting or assisting the child in meeting important needs/goals.

1	2	3	4	5
Very few or no long-term supports available. Uncertain plan regarding caregiving. Isolated, lack of acceptance of need for support, few external resources.		A few reliable support services or supportive people exist. The child accepts help and care from these supports—including friends.		Significant supports exist in the child's immediate environment. Supports are viewed as acceptable and important.

WHERE DO YOU BEGIN?
Prioritize the top-three child moderating factors (as identified above). These are factors you must consider prior to deciding how to begin/continue in a therapy session. Once you have identified the factors, you will be tracking changes in these variables such as "increased level of emotional expression."

1. ....
   ....

2. ....
   ....

3. ....
   ....

HOW DIRECTIVE SHOULD I BE? WHAT LEVEL OF CONSCIOUSNESS IS APPROPRIATE FOR THIS CHILD?

The following two scales assist the therapist to rate themselves as to how to approach their child client along the two primary dimensions.

DEGREE OF DIRECTIVENESS

1	2	3	4	5
I will begin, continue, or shift to working non-directively with the client. The client should direct the play activities.		I will begin in a non-directive manner and decide when a more directive intervention would be useful—perhaps during the same session. I will likely remain "in the play" if I do introduce an activity or idea.		I will provide the client with some activities, guidelines, or direction based on the presenting need.

DEGREE OF CONSCIOUSNESS

1	2	3	4	5
I do not believe the client is ready or able to deal with the presenting problem in a highly conscious manner.		The client may gain the ability/capacity to incorporate more conscious matters over the course of therapy. Depending on the client, I may decide to raise an issue or make a more direct and conscious reflection or interpretation.		The client has the capacity to deal with the presenting problem in a direct and conscious way. I will provide activities or opportunities for this to occur.

PLAY THERAPY APPROACHES

Please check the approach(es) you believe may be most fitting to your client need and current level of experience/philosophical belief:

☐ Child-Centered Play Therapy

- ☐ Psychoanalytic Play Therapy
- ☐ Adlerian Play Therapy
- ☐ Jungian Analytical Play Therapy
- ☐ Family Play Therapy
- ☐ Ecosystemic Play Therapy
- ☐ Object Relations/Thematic Play Therapy
- ☐ Ericksonian Play Therapy
- ☐ Filial Play Therapy
- ☐ Gestalt Play Therapy
- ☐ Cognitive-Behavioral Play Therapy
- ☐ Prescriptive Play Therapy
- ☐ Relationship Play Therapy
- ☐ Group play therapy
- ☐ Phenomenological Play Therapy
- ☐ Theraplay: Attachment-Enhancing Play Therapy
- ☐ Other ....

THE FOUR QUADRANTS

I will begin to work in Quadrant ..... based on the following (choose all appropriate):

- ☐ Child's age/stage of development
- ☐ Presenting problem
- ☐ My comfort level
- ☐ Play skill of the child
- ☐ Child need and style
- ☐ External system expectation
- ☐ Stage of play therapy
- ☐ Space availability
- ☐ Other ....

THERAPEUTIC GOAL SETTING

Considering the three child moderating factors chosen above, list three broad therapeutic goals related to those factors:

1. ....
   ....
   ....

2. ………………………………………………………………………
   ………………………………………………………………………
   ………………………………………………………………………

3. ………………………………………………………………………
   ………………………………………………………………………
   ………………………………………………………………………

INDICATORS OF THERAPEUTIC GROWTH

For each broad goal, identify factors that would indicate therapeutic growth. How will you know the child is, for instance, becoming "more adjusted" or is "better able to manage uncomfortable feelings"?

Goal 1: Factors related to growth:

………………………………………………………………………………
………………………………………………………………………………
………………………………………………………………………………

Goal 2: Factors related to growth:

………………………………………………………………………………
………………………………………………………………………………
………………………………………………………………………………

Goal 3: Factors related to growth:

………………………………………………………………………………
………………………………………………………………………………
………………………………………………………………………………

Appendix B

Degree of Immersion: Therapist Use of Self Scale

Immersion relates to the ways and degree to which you use yourself during a play therapy session with a child. Using the scales below, mark on the line the degree to which you evaluate your "immersion" on the following factors.

1) VERBAL USE OF SELF
1.1) Here-and-Now Discussion (Open Discussion and Exploration QII)
During the session, what was the degree to which you were involved in verbal discussion "about" the child's life or with the child outside of the play activity?

1	2	3	4	5
	Low	**Moderate**		**High**
Almost not at all. Stayed in play activity and/or followed child's lead.		Some discussion observed, usually led by the child. Discussion included spontaneous information sharing about school, activity, a family member, etc.		Spent significant part of session outside of metaphorical play in direct discussion.

Child's Response: Please rate the effectiveness of your use of *here-and-now discussion*.

- ☐ **Low**: Play was shut down. Child's play is interrupted and/or child ignores your questions or politely engages.
- ☐ **Medium**: Child is engaged and elaborates the discussion—may lead to re-engaging in the play.
- ☐ **High**: Child actively engaged in conversation and incorporates/assimilates language or actions facilitated by therapist, indicating a greater awareness of self or circumstances.

Provide an example that supports your rating of the child's response:

....

....

....

....

1.2) Reflecting and Tracking Statements (Non-Intrusive Responding QIII, Co-Facilitation QIV)

During the session, to what degree were you using reflecting and tracking statements? Tracking refers to what the client is doing or what the play objects are doing. Reflecting statements refer to the guesses or statements about what the therapist thinks the client is experiencing, such as, "You seem really happy right now," or what the character is experiencing, "That one is very angry."

1	2	3	4	5
Low		**Moderate**		**High**
Used few or no reflecting or tracking statements.		Some use of reflecting or tracking statements. Reflections included feelings or non-verbal action in play.		Primarily used reflecting or tracking statements related to children's emotions, non-verbal behavior, play actions, verbal content play sequences, or metaphors.

Child's Response: Please rate the effectiveness of your use of *reflecting and tracking statements*.

- ☐ **Low:** Play was shut down. Child pivoted away as a defensive response and/or child annoyed by your use of tracking and reflecting statements.
- ☐ **Medium:** Child elaborates play—i.e., adds verbalizations and/or play themes/actions.
- ☐ **High:** Child incorporates/assimilates language or actions facilitated by therapist, indicating a greater awareness of self or circumstances.

Provide an example that supports your rating of the child's response:

....

....

....

....

1.3) Restating Content (Non-Intrusive Responding QIII, Co-Facilitation QIV)

During the session, to what degree did you paraphrase what the child said during the play without adding meaning or interpretation? Children often talk in therapy directly about the play media and/or through the play media.

1	2	3	4	5
Low		Moderate		High
Used few or no restatements of verbal content.		Some/moderate use of restatements or paraphrases made to child after child's comments.		Frequent use of restatements/paraphrases of child's verbalizations during the play.

Child's Response: Please rate the effectiveness of your use of *restating content*.

- ☐ **Low**: Play was shut down. Child pivoted away as a defensive response and/or child annoyed or shut down by you restating content.
- ☐ **Medium**: Child elaborates play—i.e., adds verbalizations and/or play themes/actions.
- ☐ **High**: Child's play becomes more complex as you restate content in a variety of ways. Child is engaged and demonstrates feeling a sense of being held and followed in the play.

Provide an example that supports your rating of the child's response:

....
....
....
....

1.4) Interpretations (Active Utilization QI)

During the session, to what degree did you utilize interpretive statements? Interpretations are verbal comments made by the therapist (after observing repetitive play themes and play scenarios). It is a function of utilizing play material to assist a child to develop new understanding/meaning by bringing a link between play and the child's lived life to conscious awareness. Types of interpretations may include: reflective interpretations, linking interpretations, and/or bridging interpretations.

1	2	3	4	5
Low		**Moderate**		**High**
No use of interpretations; too soon to utilize an interpretation. Tracking and restatements used. Still formulating hypotheses/ child not ready or able to work at high levels of consciousness.		Some/moderate use of interpretations. First level: reflective interpretations used. Some soft hypotheses are formed and use of characters to test hypotheses observed. Interpretations made primarily through the play metaphor.		Used one or more types of interpretive statements (reflective, linking, or bridging). A child's current or past experience embedded in play is raised to a higher degree of consciousness through the interpretation made by therapist to child.

Child's Response: Please rate the effectiveness of your use of *interpretations*.

- ☐ **Low:** Play was shut down. Child pivoted away as a defensive response and/or child annoyed by your use of interpretive statements.
- ☐ **Medium:** Child elaborates play—i.e., adds verbalizations and/or play themes/ actions based on interpretive statements either in relation to the characters in the play or about the child.
- ☐ **High:** Child incorporates/assimilates language or actions facilitated by therapist via the use of interpretive statements indicating a greater awareness of self or circumstances.

Provide an example that supports your rating of the child's response.

....
....
....
....

2) EMOTIONAL USE OF SELF
2.1) Emotionality (Non-Intrusive Responding QIII/Co-Facilitation QIV)

During the session, what was the degree of emotional intensity that you assigned to either reflective statements or by inserting an emotion or emotional meaning to a character or characters in the play metaphor? If you were in role-play, also consider your intensity of use of emotions regarding the character that was assigned the emotion(s), including tone, prosody, duration, volume, and facial expressions (therapist).

1	2	3	4	5
Low		**Moderate**		**High**
Primarily observed the child/rarely reflected emotions of the child or the characters in the play.		Some/moderate emotional intensity utilized and focused on one or more characters or emotionality mirrored the child's emotional expression.		High use of emotionality. Many reflective statements or inserted emotional comments noted (both verbal comments and vocalizations). The overall use of self was intense on a number of levels and was either therapist led or directed by the child.

Child's Response: Please rate the effectiveness of your use of *emotionality*

- ☐ **Low**: Play was shut down. Child pivoted away as a defensive response and/or child rejected the emotionality assigned to characters and/or child corrected you.
- ☐ **Medium**: Child elaborates play—i.e., adds verbalizations/emotions and/or play themes/actions.
- ☐ **High**: Child incorporates/assimilates language, actions, or feeling states facilitated by therapist, indicating a greater awareness of self, self-expression, or circumstances.

Provide an example that supports your rating of the child's response:

....

....

....

....

2.2) Emotional Self (All Quadrants)

During the session, to what degree were you personally emotionally involved? This may include your awareness of feeling a particular intense emotion, noticing yourself shut down or become numb, or temporarily losing track of following the client. You may become aware of a personal experience or be triggered by a personal memory.

1	2	3	4	5
Low		**Moderate**		**High**
I did not feel particularly emotionally involved but remained empathic and had a clear sense of neutral but present feeling.		I felt moderately emotionally involved. I noticed I had some of my own feelings related to the client material.		I felt highly emotionally involved and affected by the client's presentation or play scenario and/or child's disclosure. I felt flooded or shut down during some part of the session.

I became aware of one or more of the following emotions:

- ☐ Anger
- ☐ Sadness
- ☐ Fear
- ☐ Confusion
- ☐ Joy
- ☐ Worry
- ☐ Frustration
- ☐ Other ....

Child's Response: Please rate the effectiveness of your use of *emotional self*.

- ☐ **Low**: Play was interrupted or shut down. Child pivoted away as a defensive response. Child sensed therapist's feeling states.
- ☐ **Medium**: Child elaborates play—i.e., adds verbalizations/emotions and/or play themes/actions.
- ☐ **High**: Child incorporates/assimilates language or actions facilitated by therapist, indicating a greater awareness of self or circumstances.

Provide an example that supports your rating of the child's response:

....

....

....

3) PHYSICAL USE OF SELF
3.1) Physical Self (All Quadrants)

During the session, to what degree were you physically involved? Physical self includes: physical movement in play activities, physical proximity or touch, and level of physical energy.

1	2	3	4	5
Low		**Moderate**		**High**
Very little physical involvement. Primarily observed the child and followed child in the space. Did not engage in activities even when approached by the child.		Engaged in physical play only when directly invited to do so. Some physical play and movement with moderate contact.		Fully engaged in the play. Physical contact part of the play. High-energy output. You may consider touch therapies as high, such as Theraplay.

Child's Response: Please rate the effectiveness of your use of *physical self*.

- ☐ **Low**: Play was shut down or interrupted. Child pivoted away as a defensive response. Therapist's physical use of self was over- or underplayed.
- ☐ **Medium**: Child elaborates play—i.e., adds verbalizations/emotions and/or play themes/actions.
- ☐ **High**: Child incorporates/assimilates language or actions facilitated by therapist, indicating a greater awareness of self or circumstances. Child uses whole body and regulates physically with the therapist.

Provide an example that supports your rating of the child's response:

....

....

....

....

4) SELF-SYSTEM
4.1) Embodiment (All Quadrants)

During the session, to what degree were you aware of your self-system in the presence of the child? Self-system includes your body/energy awareness in relation to "other" (the child). It is the ability to be consciously aware of your internal state(s) of being or having interoceptive awareness.

1	2	3	4	5
Low		**Moderate**		**High**
Disembodied: I was mostly operating from a cognitive space. I was not specifically aware of my internal state(s) of being during much or most of the session. Lost in embodiment: I became unaware of my body and internal states of self and self responses during the session.		Moderate and intermittent awareness of self-system. There were points during the process when the I-self/Me-self were operating in a reflexive and conscious way. I could identify at least one point in the session where I could identify my internal experience in relation to the child.		Highly aware of my self-system. I was mostly aware of a reflexive process of the back and forth of the Me-self informing the I-self and vice versa. Body–mind awareness "online."

Child's Response: Please rate the effectiveness of your awareness of *self-system*.

- ☐ **Low**: Play was shut down. Child pivoted away as a defensive response and/or child disengaged from you or the play.
- ☐ **Medium**: Child elaborates play—i.e., adds verbalizations/emotions and/or play themes/actions and appears to connect non-verbally.
- ☐ **High**: Child appeared highly connected in a non-verbal or verbal way. You and the child may bring conscious awareness to what is being experienced internally—heartbeat, breathing, fear state, etc.—elaborating bodily awareness and connection.

Provide an example that supports your rating of the child's response:

....
....
....
....

5) CULTURAL USE OF SELF
5.1) Cultural Self (All Quadrants)

During the session, to what degree did you acknowledge yours and/or the child's verbal cultural sharing, cultural background references, and/or representations of cultural identity either in the context of the play or directly?

1	2	3	4	5
Low		**Moderate**		**High**
Primarily observed the child. Did not introject. Did not engage in cultural opportunities, or opportunities to acknowledge or engage.		Engaged directly with a cultural reference either shared by the child or demonstrated during play. Briefly commented, shared, or inquired about the child's or child's family way(s) of being, and/or shared something of self-identity/culture. Or therapist engaged with cultural reference in the metaphor of the play.		Engaged directly with child about child's culture, way of being, identity, family identity, and rituals, and/or shared something about self-identity/culture with child. An interpersonal openness and curiosity could be described.

Child's Response: Please rate the effectiveness of your awareness of *cultural use of self*.

- ☐ **Low:** Play was not elaborated. Child demonstrated a defensive response and/or child disengaged from a play theme. Child may have looked for a response or reaction from you.
- ☐ **Medium:** Child elaborates play—i.e., adds verbalizations/emotions and/or play themes/actions or engaged in a direct or indirect cultural reference(s).
- ☐ **High:** Child appeared highly connected in a non-verbal or verbal way. You and the child may bring to consciousness a cultural play theme, action, or comment. Child engages and further explores a cultural nuance.

6) TOTAL IMMERSION SCORE

☐ 9–20 Low Immersion
☐ 21–33 Moderate Immersion
☐ 34–45 High Immersion

IMMERSION SUMMARY

1) VERBAL USE OF SELF

1.1) Here-and-now discussion ☐ Decrease ☐ Increase ☐ On track

1.2) Reflecting and tracking statements ☐ Decrease ☐ Increase ☐ On track

1.3) Restating content ☐ Decrease ☐ Increase ☐ On track

1.4) Interpretations ☐ Decrease ☐ Increase ☐ On track

2) EMOTIONAL USE OF SELF

2.1) Emotionality ☐ Decrease ☐ Increase ☐ On track

2.2) Emotional self ☐ Decrease ☐ Increase ☐ On track

3) PHYSICAL USE OF SELF

3.1) Physical self ☐ Decrease ☐ Increase ☐ On track

4) SELF-SYSTEM

4.1) Embodiment ☐ Decrease ☐ Increase ☐ On track

5) CULTURAL USE OF SELF

5.1) Cultural self ☐ Decrease ☐ Increase ☐ On track

Provide a rationale that supports your rating:

....
....
....
....

SUPERVISION FORM RE: DEGREE OF IMMERSION: THERAPIST USE OF SELF SCALE

For each area of immersion that you will either increase or decrease in degree, describe ways you will change your "use of self."

1) Verbal Use of Self

1.1) Here-and-now discussion

....
....
....

1.2) Reflecting and tracking statements

....
....
....

1.3) Restating content

....
....
....

1.4) Interpretations

....
....
....

2) Emotional Use of Self

2.1) Emotionality

....
....
....

2.2) Emotional self

....
....
....

3) Physical Use of Self
3.1) Physical Self

....
....
....

4) Self-System
4.1) Embodiment

....
....
....

5) Cultural Use of Self
5.1) Cultural self

....
....
....

Follow-up supervision session date: ....

Time: ....

Supervisor: ....

Supervisee: ....

Appendix C

Tracking and Observation Form

Child's name: ....

Therapist: ....

Location: ....

Session date: ....

Session goals:

1. ....
   ....

2. ....
   ....

3. ....
   ....

Check targeted play dimension(s) for session:

- ☐ Quadrant I: *Active Utilization*
- ☐ Quadrant II: *Open Discussion and Exploration*
- ☐ Quadrant III: *Non-Intrusive Responding*
- ☐ Quadrant IV: *Co-Facilitation*
- ☐ Pre-Imaginative Play Skills: Scaffolding

Rationale: ....
....
....

1) DESCRIPTIVE ANALYSIS
Quick View (Road Map)
Use the diagram below to draw the sequence of movement that occurred across the quadrants. Where possible, note the percentage of time spent in each quadrant.

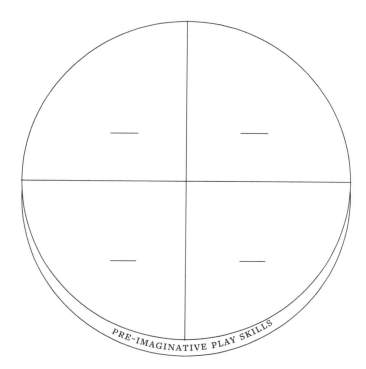

If there were therapist-led shifts creating movement between quadrants, what was the nature of the child's response?

- ☐ **Protest**: Child's actions suggested upset and protestation; they terminated play activities.
- ☐ **Ignored**: Child remained with their current play activity and passively ignored therapist's initiatives.
- ☐ **Moderate responsiveness/flexibility**: Child took time but was gradually able to shift and incorporate new play activities/themes.
- ☐ **High responsiveness/flexibility**: Child readily shifted and appeared to incorporate new play activities/themes.

Developmental Stage of Play

Check all that apply. Where possible, estimate the percentage of time spent in each stage.

- ☐ Sensory ....%
- ☐ Relational ....%
- ☐ Gross motor ....%
- ☐ Constructive ....%
- ☐ Exploratory ....%
- ☐ Cause and effect ....%
- ☐ Problem-solving ....%
- ☐ Dramatic/imaginative ....%
- ☐ Games with rules ....%

Play Processes

Briefly take note of the nature of the underlying processes that occurred.

A) *INITIATION* OF PLAY ACTIVITIES/SEQUENCES

- ☐ Child spontaneously and actively initiated play activities/sequences.
- ☐ Child occasionally initiated play activities/sequences.
- ☐ Delayed or hesitant initiation observed.
- ☐ No initiation.

B) CAPACITY TO *DIRECT AND MAINTAIN* PLAY ACTIVITIES

- ☐ **None**: Burden of play primarily rested with therapist.
- ☐ **Limited**: Child rarely directed play activities or therapist's actions.
- ☐ **Moderate**: Child frequently gave direction.
- ☐ **High**: Child issued frequent/high levels of direction.
- ☐ **Extreme**: Level of direction was so frequent that it limited/constricted most actions by therapist (verbal and non-verbal).

C) CAPACITY TO *MAINTAIN AND COMPLETE* PLAY SEQUENCES

Maintained play sequences are observed when the child represents something in a logical, complete manner. An example of an incomplete play sequence may be represented by a child repetitively playing out a bedtime scene in the dollhouse, but none of the characters are put to bed.

☐ **Low**: Child did not appear to maintain or complete any play sequence or segments; highly fragmented play.
☐ **Moderate**: Child was able to maintain or complete some play sequences or segments.
☐ **High**: Child was able to maintain and complete many play sequences; play was continuous with logical cause and effect.

D) *INHIBITIONS AND DISRUPTIONS*

Were there noteworthy instances of play that abruptly shifted, fragmented, or stopped? Did the child suddenly pivot away from the play or interrupt the play flow significantly?

☐ **None**: No inhibitions or interruptions; play scenarios appeared to flow.
☐ **Minor**: Infrequent and/or seemingly insignificant disruptions or fragmentations.
☐ **Moderate**: Play scenarios were fragmented or disrupted to the extent that it was difficult to follow the play themes.
☐ **Major/frequent**: Significant disruptions or shifts in the play field; unable to track and follow play scenarios.

If an abrupt shift or termination occurred, identify the quadrant and the surrounding context. What hypotheses do you have concerning the timing and significance of these shifts?

....
....
....
....

E) *ENDINGS*

Take note of the manner of play scenario endings. Were they gradual, such that "closure" appeared to be reached? Was there a sense of completeness or did it appear that certain feelings or impulses (e.g., anxiety, anger, fear) overwhelmed the child's capacity to regulate their experience within the context of the play?

☐ Closure appeared to be reached in a meaningful manner.
☐ Closure was realized but with tensions.
☐ Closure was only partly realized.
☐ Closure did not occur; evidence of dysregulation.

2) RELATIONAL AND AFFECTIVE MARKERS

This section is used to capture important elements of the child's relational style and observed affect. Included are important markers of the therapeutic relationship.

Emotional Range

- ☐ **Constricted**: Child displayed few emotions; affect appeared blunted; low capacity for expression.
- ☐ **Moderate expressiveness**: A moderate range of feeling states were represented in play; feeling states were congruent with play context.
- ☐ **High expressiveness**: A broad range of feeling states were represented; high levels of capacity for expression were evidenced.

Self-Regulation

- ☐ **Low**: Highly disorganized approach to planning and goal selection; poor ability to inhibit behaviors/impulses.
- ☐ **Moderate**: Somewhat disorganized and impulsive but able to initiate play activities and follow play sequences.
- ☐ **High**: Consistently exhibits ability to organize play activities/scenarios and displays tendencies to experience mastery in play.

Engagement

- ☐ **Low**: Mostly non-responsive, ignoring behavior, interpersonally disengaged.
- ☐ **Medium**: Moderately responsive, intermittently involved, and interactive.
- ☐ **High**: Highly responsive, interpersonally involved, and interactive.

3) THEMATIC REPRESENTATIONS

The following is a list of potential themes typically observed during children's play therapy sessions. While not exhaustive, it may bring forward new understandings or insights into the child's view of the world.

- ☐ Power/control
- ☐ Nurturance
- ☐ Rejection/insecurity
- ☐ Loss/abandonment
- ☐ Role reversals/identity confusion
- ☐ Loyalty/betrayal

- ☐ Secrecy/coercion
- ☐ Victimization
- ☐ Empowerment/self-esteem
- ☐ Protection
- ☐ Regression
- ☐ Confusion
- ☐ Other(s) ....

4) SUMMARY

Child's world view: Based on the information above, identify the child's view of self and others (relationships).

....
....
....
....
....

Hypotheses: Considering the child's responses and observations made about the session, are there new understandings/hypotheses that have emerged?

....
....
....
....

Plan: Consider if movement is indicated/required between quadrants. Identify strategies.

....
....
....
....

Appendix D

Parent Feedback Conceptualization Form

PRESENTING ISSUES
Describe the initial reasons for referral and any new/emerging issue:

....

....

....

....

WHAT DID YOU LEARN ABOUT THE CHILD?
Child Moderating Factors: Considerations
Integrate your knowledge of the child moderating factors into the feedback. Check the top-three areas for growth/focus in therapy. Identify your observations in the following areas:

- ☐ Play skills
- ☐ Communication skills (verbal and non-verbal)
- ☐ Development
- ☐ Emotional expression (verbal and non-verbal)
- ☐ Self-regulation
- ☐ Attachment organization
- ☐ Relational skills
- ☐ World view: cognitive schema
- ☐ Defense mechanisms
- ☐ Resilience
- ☐ Support network

Child's Presentation and Communication

Consider and comment on the following:

- ☐ Child's presentation and engagement in the process
- ☐ Play themes and shifts in themes
- ☐ Child's needs and/or view
- ☐ Child's temperament
- ☐ Child's personality
- ☐ Therapeutic growth

Point Form Summary of Findings/Observations

....

....

....

....

PARENT PRESENTATION STYLE

Parents present in a variety of ways. The following list describes a few parent styles that a play therapist might encounter. Think about your intake with the parent(s) and any ongoing contact and decide the potential style(s) of your parent(s)—check all that apply. Each parent likely presents differently.

- ☐ **Expert Parent (EP):** Knowledgeable or believes self to be knowledgeable.
- ☐ **Deflector Parent (DP):** Does not identify a particular problem—rubber fence.
- ☐ **Passive Parent (PP):** "Tell me what to do"—trouble following through.
- ☐ **Aggressive Parent (AGP):** Anger or blame focused on therapist or "other".
- ☐ **Process-Focused Parent (PFP):** Goes around and around talking about what is happening.
- ☐ **Solution-Focused Parent (SFP):** "Tell me the answer/fix the problem."
- ☐ **Collaborative Parent (CP):** "I will work with you on this and be part of process when needed."
- ☐ **Conflicted Parent (CONFP):** In conflict either with the other caregiver or inner conflict.
- ☐ **Control Parent (CONP):** Attempts to control the therapy process, or you.
- ☐ **Insensitive Parent (IP):** Does not read cues of child (or others) accurately or in a timely manner.

- ☐ **Abusive Parent (ABP):** Is a risk to the child or potential risk.
- ☐ Other(s) ....
  ....
  ....
  ....

ADJUSTING FEEDBACK TO PARENT STYLE

Modify feedback to match parent style(s). If you are meeting parents together, consider how you will manage your feedback to accommodate all parties. Identify language to use, use of self, entry points, and methods of feedback. The following list corresponds to parent presentation styles and offers a number of possible entry point choices:

- ☐ Use clear linear points and academically focused information for feedback (**EP**).
- ☐ Use visual aids to restate intake problem and pathway of treatment (**DP**).
- ☐ Connect with parent and parent issues and provide small achievable actions for parent to take (**PP**).
- ☐ Find points of intersection with parent/issues/concerns (**AGP**).
- ☐ Use process diagram and provide examples of other similar treatment situations (**PFP**).
- ☐ Use solution-focused terms (**SFP**).
- ☐ Use collaborative planning language, e.g., "we" (**CP**).
- ☐ Identify multiple issues that make things confusing and complicated (**CONFP**).
- ☐ Use language that emphasizes the role of play therapist as guide and manager of process (**COP**).
- ☐ Identify parents' early parenting experiences and personal needs first and, second, link child's cues and needs (**IP**).
- ☐ Limit feedback to surface topics only and keep all comments positive (**ABP**).
- ☐ Other(s) ....
  ....
  ....
  ....

HOW TO PROVIDE FEEDBACK

Identify key terms and methods of feedback—multi-model (e.g., use of projective activities, go to the playroom)? How will you enter the conversation? Visual presentation using drawings or metaphors/whiteboard? Provision of written materials such as info-handouts? Provision of research articles? Video feedback? Preparation of caregiver activities for home? Limit feedback due to risk?

....
....
....
....
....
....
....
....

FUTURE NEEDS/TREATMENT PLAN

Consider: Continued play therapy focusing on (area of growth) for a designated number of sessions with a review period? Home-based interventions provided by therapist to parents? Check-in sessions as follow-up, gradually tapering off? Developmentally sequenced follow-up? Referral to another service?

....
....
....
....
....
....
....
....

Appendix E

Case Conceptualization Form

RMPTI Case Conceptualization Form

CONTENT	THEMES	PROCESS	INTERVENTIONS	SELF
Cultural considerations				Cultural self
RESILIENCIES AND VULNERABILITIES	CHILD'S WORLD VIEW Child's cultural self-view	GOALS AND HYPOTHESES	SUPERVISION QUESTIONS	TRANSFERENCE AND COUNTERTRANSFERENCE

Appendix F

Playtime Exercise

Did you have toys as a child?

....

Where were they kept?

....

How accessible were they to you?

....

What kinds of toys did you have?

....

What was your favorite toy?

....

Mark on the line below the degree of control your caregivers exercised over your play.

1	2	3	4	5
Low		**Moderate**		**High**
Extremely low control, i.e., no limits or boundaries.		Moderate control.		Extremely high control, i.e., rigid limits and boundaries.

Looking back...

As a child, what was your favorite playtime activity?

....

....

Did your family take time to play together? If so, what kind of play activities did you do as a family?

....

....

Was playtime freely granted or did you have to earn the time to play? If it was earned, how?

....

....

Were you encouraged to have friends over to your house to play or did play take place mainly outside of your home?

....

....

Comparing then and now...

What are the similarities between how *your* play activities were managed as a child and how you *currently* manage play activities with the children in your care?

....

....

What is different about the way you *now* interact with children in your care?

....

....

References

Adler, A. (1937). Psychiatric aspects regarding individual and social disorganization. *American Journal of Sociology 42, 6, 773–80.*

Adler, A. (1954). *Understanding Human Nature* (W.B. Wolf, Trans.) Fawcett Premier (original work published 1927).

Adler, A. (1958). *What Life Should Mean to You.* Capricorn.

Allan, J. (1997). Jungian play psychotherapy. In K. O'Connor and L. Braverman (Eds.) *Play Therapy Theory and Practice: A Comprehensive Presentation* (pp.100–30). Wiley.

American Psychiatric Association. (2013). *Diagnostic and Statistical Manual of Mental Disorders, Fifth Edition.* Retrieved March 30 2023, from https://doi.org/10.1176/appi.books.9780890425596.

American Psychological Association. (n.d.). Circumplex. In *APA Dictionary of Psychology.* Retrieved March 30 2023, from https://dictionary.apa.org/circumplex.

Amster, F. (1982). Differential uses of play in the treatment of young children. In G. Landreth (Ed.) *Play Therapy: Dynamics of the Process of Counselling with Children* (pp.300–6). Charles C. Thomas.

Andrews, J. (1991). *The Active Self in Psychotherapy: An Integration of Therapeutic Styles.* Allyn and Bacon.

Association for Play Therapy (2022). *Play Therapy Best Practices: Clinical, Professional and Ethical Issues.* Retrieved March 30 2023, from https://cdn.ymaws.com/www.a4pt.org/resource/resmgr/publications/best_practices.pdf

Axline, V. (1947/1969/1987). *Play Therapy.* Ballantine Books.

Axline, V. (1976). Play therapy procedures and results. In C. Schafer (Ed.) *The Therapeutic Use of Child's Play* (pp.209–19). Jason Aronson.

Axline, V. (1982). Nondirective play therapy procedures and results. In G. Landreth (Ed.) *Play Therapy: Dynamics of the Process of Counselling with Children* (pp.120–9). Charles C. Thomas.

Baars, B. (2005). Consciousness is a real working theatre. In S. Blackmore (Ed.) *Conversations on Consciousness* (pp.11–23). Oxford Press.

Behan, D. (2022). Do clients train therapists to become eclectic and use the common factors? A qualitative study listening to experienced psychotherapists. *BMC Psychology 10, 183 1–13.*

Beitman, B.D. and Soth, A. (2006). Activation of self-observation: A core process among the psychotherapies. *Journal of Psychotherapy Integration 16, 4, 283–397.*

Benedict, H.E. (2003). Object relations/thematic play therapy. In C. Schaefer (Ed.) *Foundations of Play Therapy* (pp.281–305). Wiley.

Beutler, L.E. and Clarkin, J.F. (1990). *Systematic Treatment Selection: Toward Targeted Therapeutic Interventions.* Brunner/Mazel.

Beutler, L.E. and Martin, B.R. (2000). Prescribing therapeutic interventions through strategic treatment selection. *Cognitive and Behavioral Practice 7, 1, 1–17.*

Beutler, L.E., Consoli, A.J., and Williams, R.E. (1995). Integrative and eclectic therapies in practice. In B. Bongar and L.E. Beutler (Eds.) *Comprehensive Textbook of Psychotherapy: Theory and Practice* (pp.274–92). Oxford University Press.

Birch, J., Ginsburg, S., and Jablonka, E. (2020). Unlimited associative learning and the origins of consciousness: A primer and some predictions. *Biology & Philosophy 35, 56.*

Blackmore, S. (2005). Introduction. In S. Blackmore (Ed.) *Conversations on Consciousness* (pp.1–10). Oxford Press.

REFERENCES

Boyd Webb, N. (1991). Play therapy crisis intervention with children. In N. Boyd Webb (Ed.) *Play Therapy with Children in Crisis: A Casebook for Practitioners* (pp.26–44). Guilford Press.

Bratton, S. and Ray, D. (2000). What the research shows about play therapy. *International Journal of Play Therapy* 9, 1, 47–88.

Bratton, S.C., Ray, D., Rhine, T., and Jones, L. (2005). The efficacy of play therapy with children: A meta-analytic review of treatment outcomes. *Professional Psychology: Research and Practice 36*, 4, 376–390.

Bretherton, I. (1987). New perspectives on attachment relations: Security, communication, and internal working models. In J.D. Osofosky (Ed.) *Handbook of Infant Development* (2nd ed.) (pp.1061–101). Wiley.

Brewer, N.E. (1998). Computer storytelling. In H. Kaduson and C. Schaefer (Eds.) *101 Favorite Play Therapy Techniques* (pp.32–4). Jason Aronson.

Bromfield, R.N. (2003). Psychoanalytic play therapy. In C. Schaefer (Ed.) *Foundations of Play Therapy* (pp.1–13). Wiley.

Bronson, M.B. (2000). *Self-Regulation in Early Childhood: Nature and Nurture*. Guilford Press.

Burton, S. and Mitchell, P. (2003). Judging who knows best about yourself: Developmental change in citing the self across middle childhood. *Child Development 74*, 2, 426–444.

Cashdan, S. (1988). *Object Relations Therapy: Using the Relationship*. Norton.

Cates, J., Paone T., Packman, J., and Margolis, D. (2006). Effective parent consultation in play therapy. *International Journal of Play Therapy 15*, 1, 87–100.

Cattanach, A. (1992). *Play Therapy with Abused Children*. Jessica Kingsley Publishers.

Cattanach, A. (2003). *Introduction to Play Therapy*. Brunner-Routledge.

Ceballos, P.L., Post, P., and Rodriguez, M. (2021). Practicing child-centered play therapy from a multicultural and social justice framework. In E. Gill and A. Drewes (Eds.) *Cultural Issues in Play Therapy* (pp.13–31). Guilford Press.

Chalmers, D. (2005). I'm conscious: He's just a zombie. In S. Blackmore (Ed.) *Conversations on Consciousness* (pp.36–49). Oxford Press.

Chazan, S.E. (2002). *Profiles of Play: Assessing and Observing Structure and Process in Play Therapy*. Jessica Kingsley Publishers.

Chethik, M. (2000). *Techniques of Child Therapy: Psychodynamic Strategies* (2nd ed.). Guilford Press.

Chown, A. (2015). *Play Therapy in the Outdoors: Taking Play Therapy out of the Playroom and into Natural Environments*. Jessica Kingsley Publishers.

Cloninger, C.R. (1998). The genetics and psychobiology of the seven-factor model of personality. In K.R. Silk (Ed.) *The Biology of Personality Disorder*. APPI.

Cochran, J.L., Cochran, N.H., Nordling, W.J., McAdam, A., and Miller, D.T. (2010a). Monitoring two boys' processes through the stages of child-centered play therapy. *International Journal of Play Therapy 19*, 2, 106–16.

Cochran, N.H., Nordling, W.J., and Cochran, J.L. (2010b). *Child-Centered Play Therapy: A Practical Guide to Developing Therapeutic Relationships with Children*. Wiley.

Coscolla, A., Caro, I., Avila, A., Alonso, M., Rodriguez, S., and Orlinsky, D. (2006). Theoretical orientations of Spanish psychotherapists: Integration and eclecticism as modern and postmodern cultural trends. *Journal of Psychotherapy Integration 16*, 4, 398–416.

Crenshaw, D. and Mordock, J. (2005). *Handbook of Play Therapy with Aggressive Children*. Jason Aronson.

Crick, F. (2005). You're just a pack of neurons. In S. Blackmore (Ed.) *Conversations on Consciousness*. (pp.68–78). Oxford Press.

Crittenden, P.M. (1994). Peering into the black box: An exploratory treatise on the development of self in young children. In D. Chicchetti and S.L. Toth (Eds.) *Rochester Symposium on Developmental Psychopathology: Disorders and Dysfunctions of the Self* (Vol. 5, pp.79–148). University of Rochester Press.

Crouch, A. (1997). *Inside Counseling: Becoming and Being a Professional Counsellor*. Sage.

Damasio, A. (1999). *The Feeling of What Happens: Body and Emotion in the Making of Consciousness*. Harcourt

Danger, S. (2003). Adaptive doll play: Helping children cope with change. *International Journal of Play Therapy 12*, 1, 105–16.

Davies, D. (2004). *Child Development: A Practitioner's Guide*. The Guilford Press.

Davis, D.E., DeBlaere, C., Owen, J., Hooke, J.N., Rivera, D.P., Choe, E., Van Tongeren, D.R., Worthington, E.L., Jr., and Placeres, V. (2018). The multicultural orientation framework: A narrative review. *Psychotherapy 55*, 1, 89–100.

Dillman Taylor, D. and Kottman, T. (2019). Assessing the utility and fidelity of the Adlerian play therapy skills checklist using qualitative content analysis. *International Journal of Play Therapy 28*, 13–21.

Drewes, A.A. (2001). Developmental considerations in play and play therapy with traumatized children. In A.A. Drewes and C.E. Schaefer (Eds.) *School-based Play Therapy* (pp.297–314). Wiley.

Drewes, A.A. (2009). Rationale for integrating play therapy and CBT. In A.A. Drewes (Ed.) *Blending Play Therapy with Cognitive Behavioral Therapy: Evidence-Based and Other Effective Treatments and Techniques* (pp.1–2). Wiley.

Drewes, A. (2011). Integrating play therapy theories into practice. In A. Drewes, S. Bratton, and C. Schaefer (Eds.) *Integrative Play Therapy* (pp.21–34). Wiley.

Drewes, A. A. and Schaefer, C. E. (2015). The therapeutic powers of play. In K. O'Connor, C.E. Schaefer, and L.D. Braverman (Eds.) *Handbook of Play Therapy* (2nd ed.) (pp.35–60). Wiley.

Ellenberger, H.F. (1970). *The Discovery of the Unconscious: The History and Evolution of Dynamic Psychiatry.* Basic Books.

Elstein, A.S. (1988). Cognitive processes in clinical inference and decision-making. In D.C. Turk and P. Salvovey (Eds.) *Reasoning, Inference, and Judgement in Clinical Psychology* (pp.17–50). Free Press.

Erickson, M. (1966/1980) The interpersonal hypnotic technique for symptom correction and pain control. In E. Rossi (Ed.) *The Collected Papers of Milton H. Erickson in Hypnosis: Innovative Hypnotherapy* (vol. 4) (pp.262–78). Irvington Publishers.

Erickson, M. and Rossi, L. (1980). Two-level communication and the microdynamics of trance and suggestion. In E. Rossi (Ed.) *The Collected Papers of Milton H. Erickson in Hypnosis I: The Nature of Hypnosis and Suggestion* (pp.447–8). Irvington Publishers.

Erwin, E. (1997). *Philosophy and Psychotherapy.* Sage.

Fall, M. (2001). An integrative play therapy approach to working with children. In A.A. Drewes, L.J. Carey, and C.E. Schaefer (Eds.) *School-Based Play Therapy* (pp.315–28). Wiley.

Fonagy, P. and Target, M. (1997). Attachment and reflective function: Their role in self-organization. *Development and Psychopathology 9*, 4, 679–700.

Frances, A., Clarkin, J., and Perry, S. (1984). *Differential Therapeutics in Psychiatry.* Brunner/Mazel.

Frank, L. (1982). Play in personality development. In G. Landreth (Ed.) *Play Therapy: Dynamics of the Process of Counselling with Children* (pp.19–31). Charles C. Thomas.

Garber, J., Braafladt, N., and Zeman, J. (1991). The regulation of sad affect: An information processing perspective. In J. Garber and K. Dodge (Eds.) *The Development of Emotion Regulation and Dysregulation.* Cambridge University Press.

Gardner, K. and Yasenik, L. (2008). When approaches collide: A decision-making model for play therapists. In A. Drewes and J.A. Mullen (Eds.) *Supervision Can be Playful: Techniques for Child and Play Therapist Supervisors* (pp.39–68). Jason Aronson.

Gardner, R. (1971). *Therapeutic Communication with Children: The Mutual Storytelling Technique.* Jason Aronson.

Garfield, S.L. (1994). Eclecticism and integration in psychotherapy: Developments and issues. *Clinical Psychology: Science and Practice 1*, 2, 123–37.

Gaskill, R. and Perry, B.D. (2014). The neurobiological power of play: Using the Neurosequential Model of Therapeutics to guide play in the healing process. In C. Malchiodi and D.A. Crenshaw (Eds.) *Play and Creative Arts Therapy for Attachment Trauma* (pp.178–94). Guilford Press.

Gergen, K. (1996). The healthy, happy human being wears many masks. In W.T. Anderson (Ed.) *The Fontana Postmodernism Reader.* Fontana Press.

Gergen, K. (2009). *Relational Being: Beyond Self and Community.* Oxford.

Gigerenzer, G. (2001). The adaptive toolbox. In G. Gigerenzer and R. Selten (Eds.) *Bounded Rationality: The Adaptive Toolbox* (pp.37–50). MIT Press.

Gil, E. (1991). *The Healing Power of Play: Working with Abused Children.* Guilford Press.

Gil, E. (2006). *Helping Abused and Traumatized Children: Integrating Directive and Nondirective Approaches.* Guilford Press.

Gil, E. (2019). A senior therapist's observations and concerns. *Play Therapy*, September, 50–51.

Gil, E. and Drewes, A. (Eds.) (2021). *Cultural Issues in Play Therapy.* Guilford Press.

REFERENCES

Gilligan, S. (1987). *Therapeutic Trances.* Brunner/Mazel.

Ginsberg, B. (2011). Congruence in non-directive play and filial therapy: Response to Ryan and Courtney. *International Journal of Play Therapy 20*, 3, 109–23.

Ginsburg, S. and Jablonka, E. (2019). *The Evolution of the Sensitive Soul: Learning and the Origins of Consciousness.* MIT Press.

Glass, C.R., Victor, B.J., and Arnkoff, D.B. (1993). Empirical research on integrative and eclectic psychotherapies. In G. Stricker and J. Gold (Eds.) *Comprehensive Handbook of Psychotherapy Integration* (pp.9–25). Plenum Press.

Goldfried, M. (1998). A comment on psychotherapy integration in the treatment of children. *Journal of Clinical Child Psychology 27*, 1, 49–53.

Goodyear-Brown, P. (2010). *Play Therapy with Traumatized Children: A Prescriptive Approach.* Wiley.

Goodyear-Brown, P. (2019). *Trauma and Play Therapy: Helping Children Heal.* Routledge/Taylor & Francis Group.

Goodyear-Brown, P. (2021). *Parents as Partners in Child Therapy: A Clinician's Guide.* Guilford Press.

Green, E. (2009). Jungian analytical play therapy. In K. O'Connor and L.D. Braverman (Eds.) *Play Therapy Theory and Practice: Comparative Theories and Techniques* (2nd ed.) (pp.83–125). Wiley.

Greenspan, S.I. (1997). *The Growth of the Mind and the Endangered Origins of Intelligence.* Perseus Books.

Grencavage, L.M. and Norcross, J.C. (1990). Where are the commonalities among the therapeutic common factors? *Professional Psychology: Research and Practice 21*, 5, 372–78.

Guerney, L. (1983). Child-centered (non-directive) play therapy. In C.E. Schaefer and K.J. O'Connor (Eds.) *Handbook of Play Therapy* (pp.21–64). Wiley.

Guerney, L. (2001). Child-centered play therapy. *International Journal of Play Therapy 10*, 2, 13–31.

Guerney, L. (2010). Foreword. In N.H. Cochran, W.J. Nordling, and J.L. Cochran (Eds.) *Child-Centered Play Therapy: A Practical Guide to Developing Therapeutic Relationships with Children.* Wiley.

Guerney, L. and Ryan, V. (2013). *Group Filial Therapy: The Complete Guide to Teaching Parents to Play Therapeutically with Their Children.* Jessica Kingsley Publishers.

Hambridge, G. (1955). Structured play therapy. *American Journal of Orthopsychiatry 25*, 4, 601–17.

Hammarskjold, D. (1964). *Markings.* Faber and Faber.

Harris, P.L. (1989). *Children and Emotion.* Basil Blackwell.

Harter, S. (1999). *The Construction of the Self: A Developmental Perspective.* Guilford Press.

Harter, S. (2012). *The Construction of the Self: Developmental and Sociocultural Foundations* (2nd ed.). Guilford Press.

Harter, S. (2015). *The Construction of the Self: Developmental and Sociocultural Foundations.* Guilford Press.

Hayes, J.A., Gelso, C.J., Van Wagoner, S.L., and Diemer, R.A. (1991). Managing countertransference: What the experts think. *Psychological Reports 69*, 1, 138–48.

Hill, C. (2005). Therapist techniques, client involvement, and the therapeutic relationship: Inextricably intertwined in the therapy process. *Psychotherapy: Theory, Research, Practice, Training 42*, 4, 431–442

Holcomb-McCoy, C. and Myers, J.E. (1999). Multicultural competence and counselor training: A national survey. *Journal of Counseling and Development 77*, 3, 294–302.

Irwin, E. (1983). The diagnostic and therapeutic use of pretend play. In C. Schaefer and K. O'Connor (Eds.) *Handbook of Play Therapy* (pp.148–66). Wiley.

Jennings, S. (1995). Embodiment-projection-role: A developmental model for the play therapy method. In C. Schaefer, J. McCormick, and A.J. Ohnogi (Eds.) *International Handbook of Play Therapy: Advances in Assessment, Theory* (pp.65–76). Jason Aronson.

Jernberg, A. (1979). *Theraplay.* Jossey-Bass.

Jones, K.S., Casado, M., and Robinson, E.H. (2003). Structured play therapy: A model for choosing topics and activities. *International Journal of Play Therapy 12*, 1, 31–47.

Kaduson, H. and Schaefer, C. (Eds.) (2003). *101 Favorite Play Therapy Techniques* (Vol.III). Jason Aronson.

Karasu, T.B. (1996). *Deconstruction of Psychotherapy.* Jason Aronson.

Kenny, M.C. and Winick, C.B. (2000). An integrative approach to play therapy with an autistic girl. *International Journal of Play Therapy 9*, 1, 11–33.

Kiesler, D.J. (1966). Some myths of psychotherapy research and the search for a paradigm. *Psychological Bulletin 65*, 2, 110–36.

Knell, S.M. (1995). *Cognitive-Behavioral Play Therapy.* Jason Aronson

Knell, S.M. (1999). Cognitive-behavioral play therapy. In K. O'Connor and C. Schaefer (Eds.) *Play Therapy Theory and Practice: A Comparative Presentation* (pp.79–99). Wiley.

Knell, S.M. (2003). Cognitive-behavioral play therapy. In C.E. Schaefer (Ed.) *Foundations of Play Therapy* (pp.175–91). Wiley.

Knell, S. M. (2015). Cognitive-behavioral play therapy. In K. O'Connor, C.E. Schaefer, and L.D. Braverman (Eds.) *Handbook of Play Therapy* (2nd ed.) (pp.119–33). Wiley.

Kottman, T. (2003a). Adlerian Play Therapy. In C. Schaefer (Ed.) *Foundations of Play Therapy* (pp.55–75). Wiley.

Kottman, T. (2003b). *Partners in Play: An Adlerian Approach to Play Therapy* (2nd ed.). American Counselling Association.

Kottman, T. (2011). *Play Therapy Basics and Beyond* (2nd ed.). American Counseling Association.

Kottman, T. (2019). Just like a kid! Adlerian play therapy. In L. Yasenik and K. Gardner (Eds.) *Turning Points in Play Therapy and the Emergence of Self: Applications of the Play Therapy Dimensions Model* (pp.59–82). Jessica Kingsley Publishers.

Kottman, T. (2020). Adlerian Play Therapy: A Personal and Professional Journey. *Journal of Individual Psychology 76*, 2, 162–175.

Kottman, T. and Meany-Walen, K. (2016). Partners in play: An Adlerian approach to play therapy (3rd ed.). American Counseling Association.

LaBauve, B.J., Watts, R.E., and Kottman, T. (2001). Approaches to play therapy: A tabular overview. *TCA Journal 29*, 1, 104–13.

Landreth, G. (2001). Facilitative dimensions of play in the play therapy process. In G. Landreth (Ed.) *Innovations in Play Therapy: Issues, Process, and Special Populations* (pp.3–22). Brunner Routledge.

Landreth, G. (2002). *The Art of the Relationship* (2nd ed.). Brunner/Routledge.

Landreth, G.L. (2012). *Play Therapy: The Art of the Relationship* (3rd ed.). Routledge.

Landreth, G. and Sweeney, D. (1997). Child-centered play therapy. In K.J. O'Connor and L.M. Braverman (Eds.) *Play Therapy Theory and Practice* (pp.11–45). Wiley.

Landreth, G. and Sweeney, D. (1999). The freedom to be: Child-centered group play therapy. In D. Sweeney and L. Homeyer (Eds.) *Handbook of Group Play Therapy* (pp.39–64). Jossey-Bass.

Lazarus, A.A. (1976). *Multimodal Behavior Therapy*. Springer.

LeBlanc, M. and Ritchie, M. (1999). Predictors of play therapy outcomes. *International Journal of Play Therapy 8*, 2, 19–34.

Linder, T. (2008). *Transdisciplinary Play-Based Assessment* (2nd ed.) (TPBA2). Paul H. Brooks Publishing.

Lowenstein, L. (1999). *Creative Interventions for Troubled Children and Youth*. Champion Press.

McCann, I.L. and Pearlman, L.A. (1990). Vicarious traumatization: A framework for understanding the psychological effects of working with victims. *Journal of Traumatic Stress 3*, 1, 131–49.

McGuire, D.K. and McGuire, D.E. (2001). *Linking Parents to Play Therapy: A Practical Guide with Applications, Interventions, and Case Studies*. Brunner-Routledge.

McInnes, K. (2019). Being a playful therapist. In P. Ayling, H. Armstrong, and L. Gordon Clark (Eds.) *Becoming a Play Therapist: Play Therapy in Practice* (pp.98–109). Routledge.

Malchiodi, C. (Ed.) (2008). *Creative Interventions with Traumatized Children*. Guilford.

Mann, D.W. (1994). *A Simple Theory of the Self*. Norton.

Marmar, C.R. (1990). Psychotherapy process research: Progress, dilemmas, and future directions. *Journal of Consulting and Clinical Psychology 58*, 3, 265–72.

Maslow, A.H. (1982). Abstracting and theorizing. In M.R. Goldfried (Ed.) *Converging Themes in Psychotherapy: Trends in Psychodynamic, Humanistic and Behavioral Practice*. Springer.

Miller, S.D., Duncan, B.L., and Hubble, M.A. (2005). Outcome informed clinical work. In J.C. Norcross and M.R. Goldfried (Eds.) *Handbook of Psychotherapy Integration* (2nd ed.) (pp.84–102). Oxford University Press.

Mills, J.C. (1989). No more monsters and meanies: Multisensory metaphors for helping children with fears and depression. In M.D. Yapko (Ed.) *Brief Therapy Approaches to Treating Anxiety and Depression* (pp.150–83). Brunner/Mazel.

Mills, J. (1999). *Reconnecting to the Magic of Life*. Imaginal Press.

Mills, J. (2001). Ericksonian play therapy: The spirit of healing with children and adolescents. In B.B. Geary and J. Zeig (Eds.) *The Handbook of Ericksonian Psychotherapy* (pp.506–21). Milton H. Erickson Foundation Press.

REFERENCES

Mills, J.C. (2015). StoryPlay®: A narrative play therapy approach in play therapy. In D. Crenshaw and A. Stewart (Eds.) *Play Therapy: A Comprehensive Guide to Theory and Practice* (pp.171–85). Guilford Press.

Mills, J. and Crowley, R. (1986). *Therapeutic Metaphors for Children and the Child Within*. Brunner/Mazel.

Mills, J. and Crowley, R. (1988). A multidimensional approach to the utilization of therapeutic metaphors for children and adolescents. In J.K. Zeig and S.R. Lankton (Eds.) *Developing Ericksonian Therapy: State of the Art* (pp.302–23). Brunner/Mazel.

Mills, J.C. and Crowley, R.J. (2014). *Therapeutic Metaphors for Children and the Child Within* (2nd ed.). Routledge.

Milton, M. (2001). Supervision: Researching therapeutic practice. In M. Carroll and M. Tholstrup (Eds.) *Integrative Approaches to Supervision* (pp.183–91). Jessica Kingsley Publishers.

Mook, B. (2003). Phenomenological play therapy. In C. Schaefer (Ed.) *Foundations of Play Therapy* (pp.260–80). Wiley.

Moore, B. and Chow, R. (2022). Polyvagal theory in the playroom. *Play Therapy Magazine 17*, 3, 20–23.

Moustakas, C. (1955). Emotional adjustment and the play therapy process. *Journal of Genetic Psychology 86*, 79–99.

Moustakas, C. (1982). Emotional adjustment and the play therapy process. In G. Landreth (Ed.) *Play Therapy: Dynamics of the Process of Counselling with Children* (pp.217–30). Charles C. Thomas.

Moustakas, C. (1997). *Relationship Play Therapy*. Aronson.

Muller, W. (1992). *Legacy of the Heart: The Spiritual Advantages to a Painful Childhood*. Fireside.

Munns, E. (2000). Traditional family and group Theraplay. In E. Munns (Ed.) *Theraplay: Innovations in Attachment-Enhancing Play Therapy* (pp.9–26). Aronson.

Nalavany, B., Gomory, T., Ryan, S., and Lacasse, J. (2004). Mapping the characteristics of a "good" play therapist. *International Journal of Play Therapy 14*, 1, 27–50.

Norcross, J.C. (1987). *Casebook of Eclectic Psychotherapy*. Brunner/Mazel.

Norcross, J.C. (2005). A primer on psychotherapy integration. In J.C. Norcross and M.R. Goldfried (Eds.) *Handbook of Psychotherapy Integration* (2nd ed.) (pp.10–23) Oxford University Press.

Norcross, J.C. and Newman, C.F. (1992). Psychotherapy integration: Setting the context. In J.C. Norcross and M.R. Goldfried (Eds.) *Handbook of Psychotherapy Integration* (pp.3–45). Basic Books.

Norton, C.C. and Norton, B.E. (2006). Experiential Play Therapy. In C.E. Schaefer and H.G. Kaduson (Eds.) *Contemporary Play Therapy: Theory, Research, and Practice* (pp.28–54). Guilford Press.

Oaklander, V. (2003). Gestalt play therapy. In C.E. Schaefer (Ed.) *Foundations of Play Therapy* (pp.143–55). Wiley.

O'Connor, K.J. (1997). Ecosystemic play therapy. In K.J. O'Connor and L. Braverman (Eds.) *Play Therapy Theory and Practice: A Comparative Presentation* (pp.234–84). Wiley.

O'Connor, K.J. (2000). *The Play Therapy Primer* (2nd ed.). Wiley.

O'Connor, K. (2001). Ecosystemic play therapy. *International Journal of Play Therapy 10*, 2, 33–44.

O'Connor, K. (2002). The value and use of interpretation in play therapy. *Professional Psychology: Research and Practice 33*, 6, 523–8.

O'Connor, K.J. and Braverman, L.D. (Eds.) (2009). *Play Therapy Theory and Practice: Comparing Theories and Techniques* (2nd ed.). Wiley.

O'Connor, K. and New, D. (2003). Ecosystemic play therapy. In C. Schaefer (Ed.) *Foundations of Play Therapy* (pp.243–58). Wiley.

Pankseep, J. (1998). *Affective Neuroscience: The Foundations of Human and Animal Emotions*. Oxford University Press.

Parson, J.A. (2021). Children speak play: Landscaping the therapeutic powers of play. In E. Prendiville and J.A. Parson (Eds.) (2021). *Clinical Applications of the Therapeutic Powers of Play: Case Studies in Child and Adolescent Psychotherapy* (pp.1–11). Routledge.

Peavy, R.V. (1996). Counselling as a culture of healing. *British Journal of Guidance and Counselling 24*, 1, 141–50.

Peery, C. (2003). Jungian analytical play therapy. In C.E. Schaefer (Ed.) *Foundations of Play Therapy* (pp.14–54). Wiley.

Perls, F.S., Hefferline, R.E., and Goodman, P. (1951). *Gestalt Therapy: Excitement and Growth in the Human Personality*. Dell.

Perry, B.D. (2009). Examining child maltreatment through a neurodevelopmental lens: Clinical applications of the neurosequential model of therapeutics. *Journal of Loss and Trauma 14*, 4, 240–255.

Phillips, R. and Landreth, G. (1995). Play therapists on play therapy: A report of methods, demographics and professional/practice issues. *International Journal of Play Therapy 4*, 1, 1–26.

Piaget, J. (1977). *The Language and Thought of the Child*. Routledge, and Kegan Paul.

Prendiville, E. and Parson, J.A. (Eds). (2021). *Clinical Applications of the Therapeutic Powers of Play: Case Studies in Child and Adolescent Psychotherapy*. Routledge.

Prochaska, J.O. and Norcross, J.C. (2003). *Systems of Psychotherapy: A Transtheoretical Analysis* (5th ed.). Brooks/Cole.

Pynoos, R. and Eth, S. (1986). Witness to violence: The child interview. *Journal of the American Academy of Child Psychiatry 25*, 3, 306–19.

Ray, D. (2004). Supervision of basic and advanced skills in play therapy. *Journal of Professional Counseling: Practice, Theory and Research 32*, 2, 28–41.

Ray, D.C. (2011). *Advanced Play Therapy: Essential Conditions, Knowledge, and Skills for Child Practice*. Routledge.

Ray, D.C., Ogawa, Y., and Cheng, Y.J. (Eds.) (2022). *Multicultural Play Therapy: Making the Most of Cultural Opportunities with Children*. Routledge.

Repp, M. (1998). The Guess My World story game. In H. Kaduson and C. Schaefer (Eds.) *101 Favorite Play Therapy Techniques* (pp.44–5). Jason Aronson.

Ritter, K. and Chang, C. (2002). Play therapists' self-perceived multicultural competence and adequacy of training. *International Journal of Play Therapy 11*, 1, 103–13.

Rogers, C. (1951). *Client-Centered Therapy*. Houghton Mifflin.

Rogers, C.R. (1957). The necessary and sufficient conditions of therapeutic personality change. *Journal of Consulting Psychology 21*, 2, 95–103.

Rubin, L. (Ed.) (2008). *Popular Culture in Counseling, Psychotherapy, and Play-Based Interventions*. Springer.

Russ, S.W. (2004). *Play in Child Development and Psychotherapy: Toward Empirically Supported Practice*. Lawrence Erlbaum Associates.

Ryan, V. and Courtney, A. (2009). Therapists' use of congruence in non-directive play therapy. *International Journal of Play Therapy 18*, 2, 114–28.

Ryan, V. and Wilson, K. (2000). *Case Studies in Non-Directive Play Therapy* (2nd ed.). Jessica Kingsley Publishers.

Scaturo, D.J. (2012). Supervising integrative psychotherapy in the 21st century: Pressing needs, impressing possibilities. *Journal of Contemporary Psychotherapy 42*, 183–192.

Schaefer, C. (Ed.) (1993). *The Therapeutic Powers of Play*. Jason Aronson.

Schaefer, C.E. (1999). Curative factors in play therapy. *Journal for the Professional Counselor 14*, 1, 7–16.

Schaefer, C.E. (2003). Prescriptive play therapy. In C.E. Schaefer (Ed.) *Foundations of Play Therapy* (pp.306–20). Wiley.

Schaefer, C. and Cangelosi, D. (2002). *Play Therapy Techniques* (2nd ed.). Jason Aronson.

Schaefer, C.E. and Drewes, A.A. (2009). The therapeutic powers of play. In A.A. Drewes (Ed.) *Blending Play Therapy with Cognitive Behavioral Therapy: Evidence-Based and Other Effective Treatments and Techniques* (pp.3–15). Wiley.

Schaefer, C.E. and Drewes, A.A. (2014). *The Therapeutic Powers of Play: 20 Core Agents of Change*. (2nd ed.). Wiley.

Schaefer, C.E. and Drewes, A.A. (2015). Prescriptive play therapy. In K. O'Connor, C. Schaefer, and L. Braverman (Eds.) *Handbook of Play Therapy* (2nd ed.) (pp.227–40). Wiley.

Schottenbauer, M., Glass, C.R., and Arnkoff, D.B. (2007). Decision-making and psychotherapy integration: Theoretical considerations, preliminary data, and implications for future research. *Journal of Psychotherapy Integration 17*, 3, 225–50.

Seymour, J.W. (2011). History of psychotherapy integration and related research. In A. Drewes, S. Bratton, and C. Schaefer (Eds.) *Integrative Play Therapy* (pp.3–20). Wiley.

Shelby, J.S. (1997). Rubble, disruption, and tears: Helping young survivors of natural disaster. In H. Kaduson, D.M. Cangelosi, and C. Schaefer (Eds.) *The Playing Cure: Individualized Play Therapy for Specific Childhood Problems*. Jason Aronson.

Siegel, D. and Hartzell, M. (2003). *Parenting from the Inside Out: A Deeper Self-Understanding Can Help You Raise Children Who Thrive*. Penguin Putnam.

Smith, D. (1982). Trends in counseling and psychotherapy. *American Psychologist 37*, 7, 802–809.

REFERENCES

Sperry, L. and Sperry, J. (2020). *Case Conceptualization: Mastering This Competency with Ease and Confidence* (2nd ed.). Routledge Taylor & Francis Group.

Stagnitti, K. (2021). *Learn to Play Therapy: Principles, Process and Practical Activities* (2nd ed.). Learn to Play.

Stagnitti, K., Wadley, C., and Sheppard, L. (2012). Impact of the Learn to Play program on play, social competence and language for children aged 5–8 years who attend a specialist school. *Australian Occupational Therapy Journal 59*, 4, 302–311.

Stern, D. (1995). *The Interpersonal World of the Infant.* Basic Books.

Stoltenberg, C., McNeill, B., and Delworth, U. (1998). *IDM Supervision: An Integrated Developmental Model for Supervising Counselors and Therapists.* Jossey-Bass Inc.

Street, L.L., Niederehe, G., and Lebowitz, B.D. (2000). Toward greater public health relevance for psychotherapeutic intervention research: An NIMH workshop report. *Clinical Psychology: Science and Practice 17*, 2, 127–37.

Stricker, G. (2010). A second look at psychotherapy integration. *Journal of Psychotherapy Integration 20*, 4, 379–405.

Sweeney, D.S. and Landreth, G. (2003). Child centered play therapy. In C.E. Schaefer (Ed.) *Foundations of Play Therapy* (pp.76–98). Wiley.

Sweeney, D. and Landreth, G. (2009). Child-centered play therapy. In K.J. O'Connor and L.D. Braverman (Eds.) *Play Therapy Theory and Practice: Comparing Theories and Techniques* (2nd ed) (pp.123–62). Wiley.

Terr, L. (1983). Time sense following psychic trauma: A clinical study of ten adults and twenty children. *American Journal of Orthopsychiatry 53*, 2, 244–61.

Terr, L. (1994). *Unchained Memories: True Stories of Traumatic Memories, Lost and Found.* Basic Books.

Terr, L. (1999). *Beyond Love and Work.* Scribner.

Tholstrup, M.C. (2001). Supervision in and for organizations. In M. Carroll and M.C. Thorstrup (Eds.) *Integrative Approaches to Supervision* (pp.50–64). Jessica Kingsley Publishers.

Thomas, A. and Chess, S. (1977). *Temperament and Development.* Brunner/Mazel.

Turner, R., Ray, D., Schoeneberg, C., and Lin. Y. (2020). Establishing play therapy competencies: A Delphi study. *International Journal of Play Therapy 29*, 4, 177–190.

VanFleet, R. (2005). Filial therapy. In K.J. O'Connor and L.D. Braverman (Eds.) *Play Therapy Theory and Practice: Comparative Theories and Techniques* (2nd ed.) (pp.163–202). Wiley.

VanFleet, R., Sywulak, A., and Sniscak, C. (2010). *Child-Centered Play Therapy.* Guilford.

Wachtel, P.L. (1977). *Psychoanalysis and Behaviour Therapy: Towards an Integration.* Basic Books.

Weir, K.N. (2008). Using integrative play therapy with adoptive families to treat Reactive Attachment Disorder: A case study. *Journal of Family Psychotherapy 18*, 4, 1–16.

White, J., Draper, K., and Pittard Jones, N. (2001). Play behaviors of physically abused children. In G. Landreth (Ed.) *Innovations in Play Therapy: Issues, Process, and Special Populations* (pp.99–118). Brunner Routledge.

Wilson, K. and Ryan, V. (2005). *Play Therapy: A Nondirective Approach for Children and Adolescents* (2nd ed.). Elsevier.

Wilson, K., Kendrick, P., and Ryan, V. (1992). *Play Therapy: A Non-directive Approach for Children and Adolescents.* Ballerie Tindall.

Winnicott, D.W. (1965). *The Family and Individual Development.* Tavistock.

Winnicott, D. (1971). *Therapeutic Communication in Child Psychiatry.* Grune and Stratton.

Wosket, V. (1999). *The Therapeutic Use of Self: Counselling Practice, Research and Supervision.* Routledge.

Yasenik, L. and Gardner, K. (2004). *Play Therapy Dimensions Model: A Decision-Making Guide for Integrative Play Therapists* (1st ed.). Rocky Mountain Play Therapy Institute.

Yasenik, L. and Gardner, K. (2012). *Play Therapy Dimensions Model: A Decision-Making Guide for Integrative Play Therapists* (2nd ed.). Jessica Kingsley Publishers.

Yasenik, L. and Gardner, K. (2014). The consciousness dimension in play therapy: Sharpening the play therapist's focus and skills. In E. Prendiville and J. Howard (Eds.) *Play Therapy Today* (pp.29–46). Routledge.

Yasenik, L. and Gardner, K. (2019). Turning points and understanding the development of self through play therapy. In L. Yasenik and K. Gardner (Eds.) *Turning Points in Play Therapy and the Emergence of Self: Applications of the Play Therapy Dimensions Model* (pp.15–42). Jessica Kingsley Publishers.

Yasenik, L. and Gardner, K. (2020). Therapeutic use of self and the Play Therapy Dimensions Model. In S. Jennings and C. Holmwood (Eds.) *International Handbook of Play, Therapeutic Play and Play Therapy* (pp.341–59). Routledge.

Yasenik L. and Graham, J. (2016). The continuum of including children in ADR process: A child-centred continuum model. *Family Court Review 54*, 2 186–202.

Zuber, I. (2000). Patients' own problem formulation and recommendations for psychotherapy. *Journal of Psychotherapy Integration 10*, 4, 403–14.

About the Authors

Lorri Yasenik and Ken Gardner are the co-founders of the Rocky Mountain Play Therapy Institute (RMPTI) in Calgary, Alberta, Canada. RMPTI provides comprehensive approved play therapy training to those who want to be certified or registered as play therapists. Lorri and Ken are dedicated to the ongoing study and instruction of play therapy.

LORRI A. YASENIK, PhD, CPT-S, RPT-S

Lorri Yasenik, PhD, RPT-S, CPT-S, is the Director of the Rocky Mountain Play Therapy Institute in Calgary, Alberta, Canada and the Co-Director of the International Centre for Children and Family Law (ICCFL) in Australia/Canada. Lorri is a Registered and Certified Supervisor of Child Psychotherapy and Play Therapy and delivers approved training programs nationally and internationally in the areas of child and play therapy, play therapy supervision, and child inclusive practice in the family law sectors. Lorri is the co-author of the books *Play Therapy Dimensions Model: A Decision-Making Guide for Integrative Play Therapists* and *Turning Points in Play Therapy and the Emergence of Self: Applications of the Play Therapy Dimensions Model*, in addition to over a dozen chapters/ articles on the topic of play therapy, and children and family law. She is currently on the Advisory Board for Therapeutic Play and Child Play at Deakin University, Geelong Campus, Australia, and is an Honorary Fellow for the Therapeutic Play and Child Play Masters Degree Program.

KEN J. GARDNER, MSc, R Psych, CPT-S

Ken Gardner, MSc, R Psych, CPT-S is a Clinical Psychologist and Certified Play Therapy Supervisor with over 30 years of counseling experience. Through the Rocky Mountain Play Therapy Institute, Ken has presented nationally and internationally on a wide range of topics related to play therapy and supervision. Ken has served as an executive board member on the Canadian Association for Child and Play Therapy. Ken is the co-author of the *Play Therapy Dimensions Model: A Decision-Making Guide for Integrative Play Therapists*, as well as book chapters on play therapy, play therapy supervision, and play therapy techniques.

Subject Index

Sub-headings in *italics* indicate diagrams.

abuse 37, 58, 82, 99, 113, 116, 216, 223
   abusive caregivers 121–2, 213, 229
   sexual abuse 55, 229
Active Utilization 22, 54–5, 120, 136
   clinical applications 129–30
   considerations for the play
      therapy process 127–9
   defining features 120–3
   Ellis 123–6
   Haley 133–4
   therapeutic roles and activities 126–7
Active Utilization indicators
   child's drive and direction in therapy 132
   child's play skills 132
   context of presenting issue 132–3
   responses of the child 131
   therapeutic process 131
   timelines and system parameters 133
Adler, Alfred 65
Adlerian Play Therapy 16, 17, 37, 39, 76, 78,
      105, 138, 150, 161, 182, 207, 209, 211
   directiveness and non-
      directiveness 53–4, 78
   final phase of therapy 115, 145
   immersion 61
   tracking skills 80
aggression 55, 72, 158
   Ellis 92, 108, 124–5
American Psychological Association 16
Annie 52
anxiety 55, 71–2, 73, 79, 143–5
   separation anxiety 140
appendices 23–4
assimilative integration 39
Association for Play Therapy (APT) 16
autism 39, 49
autobiographical memory 66, 68, 70

bounded rationality 43–4, 45
brain function 20, 64, 65, 66–7, 139, 206, 224

caregivers 59, 130
   abusive caregivers 121–2, 213, 229
   working with caregivers 228–31
   see also parents
case conceptualization 15–17, 23
Case Conceptualization Form
      18, 24, 179–80, 266–7
   child's world view box 174
   content box 174–6
   goals and hypotheses box 167–8, 170
   interventions box 172–3
   process box 170–2
   purpose and use of the form 164–5
   resiliencies and vulnerabilities box 176–7
   self box 165–7
   supervision questions box 168–70
   themes box 173–4
   transference and countertransference
      box 178–9
case studies 25
   Ellis video 25–9
   Haley video 30–3
catharsis 38, 39, 68, 168
Charcot, Jean-Martin 65
Child Moderating Factors Scale 18,
      24, 41–2, 133, 134, 164, 236–43
   supervision 193, 198–200
Child Protective Services (CPS) 152
Child-Centered Play Therapy 37, 39,
      57, 76, 87–8, 96–7, 140, 182
   Landreth model 207–9
   non-directiveness 53, 60, 76–8
   Play Therapy Skills Checklist 205
   tracking skills 80

SUBJECT INDEX

children 50–4, 62
child's process 58–61
drive and direction in therapy
99, 115–16, 132, 146–7
importance of considering child
moderating factors 68–73
play skills 99, 115, 132, 146
pre-imaginative play skills 20–2, 34,
49–50
presenting issues 96–7, 113–14,
129–30, 144–5
responses 98, 115, 131, 146
therapeutic process 98, 114–15, 131,
146
timelines and system parameters
100, 116, 133, 147
Chowchilla kidnapping 51
client-centered psychotherapy 87
Co-Facilitation 22, 56, 104, 119
clinical applications 113–14
considerations for the play
therapy process 111–13
defining features 104–5
Ellis 108–11
Haley 117–18
therapeutic roles and activities 105–8
Co-facilitation indicators
child's drive and direction
in therapy 115–16
child's play skills 115
context of presenting issue 116
responses of the child 115
therapeutic process 114–15
timelines and system parameters 116
cognitive distortions 71, 139
Cognitive-Behavioral Play Therapy 39,
54, 61, 105, 138, 141, 150, 182, 208
common factors approach 38, 39–40
confidentiality 153, 154, 163
four hurts 30, 154
congruence 213–14
conscience 69
consciousness dimension in play
therapy 22, 50–2, 74–5
are we playing a game of hide-
and-seek? 67–8
consciousness dimension 51
historical and current perspectives
63–7
importance of considering child
moderating factors 68–73
knowledge 66

learning to embrace the game
of hide-and-seek 73–4
pre-imaginative play skills 49–50
coping skills 132, 144, 145
countertransference 60, 108,
119, 164–5, 223, 230–1
cultural background 218–19, 226–8

defenses 68, 71–3, 74
defensive exclusion 122
Degree of Immersion: Therapist Use
of Self Scale 18, 23, 24, 42, 44, 59,
82, 164, 187, 205, 219, 244–55
supervision 200–1
denial 51, 72
desensitization 70–1
developmental difficulties
20, 49, 99–100, 116
directiveness dimension in play
therapy 22, 50, 52–4, 76–9, 84–5
compass and the gauge 79–82
directiveness dimension 53
observer-participant role 83
tapping the therapeutic
powers of play 83–4
disclosure 70, 133, 142–3
domain specificity 44–5, 46
drawing 52, 53, 55, 70–1, 71–2, 82, 112, 145

eclecticism 38, 40–1, 181
technical eclecticism 39
ecological rationality 44
Ecosystemic Play Therapy 39, 54, 59–60,
105, 138, 140, 141, 150, 182, 208, 209,
211
Ellis 23, 25, 81, 179–80
Active Utilization 123–6
background 27–8
Co-Facilitation 108–11
initial impressions 29
Non-Intrusive Responding 90–2
Open Discussion and Exploration
142–3
presenting problem 26–7
see also Lynde
emotions 64, 65–7, 70–1
therapist's use of self 212–15
empathy 74, 88, 125, 191, 213, 223–4
empathic interpretations 72–3
Ericksonian Play Therapy
60–1, 106, 120–1, 182
ethnicity 226–8

• 281 •

experiential mastery play 70–1, 130
externalization 69, 71

family play 222–3
Family Play Therapy 24, 152, 223
Filial Play Therapy 68, 182
Flexibly Sequential Play Therapy (FSPT) 70
Freud, Sigmund 65

Gandhi, Mohandas 223
Gestalt Play Therapy 54, 61, 76, 105, 138, 150, 165, 182, 208, 209, 211

Haley 25, 81
  active utilization 133–4
  background 31–2
  Co-Facilitation 117–18
  initial impressions 32 -3
  Non-Intrusive Responding 100–1
  Open Discussion and Exploration 147–50
  presenting problem 30–1
  see also Susan
hypothesis testing 56, 98, 104–5, 107, 109–10, 115, 117, 178

immersion 61, 81–2, 84, 106
  see Degree of Immersion: Therapist Use of Self Scale
infants 138–9
information-processing theory 43
insertions 105, 107, 104–6, 107, 111–12, 113–14, 115, 128, 132, 144, 212
  Lynde 109, 110–11, 124
  Susan 117
integrative decision-making 22, 35–8, 46
  do decision-making theories designed for adults fit for play therapists? 43–6
  how do integrative therapists make decisions? 42–3
  need for a framework for decision-making 38–41
  Play Therapy Dimensions Model 41–2
interpretations 122–3, 136
  bridging interpretations 126, 127
  dynamic interpretations 73
  empathic interpretations 72–3
  linking interpretations 126, 127
  reflective interpretations 126, 127
  therapist's use of self 210–12
  three principles 127–9

Janet, Pierre 65
Jung, Carl Gustav 65
Jungian Analytical Play Therapy 39, 50, 60, 68, 83
  soft hypothesis testing 104–5
  therapist immersion 106

language 120–1, 123
Leibniz, Gottfried 64–5
loss 82, 99–100, 112, 129, 231–3
Lynde 90–4, 108–11, 123–7, 141–3, 180
  reflections on case of Ellis 166–7, 168, 169–70, 170, 172, 173, 173–4, 174, 176, 177, 179
  see also Ellis

mastery 37, 78–9, 91, 102, 103, 117, 118, 140, 144
  experiential mastery play 70–1, 130
meaning 221–3
Mills, Joyce 15, 220
mirroring 60, 81, 89, 106, 225
motivation 60, 106, 127
  therapists 187–8
  unconscious motivation 65
movement 18–19, 22, 24–5, 54, 58, 62, 83, 92–5
  movement between quadrants 57, 101–3, 117–18, 134–5, 147–50
  movement in supervision 190–1, 194, 196
multiculturalism 218, 226, 228
Mutual Storytelling Technique 138

Narrative Play Therapy 80, 207
National Institute for Relationship Enhancement 78
neuroscience 64–5, 68–9, 74
Nietzsche, Friedrich 65
Non-Directive Play Therapy 86, 87
  UK model 207
Non-Intrusive Responding 22, 55, 86, 103
  clinical applications 96–7
  considerations for the play therapy process 92–6
  defining features 86–8
  Ellis 90–2
  Haley 100–1
  therapeutic roles and activities 88–90
Non-Intrusive Responding indicators
  child's drive and direction in therapy 99
  child's play skills 99
  context of the presenting issue 99–100

SUBJECT INDEX

responses of the child 98
therapeutic process 98
timeline and system parameters 100
North Texas University 40

Object Relations/Thematic Play
    Therapy 105, 182
observer-participant role 83
Open Discussion and Exploration
    22, 55, 137, 150
  clinical applications 144–5
  considerations for the play
      therapy process 143–4
  defining features 137–41
  Ellis 142–3
  Haley 147–50
  therapeutic roles and activities 141
Open Discussion and Exploration indicators
  child's drive and direction
      in therapy 146–7
  child's play skills 146
  context of presenting issue 147
  responses of the child 146
  therapeutic process 146
  timelines and system parameters 147
overview of Play Therapy Dimensions
    Model 22, 47, 62
  consciousness dimension and pre-
      imaginative play skills 49–50
  degree of reorganization in the
      child's process 58–61
  factors related to movement
      between quadrants 57
  four quadrants 54–6
  *Full Play Therapy Dimensions
    Model diagram* 48
  level of therapist interpretation 61–2
  two primary dimensions 50–4
  see Play Therapy Dimensions Model

pain 74, 78, 98, 100, 231–2
parent feedback 23, 151, 163
  considering future needs and an
      ongoing treatment plan 162–3
  four steps of preparation 152–6
  parent feedback video 25
  parent presentation styles 156–62
Parent Readiness Scale 160
Parent Feedback Conceptualization
    Form 18, 24, 262–5

parents 20–1, 23, 36, 69, 121, 151
  Abusive Parent (ABP) 161–2
  Aggressive Parent (AGP) 158
  Collaborative Parent (CP) 159
  Conflicted Parent (CONFP) 159–60
  Control Parent (CONP) 160–1
  Deflector Parent (DP) 157
  Expert Parent (EP) 156–7
  Insensitive Parent (IP) 161
  Passive Parent (PP) 157–8
  Process-Focused Parent (PFP) 158–9
  Solution-Focused Parent (SFP) 159
  working with parents 228–31
  see also caregivers
Phenomenological Play Therapy 107, 182
physical self 215–17
Plato 64
play 83–4
  family play 222–3
  post-traumatic play 79
Play Therapy Dimensions Model
    15–18, 22–3, 34, 46
  decision guide for integrative
      play therapists 41–2
  Play Therapy Dimension Model diagram 21
  pre-imaginative play skills 20–2
  what is the Play Therapy
      Dimensions Model? 19–20
  see overview of Play Therapy
      Dimensions Model
play therapy training 187–91
  advanced play therapist 194–6
  bridging activities 189–90, 192–4, 194–6
  imitation of experts 191–4
  indicators of movement 190–1, 194, 196
Playtime Exercise 18, 24, 221,
    222, 223, 233, 268–9
pre-imaginative play skills 20–2, 34, 49–50
Prescriptive Play Therapy 54,
    57, 61, 182, 207, 211
presenting issues 96–7, 113–14, 129–30, 144–5
Psychoanalytical Play Therapy 72, 105, 182
psychodynamic theory 50–1, 68, 211
psychological plausibility 44
psychotherapy 15, 18–19, 35, 37,
    38–9, 65, 87, 202, 206

Quadrant I 22–3, 54–5, 120, 136
  clinical applications 129–30
  considerations for the play
      therapy process 127–9
  defining features of Quadrant I 120–3

● 283 ●

PLAY THERAPY DIMENSIONS MODEL

Quadrant I *cont.*
  Ellis 123–6
  Haley 133–4

Quadrant I *cont.*
  indications for working in
    Quadrant I 130–3
  movement within Quadrant I 134–5
  therapeutic roles and activities 126–7
  Therapist movement in Quadrant 1 135
Quadrant II 22–3, 55, 137, 150
  clinical applications 144–5
  considerations for the play
    therapy process 143–4
  defining features of Quadrant II 137–41
  Ellis 142–3
  indications for working in
    Quadrant II 146–7
  movement within Quadrant II 147–50
  therapeutic roles and activities 141
  Therapist movement in Quadrant II 148
Quadrant III 22–3, 55–6, 86, 103
  clinical applications 96–7
  considerations for the play
    therapy process 92–6
  defining features of Quadrant III 86–8
  Ellis 90–2
  Haley 100–1
  indications for working in
    Quadrant III 98–100
  movement within Quadrant III 101–3
  therapeutic roles and activities 88–90
  Therapist movement in Quadrant III 102
Quadrant IV 22–3, 56, 119
  clinical applications 113–14
  considerations for the play
    therapy process 111–13
  defining features of Quadrant IV 104–5
  Ellis 108–11
  indications for working in
    Quadrant IV 114–16
  movement within Quadrant IV 117–18
  therapeutic roles and activities 105–8
  Therapist movement in Quadrant IV 118
quadrants 54–6, 62
  factors related to movement
    between quadrants 57

Reactive Attachment Disorder 39
reflective statements 84, 89, 101–2, 103, 105
  therapist's use of self 207–10
Relationship Play Therapy 83

relationships 36, 54, 70, 95, 138, 145
repression 51, 64–5, 67–8, 72, 74, 122
resilience 182, 199, 213
rhythm 111–12
Rocky Mountain Play Therapy Institute™
  40, 97, 165, 187, 188, 190, 193, 221
Rogerian therapy 40, 52, 53, 54, 87

Schopenhauer, Arthur 64
self 63, 65–7, 69–70
  false self 121–2
self regulation 113–14, 121, 139, 144–5, 197,
  199
splitting 72
Structured Play Therapy 138, 145
supervision 23, 201
  aiding supervisees to use videos/
    video review 185–6
  bridging activities 189–90, 192–4, 194–6
  Child Moderating Factors Scale 198–200
  Degree of Immersion: Therapist
    Use of Self Scale 200–1
  developmental model of
    supervision 187–96
  how to use the videos 183–5
  indicators of movement 190–1, 194, 196
  Phase 1. beginning play therapy
    training 187–91
  Phase 2. imitation of experts 191–4
  Phase 3. advanced play therapist 194–6
  using Play Therapy Dimensions
    Model to review videos 186–7
  why use the Play Therapy Dimensions
    Model for supervision? 181–3
  Tracking and Observation Form 197–8
suppression 74, 78
Susan 33, 100–1, 117–18, 133–4, 147–50
  see also Haley
symbolization 51, 69, 72

technical integration 38–9
temperament 224–5
termination stage of therapy 82,
  95, 111, 114–15, 131, 171
themes 56, 95–6
theoretical integration 39
therapeutic process 98, 114–15, 131, 146
therapist self-awareness 23, 220, 233–4
  know yourself and your
    temperament 224–5
  know yourself as a player 220–4

● 284 ●

SUBJECT INDEX

know yourself culturally and
ethnically 226–8
know yourself when working
with parents 228–31
making meaning 231–3
therapist use of self 23, 202–4, 219
cultural use of self 218–19
emotional use of self 212–15
interpretations 210–12
physical use of self 215–17
reflective and tracking statements 207–10
restating content 210
self-system 217–18
verbal use of self 205–7
what are we looking for? 204–5
Theraplay 39, 54, 192, 208, 216
attachment-enhancing play therapy 182
Tracking and Observation Form 18, 24, 45,
113, 128, 133, 164, 170, 173, 182, 256–61
supervision 197–8
tracking skills 80–1, 101–2, 103,
107, 111–12, 119, 205
Ellis 91–2, 93–4, 124, 126, 143, 179
Haley 134
tracking comments 88–90, 101, 103, 114
tracking or reflective statements 84,
89, 101–2, 103, 105, 207–10

transference 60, 65, 73, 108, 119, 133
Case Conceptualization
Form 164–5, 178–9
transitional adjustments 129–30
trauma 20, 49, 31–2, 49, 51, 55, 70–1,
74, 78–9, 82, 86, 96, 99, 102,
113, 129, 132, 176, 191
developmental impact 130, 175
multiple traumas 95, 147
severe trauma 121–2, 171
Trauma Play™ model 70
vicarious trauma 23, 223–4

unconscious 64–5
Unlimited Associative Learning (UAL)
63
utility theory 43, 44

verbal discussion 205–7
videos 24, 34
case conceptualization video 25
case example video 24–5
parent feedback video 25
Von Hartmann, Karl Robert Eduard 64

Yasenik, Lorri 30

Author Index

Adler, A. 53
Allan, J. 83, 105, 106, 108, 111, 178
American Psychiatric Association 49
American Psychological Association 21
Amster, F. 90
Andrews, J. 202
Arnkoff, D.B. 38
Association for Play Therapy 228
Axline, V. 52, 77, 78, 87, 89, 92–3, 204

Baars, B. 64
Behan, D. 35
Beitman, B.D. 206
Benedict, H.E. 105
Beutler, L.E. 41, 42, 44
Birch, J. 63
Blackmore, S. 63
Boyd Webb, N. 130
Braafladt, N. 145
Bratton, S.C. 36, 151, 159
Braverman, L.D. 65
Bretherton, I. 122
Brewer, N.E. 138
Bromfield, R.N. 100
Bronson, M.B. 144
Burton, S. 69

Cangelosi, D. 205
Casado, M. 138
Cashdan, S. 202
Cates, J. 153
Cattanach, A. 37, 52
Ceballos, P.L. 218
Chalmers, D. 63
Chang, C. 228
Chazan, S.E. 144
Chess S. 224

Chethik, M. 37
Chow, R. 178
Chown, A. 96
Clarkin, J.F. 42. 58–9
Cloninger, C.R. 224
Cochran, J.L. 77, 78
Cochran, N.H. 77
Consoli, A.J. 41
Coscolla, A. 40–1
Courtney, A. 213
Crenshaw, D. 71, 72–3, 74
Crick, F. 64
Crittenden, P.M. 121
Crouch, A. 203
Crowley, R. 60, 106, 120, 121, 220

Damasio, A. 63, 64, 65–7, 68, 69, 74
Danger, S. 140, 144
Davies, D. 66, 72, 74
Davis, D.E. 218, 226
Delworth, U. 187
Dillman Taylor, D. 16
Draper., K. 96
Drewes, A.A. 36, 39, 40, 70, 78,
    83–4, 85, 130, 167, 218, 228
Duncan, B.L. 42

Ellenberger, H.F. 64, 65
Elstein, A.S. 43
Erickson, M. 60
Erwin, E. 202
Eth, S. 51

Fall, M. 39
Fonagy, P. 206
Frances, A. 58–9
Frank, L. 90

AUTHOR INDEX

Garber, J. 145
Gardner, K. 15, 74, 84, 115
Gardner, R. 138
Garfield, S.L. 38
Gaskill, R. 20, 49
Gergen, K. 202
Gigerenzer, G. 43
Gil, E. 17, 74, 78–9, 218, 228
Gilligan, S. 60
Ginsberg, B. 213–14
Ginsberg, S. 63
Glass, C.R. 38
Goldfried, M. 58
Goodman, P. 165
Goodyear-Brown, P. 70, 71, 79, 82. 155-6, 157, 205
Graham, J. 160
Green, E. 68
Greenspan, S.I. 138–9
Grencavage, L.M. 38, 39
Guerney, L. 77, 204

Hambridge, G. 144
Hammarskjold, D. 220
Harris, P.L. 121
Harter, S. 69, 121, 122
Hartzell, M. 161
Hayes, J.A. 230–1
Hefferline, R.E. 165
Hill, C. 15
Holcomb-McCoy, C. 228
Hubble, M.A. 42

Irwin, E. 90

Jablonka, E. 63
Jennings, S. 179
Jernberg, A. 39
Jones, K.S. 138, 143, 145

Kaduson, H. 205
Karasu, T.B. 203
Kendrick, P. 37
Kenny, M.C. 39
Kiesler, D.J. 203
Knell, S.M. 54, 61, 105, 137, 139, 145
Kottman, T. 16, 17, 35, 37, 53, 61, 77, 78, 79, 80–1, 83, 88, 89, 104, 105, 115, 145, 161, 204, 205, 208

LaBauve, B.J. 35

Landreth, G. 35, 37, 53, 57, 60, 77, 80, 84, 86, 87, 88, 94–5 96–7, 204, 207, 208, 210
Lazarus, A.A. 39
LeBlanc, M. 36
Lebowitz, B.D. 42
Linder, T. 49
Lowenstein, L. 205

Malchiodi, C. 205
Mann, D.W. 202, 203
Marmar, C.R. 43
Martin, B.R. 44
Maslow, A.H. 203
McCann, I.L. 223
McGuire, D.E. 21, 231
McGuire, D.K. 21, 231
McInnes, K. 96
McNeill, B. 187
Meany-Walen, K. 17
Miller, S.D. 42
Mills, J. 60, 106, 120, 121, 123, 130, 220
Milton, M. 187
Mitchell, P. 69
Mook, B. 106, 107, 107–8
Moore, B. 178
Mordock, J. 71, 72–3, 74
Moustakas, C. 77, 83, 95, 171, 204
Muller, W. 230, 231, 232, 233
Munns, E. 54, 216
Myers, J.E. 228

Nalavany, B. 204
New, D. 105
Newman, C.F. 41
Niederehe, G. 42
Norcross, J.C. 25, 38, 39, 41, 206
Nordling, W.J. 77
Norton, B.E. 159
Norton, C.C. 159

O'Connor, K.J. 39, 54, 59, 65, 68, 72, 73, 94, 105, 121, 122, 123, 126, 127, 140, 204, 205, 211, 226, 227–8
Oaklander, V. 54, 61, 105

Pankseep, J. 65
Parson, J.A. 84, 167
Pearlman, L.A. 223
Peavy, R.V. 202
Peery, C. 50, 60, 68, 105
Perls, F.S. 165

Perry, B.D. 20, 49
Perry, S. 58–9
Phillips, R. 35
Piaget, J. 50
Pittard Jones, N. 96
Post, P. 218
Prendiville, E. 84
Prochaska, J.O. 206
Pynoos, R. 51

Ray, D:C. 36, 77, 204–5, 205, 208, 209, 226
Repp, M. 138
Ritchie, M. 36
Ritter, K. 228
Robinson, E.H. 138
Rodriguez, M. 218
Rogers, C. 52, 87, 88, 213, 214
Rossi, L. 60
Rubin, L. 205
Russ, S.W. 68
Ryan, V. 37, 77, 213

Scaturo, D.J. 35
Schaefer, C.E. 25, 36, 37, 39–40, 54, 57, 61, 83, 84, 85, 145, 167, 205
Schottenbauer, M. 42, 43, 44
Seymour, J.W. 44
Shelby, J.S. 70
Sheppard, L. 20
Siegel, D. 161
Smith, D. 38
Sniscak, C. 77
Soth, A. 206
Sperry, J. 15, 16, 17

Sperry, L. 15, 16, 17
Stagnitti, K. 19, 20, 49–50
Stern, D. 121
Stoltenberg, C. 187, 188, 191
Street, L.L. 42
Stricker, G. 41
Sweeney, D. 53, 57, 80, 84, 96–7
Sywulak, A. 77

Target, M. 206
Terr, L. 51, 121, 130, 223, 224
Tholstrup, M.C. 181
Thomas A. 224
Turner, R. 16

VanFleet, R. 68, 77
Victor, B.J. 38

Wachtel, P.L. 39
Wadley, C. 20
Watts, R.E. 35
Weir, K.N. 39
White, J. 96
Williams R.E. 41
Wilson, K. 37, 50, 77, 87, 88, 89, 95, 121, 213
Winick, C.B. 39
Winnicott, D. 37, 111, 203
Wosket, V. 202, 203

Yasenik, L. 15, 74, 84, 115, 160

Zeman, J. 145
Zuber, I. 43